The continental connection

Manchester University Press

The continental connection

German-speaking Émigrés and British cinema, 1927–1945

TOBIAS HOCHSCHERF

Manchester University Press

The right of Tobias Hochscherf to be identified as the author of this work has been asserted by him in accordance with the Copyright, Designs and Patents Act 1988.

Published by Manchester University Press
Altrincham Street, Manchester M1 7JA, UK
www.manchesteruniversitypress.co.uk

British Library Cataloguing-in-Publication Data is available

Library of Congress Cataloging-in-Publication Data is available

ISBN 978 0 7190 9747 8 *paperback*

First published by Manchester University Press in hardback 2011

This paperback edition first published 2015

The publisher has no responsibility for the persistence or accuracy of URLs for any external or third-party internet websites referred to in this book, and does not guarantee that any content on such websites is, or will remain, accurate or appropriate.

Printed by Lightning Source

'Gingen wir doch, öfter als die Schuhe die Länder wechselnd.'
('For we went, changing our own country more often than our shoes.')
Bertolt Brecht, 'An die Nachgeborenen' ('To Posterity') 1938

Contents

List of Illustrations

Abbreviations

ABPC	Associated British Picture Corporation
ACT	Association of Cinematograph Technicians
ASFI	Associated Film Industries Limited
ATS	Auxiliary Territorial Service
BBFC	British Board of Film Censors (renamed British Board of Film Classification in 1984)
BFI	British Film Institute
BIP	British International Pictures
BTP	British Talking Pictures
DECLA	Deutsche Eclair (production company)
HO	Home Office
IPL	Independent Producers Limited
LFP	London Film Productions
MGM	Metro-Goldwyn-Mayer
MI5	Military Intelligence, Section 5 (British Security Service)
MoI	Ministry of Information
MPPDA	Motion Picture Producers and Distributors of America
NA	National Archives
NATE	National Association of Theatrical Employees
NATKE	National Association of Theatrical and Kine Employees
NSDAP	Nationalsozialistische Deutsche Arbeiterpartei (National Socialist German Workers' Party)
OSS	Office of Strategic Services
POW	Prisoner of War
RAF	Royal Air Force
RMVP	Reichsministerium für Volksaufklärung und Propaganda (Reich Ministry of Enlightenment and Propaganda)
RKO	Radio-Keith-Orpheum Pictures Inc.
TUC	Trade Union Congress
UFA	Universum Film Aktiengesellschaft
UK	United Kingdom

USA	United States of America
USC	University of Southern California
USSR	Union of Soviet Socialist Republics
WAAF	Women's Auxiliary Air Force

Acknowledgements

In undertaking my research on German-speaking émigrés I have benefitted from the support of many colleagues, librarians and others with an intellectual interest in the topic. I am endebted to the staff at the University of Liverpool, particularly to Andrew Plowman, Alison Smith and Eve Rosenhaft. At Northumbria University I would like to thank my former colleagues Peter Hutchings, James Leggott and Noel McLaughlin for the fruitful debates and suggestions on the manuscript or parts thereof. I am most grateful for the support of a number of other people, too, who have all helped at various stages of my research, including Tim Bergfelder, Christian Cargnelli, Erica Carter, James Chapman, Jan-Christopher Horak, Christoph Laucht, Bill Niven, Simon Ofenloch, the Cinegraph research group, the team at the Deutsche Kinemathek and the BFI. I thank Ronald Walker for translating some of the articles in the German trade press and the team at Manchester University Press for their editorial assistance.

Above all, however, I would like to express my deep gratitude to Friederike, Leo and Paul for their generous support and enduring patience.

1 *Catherine the Great*, 1934. Courtesy of Deutsche Kinemathek, Berlin

1

Introduction

This book deals with an aspect of British cinema from 1927–1945 that is still largely neglected: the influence of German-speaking film professionals. Although this era stands out as a prolific period in British cinema, there remain significant gaps in our understanding of these years – particularly the time before the Second World War – as few of the films and the personnel involved have been properly examined.[1] Additionally, many a general publication on British cinema has downplayed the numerous cross-cultural entanglements and relationships within the film industry and, therefore, prolonged the illusion of a self-sufficient national cinema.[2]

This study shows that, from the mid-1920s onwards, filmmaking in the UK was fundamentally affected by various migration processes, multi-faceted patterns of inter-European co-operation and the unprecedented expulsion of continental film practitioners after Hitler seized power in 1933. Such an influence can be seen in the films of the era themselves, the organisation of work and the improvement of standards. Under the leverage of German-speaking émigrés, the British film industry for the first time gained significant international recognition. The findings presented in the following, indeed, suggest that many of the achievements of British cinema are to a great extent based upon the contributions of continental talent, which introduced pioneering camera techniques, rationalised production processes and increased the importance of mise-en-scène. Not coincidentally, the most successful British film of the 1930s, *The Private Life of Henry VIII* (1933),[3] was made with the participation of numerous German-speaking film personnel. Émigré Alexander Korda, who began his career working in Vienna and Berlin, both produced and directed the film, his brother Vincent Korda designed the sets, fellow Austrian–Hungarian Lajos Bíró was co-author of the script and the German composer Kurt Schröder was responsible for its music.

Remarkably, almost all major British production companies from the mid-1920s to the early postwar years – from Gaumont-British to British International Pictures (BIP) and the Rank Organisation – employed

,onnel who had previously worked in the Weimar Republic or Austria.

: annexation of Austria, pogroms against Jews, the outbreak of the Second World War and the Nazi occupation of most of the European mainland once again significantly increased the number of German-speaking exiles who had found temporary employment in other European countries such as France or the Netherlands. Although Hollywood certainly was the final destination for most refugees after Hitler's inauguration as Chancellor, the fact that approximately 'only' 800 of an overall number of 2,000 exiled film professionals eventually landed in Southern California casts doubt on works that regarded England as a minor émigré destination.[4] On the contrary, the metropolitan area of London with its concentration of film studios must rather be considered as one of the refugee centres of the Nazi-enforced diaspora. The research undertaken for this book suggests the high figure of some 400 German-speaking film practitioners in Britain for the time-span of 1927–45. The list includes directors such as Berthold Viertel, Karl Grune, Paul Czinner and Ewald André Dupont, the actors Lilli Palmer, Elisabeth Bergner, Richard Tauber, Conrad Veidt, Fritz Kortner, Anton Walbrook (Adolf Wohlbrück), producers such as Alexander Korda, Max Schach, Josef Somlo and Erich Pommer, the script writers Wolfgang Wilhelm, Lajos Biró, Franz Schulz and Emeric (Emmerich) Pressburger, art directors such as Ernö Metzner, Alfred Junge and Hein Heckroth, the cinematographers Karl Freund, Günther Krampf, Werner Brandes, Curt Courant and Otto Kanturek, and the composers Mischa Spoliansky and Allan Gray (Josef Zmigrod). In fact, given this great number of eminent German-speaking personnel very few major British productions of the time frame observed here were made without émigrés.

Since virtually all the major studios and production companies from the late 1920s to 1945 were located in and around the English capital, it is worth noting that the British cinema of the time is English. Whilst British cinema is the established term – and is thus used in the title of this book – the story of émigré film professionals is actually the story of migrants in London. Besides the film business itself, the BBC and a high number of theatres, as alternative sources of employment, were situated in and about the English capital, making it quasi compulsory for émigré film workers and artists to reside in close proximity in order to find work. Living within the relatively small space of greater London had an influence on German-speaking refugees in many ways. Not only did it allow them to maintain numerous cultural and professional émigré networks, it also meant that they had direct access to state institutions and help organisations. By becoming the focal point and destination of many German-speaking film professionals, the English metropolis, in turn, underwent a significant cultural transformation.[5] Within less than a decade from the late 1920s to the late 1930s, its relatively small film business changed into a multicultural industry which not only made films for international consumption but also attracted many foreign staff. In the process, London's standing as a site for the production of a uniform national film culture became increasingly problematic.

Undoubtedly other foreign groups also left their mark on the London-based British film industry to varying degrees. The French cinematographer Georges Périnal, for example, was one of the most influential cameramen in England, where he shot many of Korda's acclaimed films. Yet the sheer numbers of German-speaking émigrés and their ability to fill important posts within British production companies point to their unique status. Indeed, the upward revision of the figure for the involvement of émigrés in British films to some 400 persons underlines their exceptional role as the number clearly illustrates an unprecedented development in British cinema history. This migratory movement fundamentally influenced cinematic practices and underpins wider transnational developments that make it impossible to describe 'British' film history in narrow national and candidly linear terms. As such, border-crossings, transcultural exchange, uprootings and diasporic experiences are central to British cinema from the late 1920s to the mid 1940s and beyond.

Whilst reinserting British émigré films in the historical context in which they were produced and exhibited, one must emphasize the pivotal role of motion pictures at that time. Cinema had been the paramount art form and medium of the first half of the twentieth century until television took over its role. The film industry combined entertainment with the probability of enormous dividends whilst cinemagoing was a regular habit – in particular among the interwar working class. In the late 1930s, 23 million tickets were sold in Britain each week.[6] In industrial regions like Liverpool, estimates suggest that 40 per cent of the residents attended screenings at least twice a week.[7] Yet, the popularity of cinema was not restricted to the working classes. The amusement that had begun as a fairground attraction had long become an accepted leisure time activity for all social classes. German émigré set designer Hein Heckroth had good reasons to state that 'movies are the folklore of the twentieth century'.[8]

The interwar years in Britain are generally described as marked by economic depression, mass unemployment, pessimism and the decay of the Empire. Yet, particularly in the south of England and the Midlands a number of newer industries developed and expanded – among these was the film business. The ever-increasing number of people who found employment in one of the many film studios underscores the fact that apart from its role as popular entertainment, cinema had developed into a major economic factor in the interwar years. The cultural and economic relevance of cinema again makes the reappraisal of the migrant film professionals' role one that is long overdue.

Given the importance of the German-speaking film professionals who worked in Britain as early as the mid-1920s, the large-scale emigration caused by the Nazis only intensified the already existing processes of interaction. With this in mind, the following analysis will not be strictly limited to exiles or political refugees, i.e. those who were forced out of or left Germany as a reaction to Nazi policies. Emigrants who left Germany years before the Nazis came to power, like the production designer Alfred Junge, who played a key role in the success of many English productions, will also be taken into consideration. In order to avoid confusion, the terms 'émigré', 'emigrant', 'migrant', 'alien' and 'immigrant' will be used for all of those who left the Third Reich whatever their reasons for doing so, whereas the expressions 'refugee' and 'exile' will exclusively be used to denote those who involuntarily fled countries under Nazi control.[9]

Few will argue with the principle that the émigrés' situation was distinct in every country owing to political, economic and socio-cultural differences. Nonetheless, the important term 'exile film' (*Exilfilm*) has been universally applied to the exile situation in all countries. It is defined by Jan-Christopher Horak as a motion picture produced outside Germany after 1933 by German exiles, who must fill two of the key positions of producer, director and/or scriptwriter.[10] This study, however, argues that the term 'exile film', which Horak used predominantly in his work on exiles in Hollywood, should – if at all – only be applied to the situation in Britain with care and by no means rigidly. The reason for this is that while exile films in other countries often fulfilled the above-mentioned criteria – in some cases like *Borzy* (Gustav von Wangenheim, USSR 1936) or *Hangmen Also Die* (Fritz Lang, USA 1942) nearly the complete cast and credits consisted of German exiles – only a few German-speaking directors or scriptwriters found permanent work within the British film industry. By contrast many eminent film technicians and art directors were given permanent jobs by major British film companies. What is more, many of the personnel involved in the making of films in the Weimar Republic were not German nationals. Yet they were influenced by and stood for the achievements of Weimar cinema and should also be taken into account if they had worked several years for production companies such as Sascha (Vienna), UFA (Berlin) and Emelka (Munich) before coming to Britain.

By applying Horak's criteria rigidly to the situation in the UK, a significant number of central films made with exile participation would be ignored – such as *The Life and Death of Colonel Blimp* (Michael

Powell and Emeric Pressburger, 1943) or *The Tunnel* (Maurice Elvey, 1935). The first film does not comply with Horak's criteria because Emeric Pressburger was not a German citizen. He was one of the many German-speaking Jewish film professionals who were born in the Austro-Hungarian Empire and who learned their trade working for years in Berlin before they fled when the Nazis came to power. The fact that other German-speaking émigrés participated in the making of the film (as in the case of the lead Anton Walbrook and the set designer Alfred Junge) is, according to Horak's definition, not crucial because they do not fill the post of the director, producer, or scriptwriter. As a consequence Horak's narrow definition of exile films neglects the artistic freedom and authorial input of German-speaking film professionals in other capacities. Sometimes the level of creativity of those positions sidelined by Horak could be significant. Elvey's 1935 film *The Tunnel*, for example, obviously fails to comply with Horak's criteria since neither its director nor the producer or scriptwriter were German/Austrian or had worked a significant time in Germany. Nevertheless, this study argues that the picture must be considered as an émigré film. Not only was the science-fiction film based upon a story by Kurt (later: Curt) Siodmak and a novel by Bernhard Kellermann but German-speaking expatriates were also responsible for cinematography (Günther Krampf), set design (Ernö Metzner) and costumes (Joe Strassner). Since it was in particular the contribution of cinematography and futuristic sets that characterises the film, it bears the signature of émigré artists. Acknowledging this influence helps to explain its great resemblance to *Metropolis* (Fritz Lang, Germany 1927) where the spectacular futuristic settings are concerned. Thus it seems inappropriate to describe the exile film in Britain by strictly using the definitions set out for analysing the émigré situation in the US.

Keeping in mind the great diversity of German-speaking migrant film personnel and the fact that the British film industry of the 1930s was primarily organised as a classic studio system, this study reconsiders and goes beyond previous approaches that have regarded British production of the time as authored and tend to overemphasise the work of directors. The studio films of this period are rather the outcome of complex negotiations between various film workers and cannot be limited to the certainly important positions of the director, the producer or the scriptwriter. The narrative and stylistic elements of films discussed throughout this study strengthens the thesis that German-speaking migrants changed production processes and the look of British cinema by incorporating major stylistic and organisational features of Weimar cinema. Working abroad, they continued the so-called UFA-style with its tendency to facilitate technical and stylistic innovation and improvisation. This was made possible because migrant film professionals brought with them the German version of the director-unit system which, as Thomas Elsaesser has demonstrated in his work on Weimar Cinema, allowed for a significant input of groups working independently in cinematography and art departments.[11] Consequently it seems unwise to accept as true the often quoted total number of 38 exile films produced in Britain – which according to Horak's criteria is still an impressive 18 per cent of all exile films.[12]

By acknowledging the major contributions of various professional groups to both art cinema and popular genre cinema, this investigation throws fresh light on the complex relationship between the British film industry and the German-speaking professionals within it. Given the vital role of German-speaking émigrés in Britain ever since the mid-1920s, the paucity of comprehensive works dealing with émigrés in British cinema is somewhat surprising.[13] Apart from (auto-) biographies of individual film artists,[14] the topic has only recently been discovered by a growing number of scholars after Kevin Gough-Yates has completed his pioneering doctoral thesis on the topic in 1990.[15] The two existing edited collections only serve as initial steps and need to be re-configured and amplified as many facets of the migration processes and impact of émigrés on audiovisual culture in Britain have yet to be addressed.[16]

Dealing with some of the peculiarities of the émigrés' situation in the British cinema, it is in particular Thomas Brandlmeier's and Tim Bergfelder's compelling analyses of the work of German cinematographers and art directors in London which serve as points of departure for further inquiry.[17] Bergfelder principally puts forward the thesis that the British film industry tried to establish state-of-the-art production resources and professional standards in order to create internationally successful films by recruiting American and German film workers. Their plan was to combine the Hollywood and German models, i.e. 'combining the fast-paced, fluid narration of American cinema with the mise-en-scène and visual craftsmanship of UFA'.[18] *Continental Connection* tests and further develops Bergfelder's line of reasoning by including readings of several exemplary films. Demonstrating that his argument can indeed be supported by the aesthetics of films made at the time, the findings presented here explain why there are problems in applying Horak's definition of exile films to the situation in England where a high proportion of film workers were technicians and art directors rather than editors or directors.

Including into consideration archive material and restored films that have only lately become available, this study moreover fills some of the existing gaps in the assessment of migrant German-speaking film professionals. Among other sources it builds extensively upon formerly closed files held by the National Archives on individual refugees from the Third Reich.

As representative case studies these files, which were opened during the course of the current research at the author's request to the Home Office,[19] are read against the background of wider social and political developments and offer the opportunity to compare and contrast the situation and trajectories of individual migrants. The documents are a constant reminder for the fact that exile despite all necessary generalisations is by no means a uniform condition.

Besides offering a first comprehensive synthesis of previous scholarship in English and German and original empirical research of archive material, the findings presented here, moreover, rely on readings of individual films and historical reception studies as a means of contextualisation. Among other publications, the journal of the Association of Cinematograph Technicians (ACT), *Cine-Technician*, and the trade journal *Kinematograph Weekly* make possible a detailed reading of how the migrants and their work were perceived at the time, whilst the newsletter *Pem's-Privat-Berichte* illustrates how German-speaking émigrés viewed their own diasporic situation and culture production.[20] Although some analyses of individual films covered in this book have been discussed by other scholars before, they have never related them to one another while discussing them in relation to the wider context of émigré cinema as outlined by Hamid Naficy.[21] Combining an historical approach with the more theoretical citicism of diasporic and exilic modes of filmmaking makes visible the deep-rooted interpenetration of British film culture by migrants from Germany and Austria on an aesthetic and narrative level. This outcome changes the collective understanding of the 'golden era' of filmmaking in England and adds another argument for a number of recent publications that fundamentally challenge the validity of the concept of national cinema if defined in terms of a monolithic society, cultural homogeneity and 'untained' specifity.

In an attempt to redraw crucial aspects of German-speaking film professionals' work in England, *Continental Connection* builds upon the ideas of Gerd Gemünden and Anton Kaes, who advocate a shift of emphasis in exile studies from a biographical approach 'to a more dynamic scenario of intercultural tension and negotiation'.[22] Rather than limiting its scope on trajectories of individual émigrés, this study also takes a closer look at the British films of the era that were made with German-speaking participation. By reading the films against the background of broader historical developments, this book offers findings that are of wider interest as they touch upon crucial developments in British cinema, relations within the European film industry and attempts to rival Hollywood's hegemony as well as raising general questions of cultural imagery, national cinema and intercultural exchange.

Partly informed by transnational and post-colonial theory, British and

European film studies are reacting to the various cross-cultural influences and developments by questioning and reconceptionalising the very notion of 'national' cinema.[23] The current research into the complex relationship between diasporic filmmaking and British cinema is a contribution to general debates on how far 'British' cinema was affected by foreigners. Although British cinema of the period is often and primarily associated with the documentary film movement and realist practices, the numerous successful opulent feature films suggest that it incorporated many concepts and ideas from continental Europe. On this point Andrew Moor aptly argues that the debate over stark anti-realist tendencies in British cinema of the time is to some degree linked with the question of how open British culture was to the intellectual changes marked by continental notions of modernism.[24]

Owing to the seminal works by Tim Bergfelder, Christian Cargnelli, Andrew Higson, Kevin Gough-Yates and others, British film historeography has just begun to accept the fact that the 1920s and early1930s must be seen as prolific periods of pan-European interference, transnational cross-fertilisation, and as a time when it is in general difficult to distinguish what is indiginous from what is exotic. Drawing upon a range of sources in English and German and rooted in Homi Bhabha's critique of simplistic notions of nationhood,[25] *Continental Connection* not only offers a range of case studies to support this view but also expands the time frame by including the second half of the 1930s and the wartime period. While British cinema during the Second World War has been more often than not described in terms of consensus, uniformity, national unity and as relatively centred, the influence of German-speaking film personnel persists during the war – despite numerous problems such as the internment of so-called 'enemy aliens'. Under the émigrés' influence – in terms of the personnel involved, the organisation of work, storylines and aesthetics – many films of the 1940s transcend narrow concepts of national identity and are instead characterised by difference and hybridity. So as to extensively analyse the impact of foreign film personnel it will be necessary to position the various émigrés' contributions in their complex cultural context. Or, in the words of Lutz Koepnick, only by means of mapping the work of émigrés

> against the interplay of sociocultural, industrial, technological, and ideological forces that define the history of film can we fully understand how their films opened up imaginary spaces in which different cultures and histories penetrated each other through the medium of mutual citation, interpretation, or imitation.[26]

Cultural traffic across national and geographical boundaries in general and the cinema of diaspora in particular is indeed marked by a complex integration of cultural signs and practices. Such reciprocal interactions do not simply exist as the addition of the host and home culture but create something new. It is therefore important to note, as Bergfelder does, that they should rather be understood 'as adding new discursive and aesthetic layers, which irrevocably change but also ultimately contribute to the continuing evolution of, national cultures'.[27] Since the cross-cultural contact between British cinema and German-speaking émigrés is not a global phenomenon, the term 'transnational' seems adequate to describe this very specific process of interaction. Here sociologist Ulf Hannerz offers a useful definition of the term which fits well the multitudinous, but also very specific, situation of German-speaking film personnel in England. He points out that transnationalism describes a complex contact across state boundaries without the generalisation and imprecision of phenomena that can be observed globally.[28]

Continental Connection maps the various stages and developments of German-English transnational film relations of the era – keeping in mind that the situation of film émigrés is unique in many respects. Unlike exile literature, for example, the work of expatriates in the film business did not address a German-speaking public but the audience of the country in which they found refuge. Not only did their films have to appeal to English-speaking audiences, émigré film professionals also had to subject themselves to the changed production practices of British film studios. Acknowledging these peculiarities of exilic and diasporic filmmaking, this book is structured historically covering the periods before and after the crucial year the Nazis seized power and then the war and postwar years.

The following chapter examines the ways in which artists and film workers from German-speaking countries were able to establish themselves in British film productions before the Third Reich. This first group of immigrants came to Britain during a boom period of filmmaking as a result of the implementation of quota legislation in 1927. In an attempt to raise standards, major London-based studios such as Elstree, Gainsborough or Lime Grove increasingly tried to sign up internationally acclaimed foreign personnel. All in all, about 30 film professionals came to England before 1933. Although this first group of émigrés was relatively small compared to post-1933 figures, they were very important indeed as they in many respects paved the way for later refugees. Whilst their influence can primarily be seen in the organisation of labour, camera techniques and elements of mise-en-scène, the various film projects they participated in demonstrate that storylines were also shaped by the permeability of borders in European cinema at that time.

The subsequent chapters concentrate on the years 1933–1939 (Chapter three) and wartime Britain (Chapter four). While the political situation in Germany turned many of those film personnel who came to Britain in the 1920s and early 1930s into refugees, as they could not return home, those Jewish and/or anti-Nazi film professionals who were still working in the Third Reich were forced to leave. In fact, most of the German-speaking migrants who came to Britain after 1933 were Jewish refugees – among them producer Emeric Pressburger, actress Lucie Mannheim and actor Peter Lorre. Despite the generally cosmopolitan character of the cinema industry, émigré film professionals in Britain faced an ambivalent climate as the end of the third chapter shows. As with émigré experiences in Hollywood, life and work in Britain meant both opportunities and hardships. The sheer number of German-speaking film workers who came to Britain was certainly a challenge to its relatively small film industry – even if many émigrés, all problems and drawbacks notwithstanding, were eventually able to establish themselves in the major production companies.

In fact, at one time the presence of foreign producers alone was so obvious that Georges Mikes ironically suggested in his humorous account of life in Britain *How to Be an Alien* (1946) that for anyone wanting to become a film producer in Britain a 'little foreign blood is very advantageous, almost essential'.[29] While some saw the high proportion of foreign talent as beneficial to the international aspirations of British film companies, others spoke about an 'invasion' and condemned what they regarded as an excessive number of foreign film workers. Above all, the trade union ACT viewed the ever-increasing number of refugees with concern and repeatedly campaigned for the implementation of restrictive measures designed to prevent foreigners from entering the British film business. Negative views on an influence of foreign film professionals in Britain proved very persistent indeed and eventually sieved through to scholarly works. As a prime example, Charles A. Oakley's general account of British cinema *Where We Came In*, admittedly now dated, is marred by the use of pejorative phrases in connection with foreign film personnel. He uses a military register in order to describe migration processes of the era. In so doing, the collected fears, xenophobia, and anti-Semitism of the 1930s are inscribed into his chapter-heading 'The German Invasion'.[30]

Aiming at a constructive account of immigration, cross-cultural contact and assimilation, the third and fourth chapter take into account general works of migration studies. Here, the publications by Panikos Panayi have to be named.[31] Issues addressed in his books, like racism, the structure of minority groups, questions of ethnicity, residence patterns, etc., are important because they emphasize that the many particularities, continuities and discontinuities of refugees in Britain will only be visible when read against the background of these general developments. Moreover, Louise London's fundamental study of Westminster's response to the increasing number of Jewish refugees from Nazi Germany shows that Britain was indeed far from being altruistic. Her comprehensive analysis puts forward the thesis that the plight of the European Jewry under Nazism did not have a top priority for the British government as self-interests often limited humanitarian efforts.[32] Resentments and anxiety eventually resulted in numerous restrictions and in the tragic and traumatic imprisonment of exiles on the Isle of Man, the British mainland and former British colonies, an experience that certainly left its mark on German expatriates' psyches. However, this study does not wish to limit accounts on exilic filmmaking to trauma, disenfranchisement, paranoia and loss. Both the work of those film workers who left Germany in order to escape Nazi persecution as well as those who came to work in Britain for economic reasons are being seen as a 'productive encounter and active engagement with a new culture'.[33]

In order to find employment in the competitive and, towards the end of the 1930s by and large saturated, British job market, German-speaking film practitioners had to find one of several *niches* they could occupy. They often found work in popular genres such as the spy thriller, the musical or the historical epic that often alluded to romanticised central European countries.[34] Very frequently, these films were remakes of earlier Austrian and German productions in which the émigrés could show the special talents that set them apart from their British colleagues.

In many such genre films, as discussed in Chapters three and four, émigrés played a vital role in confronting National Socialism. Even if explicitly anti-fascist films were not produced in pre-war Britain because of a rigid censorship, this does not imply that films in the UK are devoid of any political critique at all. The fact of the matter is that condemnation of Nazi ideology is often inscribed into the productions made with émigré participation. An underlying premise of reading film in such a way is that German-speaking film personnel not only had a quantitative influence on British films which can be inferred from the number of participating émigrés but also a qualitative one as they also affected the storylines.

Once the war broke out formerly stringent censorship regulations were removed. German-speaking émigrés then played a vital part in the country's war of information against the Third Reich. Many German-speaking émigrés, indeed, remained to work within the wartime film industry, despite the requisition of studio space by the armed forces and the internment of enemy aliens. Taking advantage of their new freedom, many German-speaking refugees were at the forefront of anti-Nazi film productions. One central argument put forth in Chapter four is that British films with émigré participation offer less stereotypical depictions of Germans and the Third Reich than many of Hollywood's anti-Nazi films.

In addition to the political meaning of films, the circumstances of émi-grés' lives are repeatedly inscribed into the films metaphorically. Using Hamid Naficy's framework of an 'accented cinema', the film analyses offered in the following seek to assess the ways in which geo-political mobility of German-speaking film personnel affected the aesthetics and narratives of British films. Although a reading of films in terms of diaspora, displacement, relocation and mingling of cultural traditions is only one particular of various possible readings, it is a vital method to shed light on how such conditions and developments affect processes of culture produc-tion and semantics of films. Although Naficy's findings derive in large part from work on art cinema, the reading offered here shows that they can also be related to many genre films. Naficy proposes a set of universal tropes that address issues of dislocation, claustrophobia, assimilation proc-esses and imagined homelands metaphorically through symbolic locations and objects of itinerancy such as borders, hotels, suitcases, passports, trains, buses or planes. So he reinvigorates concepts of film authorship by insisting that émigré films bear the creative imprint of the diasporic or exilic personnel involved in their making within their concrete historical circumstances.

Given that many émigrés followed the commercial imperatives of the British film industry, they were involved in the making of both 'low-brow' popular genre cinema and 'high-brow' art house films. This in mind, *Continental Connection* examines the ways in which German-speaking film professionals in Britain positioned themselves with regard to the socio-economic context as well as artistic traditions of their host country. Their status as foreigners and strangers perhaps enabled them to take alternative looks at their host country as some of the émigrés used the experience of exile as a creative impetus. In the process, they transform a condition that is typically associated with loss or distress into an illuminating examination of a new culture. By offering detailed readings of films, particular attention is drawn to the various rhetorical devices such as tropes or symbols as well as numerous historical clichés that can frequently be found in émigré films. One focus of interest is how these inscribed myths and figures of speech represent the expatriates' central concerns. By placing the work of German-speaking casts and crews within broader (film-) historical contexts this study regards émigré cinema as 'a contested space where different traditions collide [. . .] a cinema of the in-between, of creative conflict and cultural mimicry'.[35]

As an element of popular culture, exilic and diasporic filmmaking in Britain from the mid-1920s to 1945 offers valuable insights into a turbulent period of cinema history. The time-span covered by this book, however, cannot be summarised by a few generalisations, since no film period, as post-modernist thought points out, ought to be conceived as a unified entity. Unfortunately only a few English films of the era have been made commercially available as high-quality versions. Despite this dilemma, perhaps this work may contribute to leading a contemporary audience back to an often forgotten period of British cinema history – a period that cannot be accurately understood without considering the impact of émigrés.

Notes

1 See Jeffrey Richards, *The Unknown 1930s: An Alternative History of the British Cinema, 1929–1939* (London and New York: I. B. Tauris, 2000), p. vii.

2 See, for instance, Rachael Low, *The History of the British Film, 1918–29* (London: Allen & Unwin, 1971); ibid., *Filmmaking in 1930s Britain* (London: Allen & Unwin, 1985); and Jörg Helbig, *Geschichte des britischen Films* (Stuttgart and Weimar: Metzler, 1999).

3 On the international success of Korda's film see Sarah Street, *Transatlantic Crossings: British Feature Films in the United States* (New York and London: Continuum, 2002), pp. 43–69. Unless a country is given in parentheses, the films throughout this book refer to British productions.

4 The exact number of exiles is contested. Many publications, however, assume that approximately 2000 film people fled Germany after 1933. On the discussions of the overall number of German and Austrian exiles see Gerd Gemünden and Anton Kaes, 'Introduction', *New German Critique*, 89 (Spring/Summer 2003), 3–8 (p. 4).

5 On the transformation of national film cultures through migratory movements see Tim Bergfelder, 'National, Transnational of Supranational Cinema? Rethinking European Film Studies', *Media, Culture & Society*, 27.3 (2005), pp. 315–31 (especially p. 320).

6 See Philip Corrigan, 'Film Entertainment as Ideology and Pleasure: A Preliminary Approach to a History of Audiences', in *British Cinema History*, edited by James Curran and Vincent Porter (London: Weidenfeld & Nicolson, 1983), pp. 24–35 (p. 30). On the popularity of cinemas in the 1920s and 1930s see Stephen G. Jones, *The British Labour Movement and Film, 1918–1939* (London and New York: Routledge & Kegan Paul, 1987), pp. 7–12.

7 See Charles Mowat, *Britain Between the Wars 1918–1940* (London: Methuen, 1955), p. 250.

8 Cited as an epigram in Michael Powell, *A Life in Movies: An Autobiography*, 2nd edn (London: Faber and Faber, 2000).

9 It is worth noting that the British public most frequently referred to those who were forced to leave their home country as 'refugees'. A comprehensive discussion of how émigrés saw themselves and how they were labelled by the British public can be found in Jutta Vincent, *Identity and Image: Refugee Artists from Nazi Germany in Britain (1933–1945)*, Schriften der Guernica Gesellschaft: Kunst, Kultur und Politik im 20. Jahrhundert (Weimar: VDG, 2006), pp. 63–86.

10 See Jan-Christopher Horak, 'Exilfilm, 1933–1945: In der Fremde', in *Geschichte des deutschen Films*, edited by Wolfgang Jacobsen, Anton Kaes and Hans Helmut Prinzler (Stuttgart: Metzler, 2004), pp. 99–116 (p. 100). Other contributions by Horak on the issue of German exiles include among others 'Wunderliche Schicksalsfügung: Emigranten in Hollywoods Anti-Nazi-Film', *Exilforschung – Ein internationales Jahrbuch*, 2 (1984), 257–70; and 'On the Road to Hollywood: German-speaking Filmmakers in Exile 1933–1950', in *Kulturelle Wechselbeziehungen im Exil – Exile Across Cultures*, edited by Helmut F. Pfanner (Bonn: Bouvier, 1986), pp. 240–48.

11 Thomas Elsaesser, *Weimar Cinema and After: Germany's Historical Imaginary* (New York and London: Routledge, 2000).

12 See Jan-Christopher Horak, 'German Exile Cinema, 1933–1950', *Film History*, 8.4 (1996), 373–89 (p. 377).

13 Besides a lack of comprehensive works, many publications have tended to ignore or underestimate the influence of émigrés in the film industry since the mid-1920s and simply failed to simply take German fascism into consideration as the driving force behind the rapid transformation of British cinema culture. See, for instance, Christine Gledhill, *Reframing British Cinema 1918–1928: Between Restraint and Passion* (London: BFI, 2003); Robert Murphy, *Realism and Tinsel: Cinema and Society in Britain 1939–49* (London and New York: Routledge, 1989; repr. 1992), Stephen C. Shafer, *British Popular Films 1929–1939: The Cinema of Reassurance* (London and New York: Routledge, 1997); and Sarah Street, *British National Cinema* (London and New York: Routledge, 1997).

14 See, for instance, Elisabeth Bergner, *Bewundert viel und viel gescholten: Elisabeth Bergners unordentliche Erinnerungen* (Munich: Bertelsmann, 1978); Klaus Völker, *Elisabeth Bergner: Das Leben einer Schauspielerin ganz und doch unvollendet* (Beiträge zu Theater, Film und Fernsehen aus dem Institut für Theaterwissenschaften der Freien Universität Berlin, 4) (Berlin: Edition Hentrich, 1990); Lilli Palmer, *Dicke Lilli – gutes Kind* (Zurich: Knaur, 1974); a comprehensive collection of biographies can be found in *Cinegraph: Lexikon zum deutschsprachigen Film*, edited by Hans-Michael Bock (Munich: text+kritik, 1984–). Examples of anthologies are *Conrad Veidt: Lebensbilder – Ausgewählte Fotos und Texte*, edited by Wolfgang Jacobsen (Berlin: Argon, 1993); *The Cinema of Michael Powell: International Perspectives on an English Film-maker*, edited by Ian Christie and Andrew Moor (London: BFI, 2005); and *Carl Mayer – Scenar(t) ist: Ein Script von ihm war schon ein Film*, edited by Christian Cargnelli, Brigitte Mayr and Michael Omasta (Vienna: Synema, 2003).

15 Kevin Gough-Yates, 'The European Filmmaker in Exile in Britain, 1933–1945'. (unpublished doctoral thesis, Open University, UK 1990). A good summary of Gough-Yates' findings can be found in 'Exiles and British Cinema', in *The British Cinema Book*, edited by Robert Murphy, 2nd edn (London: BFI, 2001), pp. 104–13.

16 See *Destination London: German-speaking Emigrés and British Cinema, 1925–1950*, edited by Tim Bergfelder and Christian Cargnelli (Oxford and New

York: Berghahn, 2008); and *London Calling: Deutsche im britischen Film der dreißiger Jahre*, edited by Jörg Schöning (Munich: text+kritik, 1993). Brief references to the film workers' situation in England can also be found as background information in various publications that deal with different, yet related issues. Generally, however, they assume that the final destination of the vast majority of German-speaking film workers was Hollywood (see, for instance, Helmut G. Asper, 'Film', in *Handbuch der deutschsprachigen Emigration 1933–1945*, edited by Claus-Dieter Krohn and others (Darmstadt: Wissenschaftliche Buchgesellschaft, 1998), pp. 957–70). Other articles merely focus on biographical trajectories of political refugees and neglect German-speaking film staff who came to work in Britain prior to 1933 (see Waltraud Strickhausen, 'Großbritannien', in *Handbuch der deutschsprachigen Emigration 1933–1945*, edited by Claus-Dieter Krohn and others (Darmstadt: Wiss. Buchgesellschaft, 1998), pp. 251–70; and Maria Hilchenbach, *Kino im Exil: Die Emigration deutscher Filmkünstler 1933–1945* (Munich: Saur, 1982), pp. 57–61).

17   See Thomas Brandlmeier, '"Rationalization First": Deutsche Kameraschule im britischen Film', in *London Calling: Deutsche im britischen Film der dreißiger Jahre*, edited by Jörg Schöning (Munich: text+kritik, 1993), pp. 69–76; and Tim Bergfelder, 'The Production Designer and the *Gesamtkunstwerk*: German Film Technicians in the British Film Industry of the 1930s', in *Dissolving Views: Key Writings on British Cinema*, edited by Andrew Higson (London and New York: Cassell, 1996), pp. 20–37. The article is a revised English-language version of 'Rooms With a View: Deutsche Techniker und der Aufstieg des Filmdesigners', in *London Calling: Deutsche im britischen Film der dreißiger Jahre*, edited by Jörg Schöning (Munich: text+kritik, 1993), pp. 55–68.

18   Bergfelder, 'The Production Designer and the *Gesamtkunstwerk*', p. 24.

19   The following files on individual filmmakers were opened and made available at the National Archives, Kew, Richmond, Surrey (hereafter NA): Rudolf Bernauer (HO 405/2616), Lajos Biró (HO 405/2074), Paul Czinner (and Elisabeth Czinner, née Bergner, HO 405/7511), Heinrich Fraenkel (HO 405/12865), Walter Goehr (HO 405/15863), Otto Kanturek (HO 405/26547), Rudolf Katscher (Kacser, Cartier, HO 405/26875) and Conrad Veidt (HO 382/8).

20   *Pem's-Privat-Berichte* were published by émigré Paul Marcus in Vienna and London from May 1936 to September 1939 and September 1945 to May 1972. Like few other publications, Marcus' newsletter gives a vivid account of German exile culture in general and German-speaking filmmakers in Britain in particular.

21   See Hamid Naficy, *An Accented Cinema: Exilic and Diasporic Filmmaking* (Princeton, NJ: Princeton University Press, 2001).

22   Gemünden and Kaes, p. 4.

23   See, for example, Andrew Higson, 'The Instability of the National', in *British Cinema, Past and Present*, edited by Justine Ashby and Andrew Higson (London and New York: Routledge, 2000), pp. 35–47; *'Film Europe' and 'Film America': Cinema, Commerce and Cultural Exchange 1920–1939*, edited by Andrew Higson and Richard Maltby, Exeter Studies in Film History (Exeter: Exeter UP,

1999); and *Cinéma sans frontières 1896–1918 – Images Across Borders*, edited by Roland Cosandey and François Albera (Québec: Nuit Blanche Editeur, 1995).

24 See Andrew Moor, *Powell & Pressburger: A Cinema of Magic Spaces* (London and New York: I. B. Tauris, 2005), p. 9. On the period from the 1920s to the 1930s as the first phase of Modernism within British cinema see also Street, *British National Cinema*, pp. 147–9.

25 See Homi K. Bhabha, 'Introduction', in *Nation and Narration*, edited by Homi K. Bhabha (London and New York: Routledge, 1990), pp. 1–7.

26 Lutz Koepnick, *The Dark Mirror: German Cinema Between Hitler and Hollywood* (Berkeley, Los Angeles and London: California University Press, 2002), p. 161.

27 Bergfelder, 'National, Transnational or Supranational Cinema?', p. 321.

28 Ulf Hannerz, *Transnational Connections: Culture, People, Places* (London and New York: Routledge, 1996), p. 6.

29 Georges Mikes, *How to Be an Alien: A Handbook for Beginners and Advanced Pupils* 2nd edn (Harmondsworth: Penguin, 1966), p. 60.

30 Charles A. Oakley, *Where We Came In: Seventy Years of the British Film Industry* (London: Allen & Unwin, 1964), pp. 135–6.

31 See *Minorities in Wartime: National and Racial Groupings in Europe, North America and Australia During the Two World Wars*, edited by Panikos Panayi (Oxford and New York: Berg, 1993); *Germans in Britain since 1500*, edited by Panikos Panayi (London: Hambledon Press, 1996); *Immigration, Ethnicity, and Racism in Britain, 1815–1945*, edited by Panikos Panayi (Manchester: Manchester University Press, 1994); and Panikos Panayi, *Outsiders: A History of European Minorities* (London: Hambledon Press, 1999).

32 Louise London, *Whitehall and the Jews, 1933–1948: British Immigration Policy, Jewish Refugees and the Holocaust* (Cambridge: Cambridge University Press, 2000).

33 Gemünden and Kaes, p. 3.

34 On audience preferences see John Sedgwick, 'Film "Hits" and "Misses" in Mid-1930s Britain', *Historical Journal of Film, Radio and Television*, 18.3 (1998), 333–51.

35 Gemünden and Kaes, p. 5.

2

Transnational developments and migrants: the internationalisation of British studios, 1927–1933

Compared to other countries, Britain was late in developing a recognised national cinema. When American market dominance was all too obvious with only 5 per cent of films shown in the country being British in 1925, an increasing number of voices demanded governmental protection.[1] After the First World War, British cinema had to cope with a string of setbacks, which eventually resulted in the rapid decline of the industry.[2] The reasons for the crisis that engulfed the British film business by 1924 were manifold and complex, ranging from technical inadequacies to poor writing and the inability to establish a British star system. Although the frenzy surrounding the so-called 'British Film Slump' reported in the press in November 1924 was, to a certain degree, deliberately fuelled by film companies in order to increase governmental support,[3] the problems were undeniable. By the mid-1920s, approximately 90 per cent of all feature films in circulation in Britain were US productions.

Westminster reacted by the implementation of the Cinematograph Films Act in 1927. The quota legislation was designed to augment British production: it ruled that distributors and exhibitors must acquire and show a minimum number of domestic films. Gradually, the number of British films shown was to increase to 20 per cent in 1938 – a very ambitious figure given Hollywood's overall market dominance. Despite problems with the Cinematograph Films Act – like the frequent complaints that it encouraged so-called quota quickies[4] – the new law generally augmented the production of British films. It prompted investment, spread optimism and accelerated the formation of highly capitalised vertically integrated enterprises. This means that the production, distribution and exhibition of films were combined in highly capitalised companies like BIP, Gaumont-British or the Associated British Picture Corporation (ABPC).[5] In order to establish a characteristic studio style, such major production companies often sought to make films in their own studios using personnel under long-term contracts.

An increase in production went hand in hand with the internationalisation of an industry that was looking for foreign talent. As more and more film workers from around the world sought jobs in England, a significant number of German-speaking personnel found temporary or permanent employment in Britain as casts and credits of productions like *Moulin Rouge, Piccadilly* (both Ewald André Dupont, 1928 and 1929), *The Informer* (Arthur Robison, 1929) or *The Woman He Scorned* (Paul Czinner, 1929) show. This means that German-speaking film practitioners like production designers Alfred Junge and Oskar (In Britain: Oscar) Werndorff or cinematographers Karl Freund and Mutz Greenbaum were able to establish successful careers in Britain as early as the late 1920s, long before the large-scale purge of talent as a result of Nazi policies. Thus Bergfelder is right to say that 'seen from a purely industrial perspective, 1933 was in no way the beginning of a widespread emigration, but rather the politically motivated intensification of a process that had started in the early 1920s'.[6] Such an interpretation seriously questions previous approaches that solely deal with German-speaking émigrés in the context of a Nazi-enforced diaspora, 1933–1945.[7]

Many accounts of the transitional period from silent to sound cinema at the end of the 1920s refer to the poor quality of British films – especially those that were made to satisfy quota regulations. Yet the new vertically integrated major corporations mentioned above or smaller but equally ambitious companies such as Alexander Korda's London Film Productions also made many films with high production standards aimed at an international audience. In fact, the many opulent productions that were made in the late 1920s and early 1930s verify the enormous ambitions of British cinema.

German-speaking film practitioners were central to individual productions and to the industry's general objective of producing pictures for a national and international audience, as they often provided the knowledge and technical expertise needed to raise the quality of British films at a time when many production companies strove to adjusting to sound. Acknowledging the émigrés' pivotal role, Tom Ryall rightly points out that the artistic aspirations of major British studios are represented by 'the European sophistication'[8] of British films made by foreigners. In fact, it was especially the production companies' endeavour to produce films for international release that allowed the relatively few German-speaking émigrés to fill key positions in major British studios. Using the motion pictures made with émigrés from Germany or Austria in the late 1920s and early 1930s as an example, this chapter seeks to re-evaluate a period of British cinema by drawing upon its interconnections with other national cinemas. It thus advances the assumption that the post-quota era, despite all obstacles, set the agenda for Britain to create a 'viable national cinema'[9] within the network of European co-operation. In turn, pan-European joint ventures raise issues of wider interest such as the cross-fertilisation of international and European cinemas. In the course of scrutinising the ramifications of this extensive international collaboration, the following analysis raises general questions of globalisation and internationalism as it argues in favour of a broader understanding of the terms national cinema and national identity.

In order to explain adequately the complex migrations of the era one must take into consideration general international as well as national employment patterns, networks of co-operation, the organisation of work since the mid-1920s, economic factors such as the crisis of the largest German film corporation Universum Film Aktiengesellschaft (UFA), the introduction of sound and the introduction of quota legislation in Britain. While elucidating these various developments it is necessary to take a closer look not only at both the German and the British cinema of the era, but also at the various ways in which European production companies tried to compete with Hollywood by means of close co-operation. The idea of Film Europe as an attempt to create a quasi pan-European cartel has often been neglected by scholars although it is crucial for explaining the various migration processes that can be dated back to the 1920s. This in turn provides the context for an assessment of the early German-speaking émigrés to Britain in terms of employment and residence status. Out of all German-speaking film personnel, special attention is paid to set designers such as Alfred Junge and the chapter finally closes with a case study of the early émigré Ewald André Dupont. His career path helps to illustrate the strategies of major British production companies as he continuously participated in high-budget productions.

Film Europe as prerequisite: transnational networks in European cinema

In the mid-1920s, growing concerns about Hollywood's unchallenged hegemony and its aggressive market approach led to a double strategy in Europe. On the one hand, countries like Germany or England tried to protect their market by the introduction of quota legislation. On the other, they sought to compete with Hollywood by increasing pan-European co-operation. Although no equivalent of the US Office of the Motion Picture Producers and Distributors of America (MPPDA) existed in Europe, film companies were able to establish networks and personal contacts on the basis of inter-European partnerships and joint ventures. In England most of the producers either had links to Germany or Austria because of their origin or previous work experience within Weimar cinema (as is true for Alexander Korda and many other émigrés) or they worked closely with German/Austrian studios and companies for a number of economic reasons in an attempt to challenge Hollywood's overwhelming market position.

Crucial for this co-operation (commonly referred to as 'Film Europe') were a number of conferences in Paris (1923, 1926 and 1929), in Berlin (1928) and in Brussels (1930).[10] The conferences led to numerous co-operations and established pan-European networks within the industry that prompted the German trade journal *Film-Kurier* to announce: 'Film Europe – no longer just theorie' in 1928.[11] The press in England also reacted rather euphorically to such developments. In a leading article *The Bioscope*, for example, expresses the opinion that the conference in Paris in 1923

> set up a new standard of production that should so considerably widen the scope of appeal of each individual film as to bestow upon it an international appeal, which must inevitably result in the broadening of the scope of bigger and better pictures, the adopted slogan of every producer and creating an opening for every picture, no matter what the nationality of its origin, in the markets of the world.[12]

Above all, the triangle of partnerships between the biggest markets – Germany, England and France – was of the utmost importance. Among others, collaboration treaties were signed between UFA, Gaumont-British and Luce-Pittaluga, Terra, Cinéromans and BIP, Aafa and Alpha.[13] The basic idea was fairly simple: by combining their talent and sharing the costs of new projects, producers tried to minimise financial risks and simultaneously increase production values. Sometimes co-operation with, or acquisition of, foreign companies was also an effective way to gain direct access to the market despite quota regulations. In an attempt to build up distribution channels in continental Europe, for instance, BIP bought the German renter Südfilm, which had the right, under German quota regulations, to import 14 foreign films per year.[14] Furthermore, co-operation was aimed at the creation of a single European market similar to the US by making efficient use of the distribution channels of foreign companies. As a result of the increased circulation achieved in this way, profitability was augmented and higher budgets were possible. British, French and German-speaking producers of the era, like Michael Balcon, Erich Pommer, Gregor Rabinowitsch or Alexander Korda, were aware that costly high-quality films (i.e. films with high production values) could only be economically successful if they attracted an audience of at least seven or eight million before making any profits.[15] Distributing a film Europe-wide certainly ameliorated the prospects of reaching this break-even point.

Evidence that Film Europe was not just a slogan can be gathered by examining the employment patterns of film studios. Major centres of inter-European co-operation included the Elstree studios and the UFA studios in Neubabelsberg where a significant number of film workers from various countries found temporary employment. Despite their sheer number and relevance, many publications on British film history tend to play down or disregard the significance of English-language films that were shot in Germany alongside versions in other languages (commonly German and French),[16] which were films with the same plot that were shot with a different cast in a different language for varying national markets.[17] Of all the feature films produced by Michael Balcon between 1925 and 1929, for example, almost half were shot in Germany either at the UFA or the Emelka studios. The reasons for making such a high proportion of silent films and later multi-language versions in Germany were the excellent technical facilities at UFA, highly skilled human resources and a large, well-organised market.[18] The various co-productions, however, also imply that the work of British companies in Germany made the gap in standards of production in the two countries all the more obvious. In his 1934 book *Talking Pictures*, Sir John Heygate recalls his experiences in Berlin during the production of a multi-language film made with the participation of German, English and French production teams. According to his observations, the whole school-like atmosphere was clearly dominated by the outstanding skills of the Germans who 'remained permanently top of the form' at any stage of production.[19] On account of the positive experiences with continental technicians, British film companies sought to employ the very same personnel they had worked with abroad. In fact, many German-speaking film workers who had contributed to the films produced in the Weimar Republic by Michael Balcon between 1925 and 1929 were to play a role in the UK as well: Theodor Sparkuhl (cinematographer of *The Blackguard*, 1925), Otto Kanturek (cinematographer of *The Queen Was in the Parlour*, 1927, and *The Ghost Train*, 1927), Werner Brandes (cinematographer of *Moulin Rouge*, 1928, *Piccadilly*, 1929, and *The Informer*, 1929) and Oscar Werndorff (set designer of *The Queen Was in the Parlour*, 1927, *The Ghost Train*, 1927, and *The Gallant Hussar*, 1928).

The introduction of sound radically changed the whole industry and had a major influence on the various networks within the European film industry. While the intertitles of silent movies could easily be translated, the emergence of sound films brought about previously unknown limitations in the form of linguistic boundaries.[20] In their disapproval of subtitles or dubbing techniques, European producers regarded multi-language films as the most appropriate way to distribute films across borders and linguistic barriers. In *La Cinématographie Française*, producer Gregor Rabinowitsch explicitly linked the survival of the European industry to their ability to produce at least three or four language versions of each talkie by close co-operation.[21] Joint film projects were a possibility for the making of successful high-quality films despite their high costs after the introduction of sound. Albeit a relatively short-lived phenomenon, the relative economic success of pan-European productions can be inferred from the significant overall proportion of multi-language films in the first years after the introduction of sound: in the transitional period between 1929 and 1935 almost one third of all talkies in Germany were produced as multi-language versions.[22]

Notwithstanding the prime position of the Weimar Republic, southern England increasingly developed into a multi-language film centre. One of the pioneers of the production of multi-language films there was BIP. The company's managing director, American entrepreneur J. D. Williams, argued that multiple-language production was an adequate response to the language barriers created by the coming of sound in 1929.[23] For this purpose he wanted to build new studio facilities at Elstree in an attempt to rationalise the then fragmented film industry and make London the centre for multi-language film production. Williams claimed that this way of producing films for more than one market could, by using many stages simultaneously and leaving sets standing, save 30 to 40 per cent of the costs per picture.[24] Others were just as enthusiastic. In the face of the success of the German multi-language production *The Congress Dances* (Eric Charell, 1931), its producer Erich Pommer, for instance, expressed his opinion that the 'Esperanto of the talking screen has been discovered'.[25]

Whilst every scene was filmed anew with a different cast in the respective target language, inter-European and international film corporations and casts from different countries commonly worked together for the time of production. The demand for an increasingly mobile workforce, as a direct result of the growing pan-European co-operation in the 1920s and 1930s, led to a new kind of film professional: the mobile freelancer.[26] In 1930, Ernst Jäger, like many others in the industry, unpretentiously comments on the increasing globalisation of employment in the film business: 'Paris or London are not further apart from Berlin than Berlin-Tempelhof is from Geiselgasteig near Munich.'[27] Michael Balcon later states in his autobiography that in the five years he was in charge of the Gaumont-Gainsborough studios, Anglo-German films were one of the cornerstones of production.[28]

After the great box-office success of the English versions of *Sunshine Susie* (1931, a remake of the German *Die Privatsekretärin*) and the multi-language production *The Congress Dances* (1931, *Der Kongreß tanzt*), which was praised by the *Daily Mirror* as a 'magnificent picture',[29] Gaumont-British under the aegis of Michael Balcon agreed to foster the company's co-productions and joint ventures.[30] In the following years, Gaumont-British made a series of versions based on selected UFA productions deemed suitable for Britain and its overseas territories. Realised projects, many of which were made as German, French and English versions, include *The Ghost Train* (Geza von Bolvary, 1927), *Happy Ever After* (1932), *F.P.1*

(Karl Hartl, 1933), *Early to Bed* (Ludwig Berger, 1933) and *The Only Girl* (Friedrich Hollaender, 1934). Although a number of British filmmakers were involved in the making of the respective English versions, Gaumont-British failed to register them as British films under the ruling of the quota legislation – a problem that contributed to the end of multilingual productions in the course of the 1930s. In the short term, however, when the Cinematograph Act provided more stringent criteria for what constitutes British films at the end of 1927, British companies responded by relocating pan-European productions to Britain. This change in the organisation of British and continental European joint ventures, as Lawrence Napper has shown in connection with *The Ghost Train*, has 'heralded the golden age of the German-speaking émigré in the British film industry'.[31]

Apart from Gainsborough and Gaumont-British, the BIP production facilities at Elstree developed into a European centre for the production of multiple-language films. The village of Elstree, with its six adjoining studios, thus became the temporary or permanent home for many German-speaking émigrés in the course of filming versions for various different national markets. Among other important productions, Dupont's lavish production about the tragic sinking of a liner, *Atlantic* (1929), was shot as a tri-lingual film at Elstree. In 1930 an article in the German trade journal *Film-Kurier* takes note of the increasing European co-operation at Elstree and the vital role German film professionals played in this process:

> In Elstree all the English people speak broken German and all the Germans broken English. There are moments when one senses the potential film has for promoting understanding among nations. The enormous iron studios . . . prominently display the word "International" in huge letters on their facades. At the time they were being painted, no one could have realised just how appropriate they were. Now films, and not just those made there, are seen all over the world. And it seems, too, as if the whole world comes to Elstree.[32]

The enormous optimism of the time is also reflected here when film is seen as a utopian universal language able to transcend national boundaries. However, while some underlined the possibility of an 'understanding among nations' through films, as in the above quote, others disliked the internationalisation of the British film industry (see Chapter 3). In fact, the more continental filmmakers came to Britain, the more critical voices uttered concerns. For the critic Lionel Collier, the international, exotic style of films made by German-speaking personnel such as Dupont's *Piccadilly* or *Moulin Rouge* was grist to the mill of the general campaign against foreign influence that he ran as review editor of *Kinematograph Weekly*. He repeatedly expressed his disapproval of multinational co-productions and overseas personnel and thus set the tone for an increasingly critical rhetoric in the years to come when an ever-greater number of filmmakers from the continent came to Britain because of National Socialism.[33] In September 1928 he wrote a programmatic article in which he speaks out against the tendency of British cinema to 'Continentalise or Americanise'.[34] In a similar way, a review of *Piccadilly* in *Close-Up* concludes with more than a hint of xenophobia:

> This is the perfect British film. That means to say it was made by a German, with a German cameraman; its leading lady is an American of Polish extraction and its second lady an American of Chinese extraction; the leading man is English and the second man Chinese. . . . For the remainder, it is authentically rumoured that the great aunt of one of the men who trimmed the lights came from Aberdeen.
>
> So you see, a typical British film. . . . There must be something wrong somewhere.[35]

Although critical voices – with or without jingoistic undertones – were common at the time, responses toward foreign personnel in Britain were at large rather ambivalent. Indeed, German-speaking film professionals also had many advocates within the industry or editorial departments of trade journals. Under the evocative heading 'Let Them All Come', critic John K. Newnham, for instance, argues in favour of the increased immigration of foreign talent and of international co-operation.[36] If Britain wanted to compete with Hollywood, Newnham claimed, then English producers had to follow the American practice of signing excellent international filmmakers. Thus, he calls for the turning of 'Elstree into a miniature international world on its own, with wide-awake brains from all countries playing important parts'.[37] Drawing attention to the great opportunities for British producers offered by multi-language productions, Maurice Cowan writing for *Picturegoer Weekly* also argues in favour of increasing pan-European co-operation. He explicitly mentions the close and fruitful ties of Michael Balcon's Gaumont-British with German UFA. Interestingly, Balcon himself uses almost the same line of argument in a letter to Isidore Osterer. Outlining his production plans, he expresses his belief that 'continental artists form a large part of the successes of the American and English box-office attractions'.[38]

Besides the co-operation of major German and British production companies or the contributions of German-speaking personnel to individual films like *Atlantic* or *The Informer*, the great extent of Anglo-German co-operation also becomes obvious in the history and profiles of pan-European ventures. One such example is the amalgamation of German Orplid and Messtro with the London-based British & Foreign Films Ltd.[39] Above all, however, the attempts of the German Tobis Klangfilm conglomerate to establish itself as a provider of film recording equipment in Britain opened a new chapter in German-British co-operation. While most French and German studios struggled to make the costly transition to sound, the affluent major British studios were quick to install fully equipped sound stages. Indeed, the large sums that were available as a result of the contingent legislation of 1927 helped the British industry to lead the way in becoming the first country to convert its cinemas and production facilities to sound.[40]

With most British studios and cinema chains preferring the American systems provided by Western Electric and R.C.A.,[41] the newly merged Tobis Klangfilm conglomerate set up its own production company Associated Film Industries Ltd. (ASFI) together with its partners British Talking Pictures (BTP) and the Dutch company NV Küchenmeister.[42] The company's international nature was reflected in its management. The American head of BTP, I. W. Schlesinger, became chairman, the German Rudolph Becker was appointed general manager and the German-speaking Hungarian Arnold Pressburger supervised all studio processes as production manager.[43] Given their previous engagements in Germany and Austria, both Becker and Pressburger maintained excellent contacts with filmmakers from the two countries. Under their aegis, ASFI intended to produce talkies in multi-language versions by means of close co-operation and exchanges of personnel through the German parent company Tobis Klangfilm. Though such networks films as *City of Song* (Carmine Gallone, UK/Germany, 1931) and *The Bells* (Oscar Werndorff and Harcourt Templeman, 1931) were made in Britain almost exclusively with participation of senior continental personnel (except for native English-speaking actors).[44] Reviewers deemed the sound recording a great success. *The Times,* for instance, praised the 'beautiful clear voice' of the Polish-born tenor Jan Kiepura in *City of Song*.[45] The editor of the trade journal *Lichtbild-Bühne*, Hans Wollenberg, explicitly stresses the successful co-operation between the British ASFI and the German Allianz Tonfilm GmbH in a rather florid review that particularly draws attention to Kiepura's voice and the Naples setting:

> This film is a true feast for the eyes and ears. And in Jan Kiepura and the infinite beauty of Naples and its gulf, it introduces us to two veritable wonders of nature. Thus it continues to prove an unusual and alluring delicacy that never fails to delight the artistic palates of its audiences. If sound cinematography had done nothing else but make it possible to bring the consummate reflection of such beauty as we find in these opulent landscapes and that beautiful singing into the dull everyday lives of millions of people it would already have justified its incalculable value to humankind. . . . The cooperation with the "Asfi" in London has been rewarding: With not the slightest hint of any technical shortcomings, Jan Kiepura's world-famous voice comes over crystal clear in its unimpaired brilliance.[46]

25

Yet, for all the critical praise, *The Bells* – all copies of which seem to be lost today – and *City of Song* were only partially successful in attracting large crowds at the box office. While the meagre revenues were responsible for the short-lived presence of Tobis Klangfilm in the British Isles, many of the German-speaking personnel involved in the company's ASFI enterprise later became central figures among the German-speaking filmmakers in the diaspora. Apart from the set designer Oscar Werndorff, Arnold Pressburger set up the production company British Cine-Alliance in 1934 and produced the émigré films *The Return of the Scarlet Pimpernel* (Hanns Schwarz, 1937) and *Prison without Bars* (Brian Desmond, 1938) for Alexander Korda before he left for France and later the US. Moreover, despite the films' insufficient profits, the storyline and the chic and atmospheric Mediterranean European settings of *City of Song* reappeared in slightly varied form as a successful multi-language formula in numerous later productions such as the 1932 *Tell Me Tonight*.[47] Once again, the many German-speaking and other central and southern European filmmakers contributing to its production added the required continental feel to the film.

The thriving film industry in the UK and the UFA crisis

Whilst European production companies increasingly worked together, two contrasting developments took place: whereas the German film industry suffered a number of severe crises, film production in the UK was thriving. Because of exploding costs, German firms lost money despite the many highly acclaimed films and successful productions which had established Weimar cinema as the only serious challenge to Hollywood at the time. As a consequence the film industry suffered a series of financial setbacks starting in the mid-1920s.[48] The acute problems were the result of the expensive introduction of sound in 1929 and of gross financial mismanagement owing to UFA's desire to compete with Hollywood by producing immensely costly, lavish prestige pictures such as Fritz Lang's *Metropolis*. Despite its acclaimed set design and special effects, the film proved to be a financial disaster for the already stricken industry. At one point the difficulties were so acute that the company was not able to pay its 5,000 employees without third-party financial help. In order to avoid bankruptcy UFA was forced to sign an unfavourable contract with Paramount and Metro-Goldwyn-Mayer (known as the 'Parufamet' deal), which helped to ease the crisis temporarily but ultimately caused further problems.[49]

In Britain, however, the situation was notably different. The many difficulties of British production companies were by and large overcome after the implementation of a quota system in 1927. By the end of the year, as Horst Claus observes, 'developments had accelerated to such an extent that foreign observers expressed concern over the gold-rush atmosphere, pointing out that neither capital nor big names would guarantee the success of a film, but only experience, hard work and organisational talent'.[50] With large sums available, British companies like BIP increasingly began to invest in continental European companies and, long after the German film companies which had been involved in European co-productions and joint ventures in the mid-1920s, became key players in the effort to establish a pan-European cartel powerful enough to challenge Hollywood's hegemony.[51] The more British companies co-operated with foreign partners, the more the situation outside Britain had an effect on the home market. In particular the problems of the most important British partner in Germany, UFA, caused British production companies to make more and more films independently. Gradually joint-financed multi-language versions were replaced by remakes of successful German films (see Chapter 3).[52]

If Rachael Low is right to explain the various migration processes of the late 1920s and early 1930s with state-of-the-art British production facilities that were able to attract foreign film workers, then the British studios of the time must have offered at least similar, if not better, standards of production than their German or American counterparts.[53] However, Kevin Gough-Yates shows that Low's argument regarding superior production facilities was an unlikely *raison d'être* for German-speaking film professionals to participate in English productions. While the British film business was, with few exceptions, still organised as a cottage industry at the beginning of the 1930s, the spacious and technically advanced Sascha, UFA and Emelka studio complexes provided excellent resources.[54]

What can be ascertained from personal accounts, reports in the trade press and technical data on British production facilities is that it was the backwardness and substandard nature of the British film industry in terms of technical facilities and labour that prompted the migration. Although the quota legislation made large sums available to British production companies, the studios' capacity and technical standards were still very poor and they suffered from the lack of a skilled workforce. In other words, British production companies had the financial background that allowed them to open new production facilities such as the Whitehall Studios in 1928 or to install costly state-of-the-art sound equipment but not the human resources to increase both the quality and quantity of film production. Thus production companies increasingly sought to employ foreign film professionals in order to raise standards and fill posts with experienced workers. The crises of the German film industry therefore certainly played into the hands of British companies to lure away talent from Germany and Austria, which, as its most important market, was also affected by the crisis in the Weimar Republic. At the same time, personal contacts that were established during projects of inter-European co-operation and joint ventures helped German-speaking film workers to find employment within the British industry. It was therefore no coincidence that German-speaking filmmakers such as Otto Kanturek, who had been employed as a cinematographer in Germany since 1920 where he worked repeatedly with Georg Jacoby, Robert Wiene and Joe May, shot his first British film *The Wrecker* (Géza von Bolváry, 1929) when financial problems in Germany were at their worst.

Since economic factors were the incentive for German-speaking film practitioners to move and not political reasons, the émigrés who came to Britain before 1933 did not share a common experience of political exile. Nevertheless, we can, following Tim Bergfelder, distinguish between émigré groups by identifying their different employment and residence status.[55] The first group are freelance film workers who were employed by various European production companies for the making of a limited number of films or for a single project. Instead of having binding contacts they were temporarily employed. As a consequence they had to be very flexible and mobile. Although many of these 'professional travellers'[56] would still have preferred work in the States, the belief in Britain as a springboard for a Hollywood career, once they had improved their language skills and established themselves in an English-speaking cinema, reinforced their decision to move to the UK. For many, this plan seemed to have worked as they successfully managed to find employment in Hollywood by the end of the 1930s when impending war hindered the mobility of Jewish freelancers. Curt Courant's career path can be regarded as exemplary for this group: after having worked as cinematographer in the German film industry since 1916, he also worked in England and France from 1930 to 1932. In 1933 he then emigrated to France and a year later to England where he participated in the making of ten films (including Hitchcock's *The Man Who Knew Too Much*, 1934). In 1937 he again returned to France before finally going to Hollywood in 1941. As this example shows, the years before the mass purge of political exiles has already been characterised by migration and transnational careers. Indeed, the itinerary from the Weimar Republic to Hollywood via Paris or London was a common phenomenon and typifies many career paths including those of the cinematographers Franz Planer, Eugen Schüfftan and Curt Courant as well as those of the author Curt Siodmak, the directors Leo Mittler and Anatole Litvak and the actress Dolly Haas, to name but a few. Next to this mobile workforce a second group of German-speaking filmmakers in Britain consisted of those who envisaged a long-term if not permanent stay. Frequently these film practitioners had gained their experience in Weimar cinema's silent films and had been in Britain since the late 1920s.[57] Because many of those who had previously participated in European co-productions had the necessary personal contacts as well as considerable experience in producing films in a language other than German, it is not surprising that these very same workers were those who found temporary or permanent jobs in the UK.

A typical example, besides cinematographer Werner Brandes who worked regularly at the UFA studios before joining BIP in 1927,[58] is the Austrian Oscar Werndorff, who worked as set designer in Germany since 1921, among others together with Dupont (*Varieté*, Germany, 1925) and Alexander Korda (*Madame wünscht keine Kinder*, Germany, 1926). Both were important contacts if one wanted to find employment in the UK. In 1927–28 he created sets for English-German co-productions (*Die letzte Nacht/ The Queen Was in the Parlour, Der fesche Husar/The Gallant Husar, Der Geisterzug/The Ghost Train*) before he found permanent employment in the UK at the peak of the UFA crisis in 1929. In 1933 Werndorff was given the post of art director at Michael Balcon's company Gainsborough in Islington where he was responsible for the set design of Hitchcock's *Sabotage* (1936), *Secret Agent* (1936) and *The Thirty-Nine Steps* (1935).

Elstree as centre of immigration: Ewald André Dupont and BIP

Although every émigré biography is different, one can nevertheless observe different intensities in the migration processes and patterns of employment. Examples of individual filmmakers' itineraries clearly reveal the lively migration processes that existed across national boundaries. Besides art directors and cinematographers, the complex European and transatlantic interactions and co-operations of the 1920s and 1930s, including the common exchange of personnel, can be described well by following the career path of Dupont. He worked for UFA in Germany, Universal in the USA and BIP at Elstree since 1927. Although Dupont has to be named among the most innovative directors of British silent and early sound cinema alongside Alfred Hitchcock, Victor Saville, Anthony Asquith and Graham Cutts, he is little known today. Only in 2003 did the BFI's National Film and Television Archive make available a restored version of Dupont's silent film *Piccadilly* (1929). In so doing, the archive acknowledges the aesthetic qualities of the film and the influence it had on productions to come. Given Dupont's expressive style and innovative design, such critical rehabilitation was long overdue. Those of his British films made with constant participation of German film personnel, moreover, serve as good examples of an early German influence on British cinema. Indeed, Dupont's journeys between Berlin, Hollywood and London illustrate the increasing internationalisation of the film industry at the end of the 1920s.[59] While some might have seen this development with concern, Dupont viewed it as an opportunity rather than a problem:

> [A]rtistically speaking, I am not a continental European; rather, I try to produce pictures according to international taste. Europe has a lot to learn from America and America could learn some things from Europe. It is not impossible to unite both of the film industry's endeavours, namely to succeed not only with audiences and critics, but also at the box-office.[60]

Born in Germany in 1891, Dupont became a film critic in 1911, writing for the *Berliner Morgenpost* and the *Berliner Allgemeine Zeitung*. He started to work in the film industry as a scriptwriter in 1916, and published his experiences as a book in 1919,[61] before directing 12 episodes of the popular series *Europa Postlagernd* (1918). After Dupont gained his first acclaim with the *Heimat*-genre film *Die Geier-Wally* (1921) he became a well-known director of the Weimar cinema. His biggest German success and his international reputation, however, was based on his film *Varieté*. The film was admired above all because of its set design and cinematography, featuring Karl Freund's 'unchained camera' which gave the film its distinctive style through the fluidity of its camera movement and the use of the subjective camera. The film's positive critical reception euphorically labelled the German filmmaker a 'genius' and *Film Daily* included him in a list of the ten best directors.[62] Dupont, as Bergfelder notes, stood less in the tradition of high-brow non-realist traditions. Together with Richard Eichberg, Reinhold Schünzel, Joe May, Geza von Bolvary, Friedrich (Frederic) Zelnik and others he rather represented a popular Weimar cinema, 'a cinema dedicated to popular generic conventions, stars, and couched within the demands of an industrial mode of production'.[63]

After a brief and unsuccessful stay in Hollywood, where he was initially offered a three-year contract, Dupont had the misfortune to return to Germany at the time of the UFA crisis. In order to revive his struggling career, he relocated to England where film production was thriving and where he found employment as author, production manager and director at the new Elstree studios for BIP after the company had absorbed British National Pictures. His arrival was heralded by *Kinematograph Weekly* as a scoop and seen as further proof of the production company's intention to produce pictures 'of world calibre'.[64] In a similar way, a journalist writing for *The Bioscope* interpreted Dupont's employment as 'an important event in British film history'.[65]

Moulin Rouge, Dupont's directorial debut in England shot at the Elstree studio in 1927–28, is a typical pan-European project jointly funded by

Dupont's own production company Carr-Gloria-Dupont,[66] the Munich-based Emelka and BIP. Its plot revolves around the setting of his favourite subject: the variety theatre and the world of show business. *Moulin Rouge* was an exceptional production for the British industry insofar as it was labelled the most ambitious and most lavish British picture ever.[67] Since Dupont was still held in high regard on account of his success with *Varieté*, the international rights for his first British production were sold for record sums even before a single scene had been shot. This success certainly contributed to the overall very positive impression Dupont had of his new country of residence. In London, where he was able to revive his career, he was understandably more at ease with working conditions than in the US:

> There is no shortage of opportunities for producing, as England currently has world-class filmmaking facilities. The modern studios in Elstree, in particular, can more than hold their own with facilities anywhere in the world. There is no doubt that the appointment of experienced film workers would quickly boost the ambitious plans, especially since Elstree, the British Hollywood, is a place of almost unlimited possibilities.[68]

Although an unbiased observer would have noticed that not all was ideal in England, and that the facilities were certainly not comparable to studio complexes in the US, the Elstree studios, built in the 1920s, offered the largest state-of-the art filmmaking facilities in Britain before Denham was built in 1936. And even Dupont notes above that there was indeed a great need for experienced and skilled film workers if the studio was to expand and produce films for an international audience. Aiming at a domestic as well as worldwide market, the employment of Dupont by BIP may therefore also be seen as an attempt to use his excellent contacts in order to get in touch with some of Weimar's foremost film professionals. Accordingly, his employment was considered an important event in British cinema history by the trade press.[69] In filling important positions with persons suitable for the production of first-class pictures, Dupont (in addition to producers like Michael Balcon or directors like Alfred Hitchcock) could indeed rely on his previous experiences and his reputation, which enabled him to find excellent personnel for BIP. In fact the credits of his German films up to *Varieté* read like a 'who's who' of German émigrés in the UK in the second half of the 1920s, including as they do actors like Conrad Veidt, the cinematographers Werner Brandes, Karl Freund, Curt Courant and Theodor Sparkuhl as well as set designers such as Werndorff and Junge.

It was especially the partnership between Dupont and Junge that seemed to have worked very well. Having previously worked together in Berlin during the production of *Die grüne Manuela* and *Das alte Gesetz* (both films directed by Dupont in 1923) they made two silent films (*Moulin Rouge*, 1928 and *Piccadilly*, 1929) and three talkies, each in an English, French and German version (*Atlantic*, 1929, *Two Worlds*, 1930, and *Cape Forlorn*, 1930). For his last silent film *Piccadilly*, with its gigantic and expensive setting of a glamorous London nightclub that for weeks filled up most of the Elstree studios,[70] Dupont again selected German film practitioners (namely Alfred Junge and Werner Brandes) for the vital posts of set designer and cinematographer.[71]

Besides Dupont, other directors also relied on the expertise of German-speaking film professionals, particularly for productions that were intended for international release such as Alfred Hitchcock's British films, Arthur Robison's *The Informer* (1929) or Walter Forde's *Rome Express* (1932), all of which featured German-speaking émigrés in decisive posts. The favouritism towards German-speaking personnel was not only tolerated by the production company but was actually an integrated part of the strategy of raising standards and an indicator of the British companies' international aspirations. These endeavours are illustrated well in the programme booklet for the premiere of Dupont's British picture *Moulin Rouge*, which explicitly mentions the international appeal of the film for BIP marketing purposes:

> The eyes of the world are on Dupont and his big effort to make for British International a film which will go to every country and show what a British film producing organisation can do when it attempts to be really international and masses the artistic resources to Europe to make one picture. . . . This is veritably an international film.[72]

Because of their previous work experience for the sumptuous productions of Weimar cinema, the trio of Dupont, Sparkuhl and Junge made them the first choice for BIP. By hiring a number of talented and experienced film workers from Germany and Austria as well as some Americans, BIP, like other major companies in the UK such as Gaumont-British or Gainsborough emulated both Hollywood's productivity, fluid narration and editing techniques as well as Weimar Cinema's visual craftsmanship and innovative style.[73] In so doing, British studios, for instance, adopted the director-unit-system that Erich Pommer had developed and refined at UFA as Kelly Robinson argues in connection with Werner Brandes work for BIP in the late 1920s.[74] BIP, which was at the centre of such developments, however, was a unique centre of early British émigré cinema insofar as the company was one of the first to develop an international sales strategy, employing not only film technicians and art directors but also a number of German directors – a fact often overlooked. Besides Dupont, Arthur Robison, F. W. Kraemer and Richard Eichberg were also on the company's payroll. The latter, for example, had previously worked for

UFA to make several Anglo-German films in the UK like *Song/Show* Life/ *Schmutziges Geld* and *Pavement Butterfly/ Großstadtschmetterling* (1928 and 1929, both films starring Anna May Wong) as well as multi-language films for BIP in Elstree from 1930 to 1931 (*The Flame of Love/ Hai-Tang-Der Weg zur Schande, Let's Love and Laugh/Die Bräutigamswitwe, Night Birds/ Der Greifer*). Often dubbed the British Hollywood, the now well-equipped BIP studio complex at Elstree had the resources to produce a variety of different multi-language films and German-English co-productions for which the German-speaking directors were needed. Seen from a broader perspective, reciprocal distribution deals and co-operation treaties between German and English production companies as well as the presence of Dupont, Eichberg, Robison and Kraemer in Britain were all 'symptomatic both of developments in the British film industry and the attempts in the late 1920s to establish a pan-European cinema capable of competing with Hollywood on its own terms'.[75] Consequently it is wrong to claim that Anglo-German co-production began in 1932 with films like *Happy Ever After* (1932) and *F.P.1* (1933) as one recent publication did.[76] Joint ventures and co-operation treaties can be dated back at least to the production of Dupont's *Moulin Rouge* in 1927–28 which was not a single development but part of Film Europe's pan-European strategy of combining forces against Hollywood's market hegemony.

After having worked in Britain since 1927, Dupont again relocated and returned to Germany where he made three films: *Salto Mortale*, 1931, in a German and French version, *Peter Voß, der Millionendieb*, 1932 and *Der Läufer von Marathon*, 1933. Whereas Dupont struggled to repeat his early successes with these films, many of the German-speaking personnel working with him in Britain were able to launch illustrious careers abroad. This is particularly true for his long-term set designer Alfred Junge. Being born in Görlitz, Germany, in 1886 and having started off working for UFA in 1920, he owed his subsequent career to the elaborate design of his early collaborations with Dupont.

All in all, Dupont's last German films are interesting insofar as they brought together many talented film professionals who were forced into exile shortly afterwards. Among others, *Salto Mortale* stars the young Adolf Wohlbrück (who in Britain later changed his surname to Walbrook for phonetic reasons and his first name to Anton because he did not want to share a first name with Hitler) and the dialogues were written by Carl Zuckmayer. Together with cinematographer Eugen Schüfftan and set designer Ernö Metzner, who worked with Dupont on *Der Läufer von Marathon*, they all left Germany after the Nazis seized power. Dupont himself fled to Hollywood where his failure to repeat his former achievements underlines the fact that despite the successful career paths of some émigrés,

the German-speaking film workers and other refugees who were
leave Germany were never able to re-establish themselves in
 ᴄᴀᴍe. As a matter of fact, Hollywood was indifferent to the past acclaim of
European professionals and Dupont gained a bad reputation for his difficult character and his tendency to make overly costly pictures when his
first two films proved far from being successful. Although many of the early
film émigrés were generally those who best came to terms with the foreign
studio system, Dupont failed as he had never been able to adapt to his new
environment. Going from Universal to MGM to Paramount and finally
Warner Brothers, he never revived his struggling career. His work then
mainly consisted of the production of 'B' pictures before he was declared
a *persona non grata* by the Hollywood studios after he was sacked for slap-
ping an actor on the set of *Hell's Kitchen* (1939) who had made fun of his
accent.[77] Life in the diaspora had made him sensitive to verbal attacks and
ill-mannered jokes about his foreignness.

A new job for everyone? Immigration and the employment strategies of British production companies in the late 1920s

The significant number of German-speaking film personnel in London
poses the question of whether Britain offered jobs across all employment
groups within the cinema industry. A closer look at the casts and credits
suggests that some émigré groups such as actors had it significantly easier
in finding employment. In the endeavour to become international stars,
several German-speaking actors and actresses were able to appear in leading roles in British feature films – most of them directed by émigrés as
well: Olga Tschechowa in *After the Verdict* (Henrik Galeen, UK/Germany
1928), Pola Negri in *The Woman He Scorned* (Paul Czinner, 1929), Lya de
Putti in *The Informer* (Arthur Robison, 1929) and Conrad Veidt in *Rome
Express* (Walter Forde, 1932). This seems somewhat surprising given the
language barriers that emerged with the introduction of sound and can only
be explained by the special situation of the film industry. British cinema in
the 1920s initially failed to establish a significant home-grown star system
in the Hollywood mould.[78] As a result, the British job market of the late
1920s and early 1930s was not yet saturated for émigré actors. Especially
the general lack of outstanding female stars, apart perhaps from Chrissie
White, Alma Taylor and Betty Balfour, represented an opportunity for
foreign actresses from the European continent and America. Apart from
the polyglot actress Lilian Harvey, who appeared in the British, French and
German versions of films like the Gaumont-British-UFA co-production
Happy Ever After (*Ein blonder Traum/Un rêve blond*, Paul Martin/Robert
Stevenson, 1932), Elisabeth Bergner was also able to establish herself in

the British cinema before 1933 where she soon became one of the most important female stars. In addition to her great personality and acting ability, which prompted Michael Balcon to the euphoric statement that she 'is better than Greta Garbo, better than Marlene Dietrich',[79] her exceptionally good English allowed her to play a variety of British roles. In a similar way, the British press admired Renate Müller's performance in *Sunshine Susie* (Victor Saville, 1931) despite the fact that her accent was noticeable: 'She speaks English with a delightful broken accent (and broken accents are becoming all the rage now).'[80]

Compared with actors who relied heavily on language and thus needed to fill certain *niches* (often playing the roles of foreigners in British films), the situation of technical personnel and art directors was notably different. They by and large formed the biggest émigré group in Britain before 1933; and continued to be important thereafter as the following chapters show. Although some German-speaking film staff were only employed for the production of one particular picture and often, as freelancers, had to travel back and forth between sets in Germany, Austria, France and England, many cameramen and art directors were given long-term contracts. This, however, is remarkable insofar as the more common practice of the time was indeed to 'sign technical crews for individual films only – thereby actively encouraging internationally mobile film technicians', as Bergfelder states.[81] Although temporary contracts were a constant source of discontent among film workers, production companies could save large sums by not granting employees security of tenure.[82] The central question here is why British major studios were acting contrary to common practice and despite higher expenses. In order to answer this question, it is necessary to place the long-term employment of eminent German-speaking film personnel into its historical context.

Although the introduction of the 1927 quota legislation helped to attract investors, the newly available financial resources alone could not revolutionise the overall less than mediocre standards of British production. In 1929, the film critic Patrick L. Mannock, for instance, wrote a devastating appraisal of the British cinema in which he harshly blamed the studios' facilities, directors and producers for the poor production values.[83] The main problem the British industry was facing was a shortage of highly skilled film workers. Often major production companies offered long-term employment, which suggests that they not only had a particular production in mind when offering these contracts but rather followed long-term development plans. In an attempt to augment standards and to compete with Hollywood, companies such as BIP, Gainsborough, or Gaumont-British increasingly tried to rationalise both their production and distribution as well as to harness the stylistic qualities of films. The purpose was to create recognisable and distinctive motion pictures for a national and international audience.[84] To achieve this, artistic craftsmanship, creative ability and organisational talent were needed. A sufficient number of human resources, however, could not be found in Britain as Shepperton employee Martha Robison underlines:

> [E]ven with the absorption of an allowed number of foreign technicians, there was a shortage. The film companies were forced to take on apprentices who were rushed through a rapid training and pushed into positions they were totally unqualified to occupy. Those who showed any special technical or artistic ability found themselves filling two or three positions at once merely because of the incompetence around them.[85]

With this in mind, British majors needed to employ an increasing number of foreign film workers if standards of productions were to be improved. Rather than to raise the production values of individual films, German-speaking technicians, most of whom had previously worked for the largest studio facilities in Europe such as UFA, DECLA or Emelka, were employed to modernise the studios themselves by reconstructing the art and cinematography departments and by providing training for future technicians with their know-how and professional expertise. Especially as the close co-operations with German companies had made obvious the enormous deficits of British production processes that resulted in poor stylistic standards. Having been involved in numerous Anglo-German cooperations, the script supervisor and later director Robert Stevenson suggested German studios – in particular their technical departments and organisation of labour – as a role model for production facilities in Britain. In a lecture to representatives of the cinema industry that was subsequently included in *The Proceedings of the British Kinematograph Society*, he explains how UFA's excellent technical facilities and efficiency of the unit production system could serve as a role model for British studios. Yet, he also advised British companies to be mindful of cultural differences regarding multi-national teams and the inflexibility of organisational structures he had experienced in Germany.[86] Although many British producers were aware of problems for some time and might thus have well agreed with Stevenson's account, change could not happen overnight. In a spirit of resignation and, in contrast, with his contemporary Dupont, Werndorff asserted that the British film industry was years behind developments and production standards in Germany. Having already worked in London for three years at the time, he wrote a special report about his experiences for the *Film-Kurier*: 'Step-by-step, I went through all the stages of development in filmmaking here once more. Everything was just altered, shifted back a couple of years.'[87]

The interest British production companies had in attracting foreign experts did not apply equally to all jobs. Despite exceptions like Dupont, employment patterns of the time show that while German-speaking film workers often found employment as production designers or cinematographers, hardly any continental editors and few directors and scriptwriters came to Britain. From this it can be concluded that migration to Britain in the late 1920s was by no means accidental but rather the outcome of specific recruitment strategies. Looking towards America and Germany, major British producers such as Michael Balcon sought to replicate successful filmmaking models, namely Hollywood's fast-paced, fluid narration and UFA's sense for décor and visual craftsmanship.[88] Such a dual orientation towards the US and Weimar cinema prior to 1933 resulted in the recruitment of a significant number of American and German film workers in order to acquire continental and overseas know-how. Whereas posts for editing, scriptwriting and directing were frequently taken up by US citizens, the art and cinematography departments restructured themselves using German studios as role models. Accordingly it can be explained why these departments were staffed with technicians who had gained experience in the production teams of UFA or DECLA in Berlin.[89] These German-speaking film workers were held in high regard, as they were associated with internationally successful and admired films like *Madame Dubarry* (Ernst Lubitsch, Germany 1919), *Das Cabinet des Dr. Caligari* (Robert Wiene, Germany 1920) and the lavish and exotic British-Austrian-German co-productions by Mihály Kertész (who later became Michael Curtiz in exile in Hollywood), *Das Spielzeug von Paris/Red Heels* (1926) and *Einspanner Nr. 13/Fiaker Nr. 13/Road to Happiness* (1925). In view of 'the commercial clout, artistic prestige and technical innovations of Weimar Cinema in the 1920s',[90] film professionals who had previously worked in Germany and Austria were expected by British production companies to improve technical standards, harness stylistic innovations and draw more attention to elements of mise-en-scène and camera techniques. In fact, the most prolific period of German film, Weimar cinema, owes much of its reputation to its use of low-key lighting, chiaroscuro techniques, stylised sets, costume design and make-up which were more than mere background but part of the narrative itself. In addition to the mise-en-scène, innovative camera techniques were also employed as a narrative device by camera pioneers such as Karl Freund, who was famous for his 'unchained camera' or Eugen Schüfftan, who developed the special effect named after him, the 'Schüfftan process': a complex optical effect which combined miniature sets and full-size action in a single shot with the aid of mirrors.[91] Based on such innovations, Michael Powell expresses an opinion shared by many when he points out that the German cinema had the best technicians . . . I had ever seen. . . . The Americans, the French and the English couldn't hold a candle to them. First of all the early great days of UFA and then the people who came over to British International Pictures . . . like Dupont . . . and Alfred Junge, his art director with this fabulous control of the whole organization of making films.[92]

Likewise, the documentary filmmaker Paul Rotha acknowledges the great achievements of Weimar cinema in his comprehensive 1930 film history *The Film Till Now*. In this he claims that the German cinema 'has produced the principles and processes that have been all-important contributions to the cinema of the world'. Again, he emphasised particularly the importance of the mise-en-scène and innovative cinematography by stating that 'from its individual development there have come the freedom of the camera, the feeling of completeness and the importance of architectural environment as part of realisation'.[93] Full of admiration for Weimar Cinema's visual achievements, a number of British cinematographers such as Jack Cardiff, who began his career working with Werner Brandes on *The Informer* (Arthur Robison, 1929), welcomed the arrival of continental experts.[94]

The accomplished skills of German émigrés, which had implications for their incomes, explain why almost none of the émigrés participated in the making of so-called quota quickies, films that were solely produced to meet quota requirements. On account of budgets as low as £4,000–6,000,[95] the labour of German-speaking émigrés was simply too expensive. As a result émigrés predominantly contributed to big-budget prestige films. Accordingly it was almost exclusively the major British production companies like Gaumont-British, Gainsborough and BIP that could afford to hire them and were willing to do so.

Combined with other measures, the employment strategy to recruit foreign talent proved very successful. Owing to the assimilative powers of British cinema at that time, German-speaking film workers contributed to the economic success of films by major British production firms despite the significantly high costs of films such as Walter Forde's *Rome Express* (1932). Produced with participation of Günther Krampf as cinematographer and starring Conrad Veidt, the film attracted an audience of 11 million.[96] *B.W. Cinema Quarterly*, which welcomed the commitment of Gaumont-British to produce quality films, attributed the box-office success of *Rome Express* primarily to its high production values. Günther Krampf's skilful cinematography is explicitly highlighted as one of the strengths of a technically sound and entertaining film.[97] The commercial success of films like *Rome Express* underlines the fact that British pictures at the time were able to attract the cinema-going public. In particular large-budget British films of the time with significant émigré participation therefore help to explain why the exhibitors' quota was exceeded from 1932 onwards, indicating that cinemas around the country were voluntarily showing many more films than the 1927 Cinematograph Films Act required of them.[98]

The employment records of early German-speaking émigrés show that they were given permanent senior posts within studios – against the grain of the usual terms of employment. This was done not least because they were seen as vital for the development of the studios and for the training of future staff. Michael Balcon, who had links with UFA and much admired German film practices, later notes that at Shepherd's Bush, which may well be seen as exemplary for apprenticeship training in other studios, '[w]e also started training schemes at a local technical school and many of the first-class British technicians received their early instruction under the supervision of the men we had brought in from the Continent'.[99]

Besides the aforementioned Oscar Werndorff, who became the head of the costume and set design department at the Gainsborough studios in Islington, two other examples are Alfred Junge and Mutz Greenbaum, who were both important for the development of the British cinema. As supervising art director at the Lime Grove studios at Shepherd's Bush, Junge trained a whole generation of British workers, thereby guaranteeing high production standards in the years to come. Arguably the most prominent of his apprentices was Michael Relph; having started as Alfred Junge's assistant, he became one of the predominant British film architects of the 1940s and 1950s while much of his work bore great resemblance to the designs of his teacher.[100] One of the characteristics of Junge's work was an exact professionalism that gained him respect but was also responsible for a certain coldness that marked his relationships at work. Powell later recalls in his memoirs that 'Alfred was a Prussian, a great disciplinarian as well as a great organiser. He hadn't a second to waste. . . .'[101] While Powell's statement can be read as a slight disapproval of Junge's meticulous work ethic and methods, his organisational talent was admired all the more. Writing for *Kinematograph Weekly* in 1932, the Hollywood art director Paul Holmes noted the major changes and improvements that came with Junge and his fellow German-speaking filmmakers who were working in the art departments of British studios:

> A valuable advance in realism has been attained [in Britain] through the closer co-operation of the director and the cameraman with the art director. . . . German producers, ever in the forefront where scenery is concerned, have always insisted on the closest attention to building of sets which are intended to help the camera to secure the utmost realism. . . . The German studios have always realised that large sums of money and a great deal of time can be saved if the director, camera staff and art director work in the closest harmony.[102]

Greenbaum's role was equally important. Like many of his compatriots the camera expert first worked at Elstree before he joined Gaumont-British. Following the same employment strategy as with Junge, Michael Balcon appointed him as director of photography at their Lime Grove studios at Shepherd's Bush where he shot many lavish large-scale pictures before the closure of the studio in the late 1930s, such as *Chu-Chin Chow* (Walter Forde, 1934) and *Tudor Rose* (Robert Stevenson, 1936). His job description as 'director of photography' is as significant as Junge's as 'art director'. While cameramen and designers in 1920s England were still widely perceived as 'camera operators' and various decorating craftsmen (joiners, painters, etc.), their German and Austrian counterparts were called 'art director' and 'director of cinematography' because they were seen as creative artists managing a team of film staff. For Gaumont-British, Greenbaum and Junge stood for an idea according to which the cinematographer and the art director on the one hand played a major creative role in the filmmaking process and on the other incorporated the idea of a German/Austrian-style apprenticeship scheme. So it can be partially explained that they were given a long-term contracts as they were regarded vital for the future artistic development of films made by Gaumont-British and for the training of prospective staff.

Internationalism and the 'unpleasant emotional appeal': Cosmopolitan émigré films and their reception in Britain

In their endeavour to produce transnational films, European film companies toned down national characteristics in favour of a more universal and spectacular appeal. In 1928, German producer Erich Pommer defined some of the directives he thought necessary to make internationally successful European movies:

> In the same measure as one finds subjects, motives and happenings which are of a typically local character, so may one encounter thoughts and events which will equally impress the feeling and thinking of all nations and countries. Only if a picture complies with this condition can it be properly called an 'international film'. . . .
>
> Such [international] productions always have a simple story of universal appeal. . . . The splendour in such production is not merely created for decoration – it is its outstanding purpose. So, quite naturally, the splendour is always in the foreground and suppresses the human element. But splendour means show and a show is always and everywhere easy to understand.[103]

The implications of Pommer's remarks and their implementation on various levels were far-reaching and fundamental. 'Film Europe', which was launched as a means to ward off Hollywood's market supremacy by fostering pan-European distribution channels and co-operation on multi-ple levels, soon became more than a commercial enterprise. It acquired a significant cultural dimension by seeking to transcend national boundaries. Andrew Higson and Richard Maltby therefore emphasise that the his-tory of pan-European co-operation had both an economic and a cultural dimension in that it was born out of pragmatic notions of trade collabora-tion but soon developed into a cultural project that embedded ideas of internationalism.[104] As a result, the network of European co-operation not only had a major influence on the organisation of labour but also funda-mentally changed the visuals of films – often by adding a cosmopolitan feel to national cinemas. Such fundamental changes can be observed in the storylines of individual films, the use of innovative camera techniques, the elements of mise-en-scène and performance – especially in the film's display of exoticism combined with scenes of a sexual nature. Whilst the films were to be released throughout Europe, the approach was not to offer global films that conceal their foreignness. Although producers strove to ensure that the films themselves as well as their marketing and distribution would tally with audience expectations in the respective markets, the films maintained many a foreign and exotic element as a means of product differ-entiation. As Higson argues, the films were born less out of 'an international spirit or a European sensibility, and more [of] a fascination with cultural difference, a voyeuristic fascination with an exotic other'.[105]

The transformation of British films as a consequence of increasing pan-European co-operation and of the many émigrés who worked in Britain from the late 1920s onwards was immediately recognised by critics. Among other things they explicitly pointed to the technical excellence of foreign personnel in the fields of cinematography and art direction. British reviewers were particularly impressed by the way film personnel who had previously worked for major German or Austrian studios was commonly combining technical perfection with lavishly decorated sets that comprised elements of grandeur and otherness. In an otherwise negative review *The Daily Mail*, for instance, eulogised Werner Brandes' camerawork and Alfred Junge's set design when it described Dupont's film *Moulin Rouge* as 'sumptuously mounted and exquisitely photographed' and another review in *The Daily News and Westminster Gazette* called it 'the most glittering thing that has came out of an English studio', noting that the film's car chase in particular stands for 'a triumph of suggestive and spectacular achievement' while the *Daily Mirror* suggest that it could well be 'the greatest film yet produced by a British company'.[106] In a similar way, the review editor for *Kinematograph Weekly*, Lionel Collier, regarded another of Dupont's motion pictures, *Piccadilly*, – again made in collaboration with Brandes and Junge – a visual masterpiece by claiming that 'pictorially no British picture has ever been better'.[107] Full of admiration for Junge's work in particular, Paul Rotha even claimed that the set design for *Piccadilly* is 'the only creative work being executed in this country' and that it 'is amongst the best yet done in any studio'.[108]

However, films with participation of German-speaking personnel did not only differ from most other British productions of the time in terms of mobile camerawork and meticulously constructed sets. A further notable feature of major productions including *Rome Express*, *Moulin Rouge*, *Road to Happiness* and *Pavement Butterfly*, the English version of *Großstadtschmetterling*, was that they were commonly set on foreign soil. As can be seen in the many multi-language films like *City of Song* that were commonly defined by multiculturalism and notions of nostalgia, German-speaking filmmakers often chose a Viennese, Parisian or Mediterranean setting in an endeavour to combine elements of scenic realism with romanticised depictions of tourist attractions. At a time when (overseas) travel was still difficult and simply not affordable for the vast majority of Britons and other Europeans, the films therefore offered an escape from the everyday by taking the audience on trips to cosmopolitan places. On a deeper level, the films refrain from depicting monolithic national identities and unchanging places. Instead, the narratives frequently focus on margins, boundaries and cosmopolitan meeting places all representing hybrid, polyglot and multivalent cultural sites.

In fact, as many of the plots include extensive transnational journeys, the settings of these films often correspond stylistically and thematically with the émigré situation as cosmopolitan settings, foreignness and uprooted living conditions are recurring features of the narratives (see also the following chapters). Higson thus stresses that the 'internationalism of the films was not simply a question of personnel but was embodied too in the spectacular scale and the self-conscious exoticism of the films'.[109] Moreover, the international settings allowed German-speaking actors who generally spoke with a noticeable accent to play the roles of foreigners appearing in one of the numerous overseas settings of films.

The change in the style of these films was quickly referred to in the British trade press. *Kinematograph Weekly*, once again, noted that the set design of *Piccadilly* by Alfred Junge was excellent and wonderfully composed but appeared to create a continental atmosphere rather than the illusion of sites in London.[110] Where critics commented unfavourably upon the plots, which tended to have a somewhat slower pace than comparable American productions, the assessment of the exoticism that was a pivotal characteristic of British films made with the participation of German-speaking personnel was rather divided. Some reviews praised the international appeal of the films through exceptional camera work and set design while others regarded them as too continental. Writing for *The Picturegoer*, Lionel Collier even argues that *Moulin Rouge* was 'as un-English as a film could be'.[111] Others called it 'euphemistically British' (*Kinematograph Weekly*), 'the most un-British film ever made in Britain' (*Daily Express*) and a film that 'one would not suspect that it had any connection to this country' (*Daily Telegraph*).[112] Above all, however, British critics were particularly irritated by the film's eroticism, or, as it was formulated then, by the way in which scenes 'could only be described as unpleasant in their emotional appeal'.[113] In another article, again by Lionel Collier the review editor of *Kinematograph Weekly*, the sexual content of *Moulin Rouge*, which shows cancan girls dancing in Parisian entertainment revues, is once more criticised: '[Dupont has] introduced a sense of unpleasantness in his presentation of what is at base a "leg" show.'[114] In a similar way, others pointed out that some of the lavish scenes were so 'daring that they are lucky to have survived censorship'[115] and the *Daily Express* made the case that *Moulin Rouge* 'should please Continental audiences, who like this kind of erotic nonsense'.[116]

In contrast, continental reviews regretted that multinational productions seem to tone down scenes with sexual content. Published in 1929, a German critic for instance argues that the unconvincing prudery in *Großstadtschmetterling* (Richard Eichberg) that was released in Britain as *Pavement Butterfly* could have had English roots: 'The Eichberg team did not dare to let a happy white man share the same bed as the undressed body of a Mongolian woman. The erotic hypocrisy could have originated in an English boarding school for girls.'[117] One year later, in an ironic review of Richard Eichberg's *The Flame of Love*, which was released in Germany and France under the less romantic titles *Hai-Tang-Der Weg zur Schande* and *Hai-Tang-L'Amour maître des choses*, the journal *Film-Kurier* argues:

> It is interesting to see how well the producer Eichberg has understood the English mentality: eroticism without sex-appeal, exoticism without miscegenation; instead, tender melodies are played on the piano in a homely setting. Hai-Tang's lover is her brotherly friend, he watches her dancing, alluringly undressed, but apart from that – nothing happens between them. This is truly English.[118]

Such reviews illustrate an undeniable discrepancy between the UK and continental Europe regarding the display of sex and nudity in films. Writing about the problems of Arthur Robison, who came as a director from Germany to Britain in the late 1920s, Patrick F. Sheeran notes: 'From the time of Chaucer's domestication of adulterous French *amour courtis* into glad marital affection, the English have had a genius for taking the wider impulses of Continentals, lowering the voltage and making them more humanly tolerable.'[119]

However, this had less to do with 'the English mentality' itself as argued in the *Film-Kurier* review above, but was more accurately the result of restrictions imposed by the censors. Owing to strict content control, few films actually included scenes depicting sexuality other than by way of implicit remarks or veiled hints. Here, 'Film Europe' brought about some significant changes. Although it was still unthinkable to promote films such as *Piccadilly* using a poster with an image of the leading actress dancing topless – as in the film's Austrian release – many strong references to sexuality, nudity and eroticism can be spotted. Made as a European co-production by the Carr-Gloria-Dupont group, BIP and the German Emelka, Dupont's *Moulin Rouge*, for instance, tells the story of a *ménage à trois* involving an engaged couple and the fiancée's mother who is a revue show star. Apart from the provocative story itself, the film features numerous dancing show-girls in revealing dresses. Confirming Laura Mulvey's notion of how narrative cinema positions the viewer to take the 'male gaze',[120] the subjective point of view recreates the perspective of the show's audience and thereby offers glimpses underneath the dancers' dresses. The voyeuristic camera also plays a key part in the first scene that introduces Parysin, played by the Russian-born star Olga Tschechowa (sometimes spelled Chekhova in Britain) who had appeared in German films since 1920. The first image of her is a medium shot of her legs with a bare-breasted statue in the background that forms the centre of the scene when Tschechowa dances out of the frame. Moreover, her sexual attributes also play a key role in a scene in which the daughter helps Parysin to get dressed. Whilst the mother insists that she should not worry because her dress 'isn't so revealing and so short' and that tonight she will 'play the mother-in-law', her provocative outfit neither fails to attract the diegetic fiancée nor the audience of the film.

Tschechowa's role as seductive *femme fatale* was by no means the exception but rather exemplary for many parts played by actresses who came to Britain via Berlin. This holds especially true for the Polish-born Pola Negri, Lya De Putti and the Chinese-American Anna May Wong, all of whom were well-known actresses in Austria and Germany before coming to London. Once in Britain, they were cast as exotic and erotic vixens – particularly in storylines set in a French environment. Negri, for instance, stars as a French prostitute who marries an English lighthouse guard in the 1929 British film *The Woman He Scorned* by Austrian–Hungarian director Paul Czinner. The film is partly set in a small amusement precinct of a fishing village and displays the open promiscuity of the fallen women who frequent the bars.

Moreover, the female stars coming to London from Berlin imported a new type of woman to British films. In the 1920s, American 'flappers', who perhaps found their most prominent fictional representation in the character of Jordan Baker in Fitzgerald's popular novel *The Great Gatsby* (1925), influenced many women in the European capitals. Proclaiming a new kind of female, Victor Margueritte published his disputed book *La Garçonne* (1922) in France and in Berlin, Marlene Dietrich's blunt performances in male outfits made her the model for Weimar's *neue Frau*. Representing a modern female as emancipated, independent, seductive and sexually liberated, this New German Woman challenged many traditional gender roles.[121] Featuring many actresses from Berlin in roles of ardent lovers and showgirls, British films such as *The Informer, Moulin Rouge* or *Piccadilly* do not conform to the conventional social definitions of women as devoted wives and mothers usually associated with filmic representations in the melodramas of the time. The films repeatedly break the taboo about female sexuality while consciously using their seductive powers for their own purposes. However intriguing these new female roles might be, the fact that the characters all fail in the end once again confirms the status quo. Yet, rather than portraying women according to the paradigm of 'the whore' and 'the saint', the films allow for nuanced descriptions. In this regard, several British films by German-speaking filmmakers anticipate the role of women in the *film noir*.[122] Although they can be criticised for violating many cultural conventions, the narratives suggest a great sympathy for the stricken female leads.

When the director Arthur Robison came to Britain in the late 1920s to turn the Irish novel *The Informer* (1925) by Liam O'Flaherty into a movie, he initially sought to contract two stars of Weimar Cinema as leads: Emil Jannings and Lya de Putti. Robison, who was born in Chicago of German-American-Jewish parentage and became a well-respected filmmaker in the Weimar Cinema after the First World War, wanted to work with artists he knew from past experience. Although he failed to contract Emil Jannings, he was able to win de Putti for his project alongside the German cinematographers Theodor Sparkuhl and Werner Brandes. The Hungarian-born de Putti seemed ideally to fulfil the requirements of the original story. Born in Hungary, her early film roles fostered her image as the Weimar vamp incarnate. Acting in line with her star image, her performance as Katie in *The Informer* deliberately utilises her seductive powers to help her lover Gypo (Lars Hanson).

Besides Negri, de Putti and Tschechowa, the American-Chinese leading actress of *Piccadilly*, Anna May Wong, ideally personified what many multinational European productions of the period aimed at: the combination of the modern woman with an exotic look.[123] Whilst her extraordinary performance as Shosho, an Asian scullery maid who becomes the star act in a fashionable City nightclub where she finds herself in the middle of a tragic story of love intrigues and seduction, helped the film to receive an overall positive echo in the press,[124] some reviews were nevertheless concerned about its display of sexuality. The journal *Close-up* expressed a great dislike for the actress who dances in an erotic manner throughout a film which generally contains 'more close-ups of legs, knees and the like than almost any other film'.[125] However, despite the small number of negative reviews, the general rule that 'sex sells' regardless of borders or historical contexts helps to explain why producers relied heavily on its appeal in films and publicity pictures of the era. In fact, it was especially the mixture of exoticism and eroticism that was a fad of the time. Bergfelder, for instance, argues that Wong's career bears many striking parallels to her black contemporary Josephine Baker, who was able to establish herself as a *niche* star in the French film industry after her initial fame as cabaret performer.[126] In both cases the erotic feminine appeal was intrinsically associated with the fascination of mysterious otherness. Wong's ethnic eclecticism, Bergfelder continues, appropriated the attempt of Film Europe to take up 'Hollywood's aesthetic of stylising the exotic into a global consumer product'.[127] The same also applies, arguably to a lesser degree, to Olga Tschechowa, Lya de Putti and Pola Negri. By playing on exoticism, sexuality and cultural internationality, the ambivalent atmosphere of sets that include nightclubs, revue shows or bars formed what can be dubbed as the 'continental British film'.

Above and beyond the performance of German-speaking female actresses, a German influence is particularly obvious in the constant use of low-key and chiaroscuro lighting and in the opulent, exotic and meticulously crafted sets. What is more, many of the elements of mise-en-scène, some of which are explicitly mentioned in Barbara Steinbauer-Grötsch's work on the influence of German exiles on the American *film noir*, were typical of Weimar iconography.[128] In this regard, films such as *Piccadilly* and *The Informer* foreshadow key characteristics of American *film noir*. Examples here are the recurring use of mirrors, transparent materials and shadows that create an atmosphere of uncertainty and ambivalence. One important Weimar-inspired feature, as Patrick F. Sheeran argues with regard to *The Informer*, is the 'pervasive sense of surveillance, a sense that everybody is being watched. (Two years on, Fritz Lang's *M* (1931) would give the theme its classic treatment.)'.[129] In a similar way, the attempt of the Chinese scullery maid to gain back her job by offering her body to the white British nightclub owner in *Piccadilly* does not remain unnoticed as an employee observes the two going to the manager's bureau well after office hours. In another scene, a policeman's gaze through the window of a bar symbolises the great degree of close official surveillance.

Other influences include the use of a mobile camera, an important narrative device in German films such as Friedrich Wilhelm Murnau's critically acclaimed *Der letzte Mann* (The Last Laugh, 1924),[130] throughout the film. Often in the form of point-of-view shots, the use of this voyeuristic 'unchained camera' bears great resemblance to that in Dupont's early world success *Varieté*. Accordingly, John Gillett records in a programme leaflet for a screening of *Piccadilly* in 1982 that the film 'looks more German than British. Dupont turned Bernett's rather novelettish story . . . into an exotic, nightmarish affair whose visual panache places it squarely in the Sternberg/ Pabst bracket'.[131]

Using chief characteristics of Weimar cinema and earlier British-Austrian co-productions such as *The Golden Butterfly* (Michael Curtiz, Austria/ Germany 1926), Dupont's *Piccadilly* offers a grandiloquent visual imagery that deems elements of mise-en-scène to be more than merely decorative. By depicting the world behind the glitzy facades of the show business, the film draws a rather sinister picture of multi-cultural London. The gloomy environment also serves as an appropriate backdrop for dealing with issues such as race and inter-racial relationships – topics that were widely regarded as taboo in 1920s British culture. The British Board of Film Censors (BBFC), for instance, generally forbade storylines dealing with miscegenation. Yet, being a truly international film with a multi-national cast, *Piccadilly* repeatedly alludes to mixed-race relationships. Apart from the affairs and love adventures of the leading female protagonist (Anna May Wong), the movie features a scene in which a white woman has to leave a club because she danced with a black man.

Although 'continental British' films such as *The Informer*, *Piccadilly* and *Moulin Rouge* were oddities within the context of British cinema, they became role models for other films as they featured many of the elements that can thereafter constantly be found in British cinema – not least because of the increasing number of German-speaking film personnel. Among other things they comprise innovative camera techniques, inspired elements of mise-en-scène that formed an important part of the plot, diasporic settings, displaced characters, racial conflict and depictions of sexuality. Apart from the constant use of shadows, mirrors or other recurring elements of expressionist films, they more importantly introduced a universal uncertainty, ambiguity and multi-national diversity that were chief characteristics of Weimar Cinema. Paul Rotha's comment that 'Arthur Robison, Dupont and Henrik Galeen, three directors of talent, have had no effect on the Elstree school' and that '[f]oreign directors failed to discover in Britain the collectivism and teamwork so vital to film production [and that] they were unable to understand our ideas of picture-sense' may well be questioned.[132] Rather than a lack of teamwork, the evident 'continentalism' of films such as *The Informer*, *Moulin Rouge* or *Piccadilly* – all of which looked similar to films produced in the Weimar cinema – resulted from the intention to mount big-budget films able to penetrate global markets rather than the failure of directors to assimilate to British modes of production. Patrick F. Sheeran thus suggests that 'perhaps the best way to approach [a film like] Robison's *Informer* is to view it not as a British . . . film at all, but as a late outrider of Weimar expressionism foundering in the "porridge factory" of Elstree'.[133]

While Rotha denies an influence of directors in the late 1920s, he nevertheless had acknowledged the fact that German-speaking émigrés such as art director Alfred Junge had an impact. Even if it might be true that British and German traditions – however these may be defined – did perhaps not initially mingle, they increasingly did so in the years to come; in particular after the mass purge of the German film industry after 1933 when the British cinema benefited from the intensifying cross-cultural fertilisation. Arguably it was the foreigners who ultimately made possible the consolidation of the film industry, which had begun with the import of foreign film personnel and the modernisation of studios in the late 1920s and culminated in the sophistication of many films made in the 1930s and 1940s. In fact, given the importance of the German-speaking film professionals who worked in Britain as early as the 1920s, the large-scale emigration caused by the Nazis only intensified the already existing processes of interaction.

Notes

1 See Sarah Street, 'British Film and the National Interest, 1927–39', in *The British Cinema Book*, edited by Robert Murphy, 2nd edn (London: BFI, 2003), pp. 20–37 (p. 28).

2 On the problems of the industry see, for instance, Michael Chanan, 'The Emergence of an Industry', in *British Cinema History*, edited by James Curran and Vincent Porter (London: Weidenfeld and Nicolson, 1983), pp. 39–58; and John Hawkridge, 'British Cinema from Hepworth to Hitchcock', in *The Oxford History of World Cinema*, edited by Geoffrey Nowell-Smith (Oxford and New York: Oxford University Press, 1996), pp. 130–6 (pp. 132–6).

3 See Jon Burrows, 'Big Studio Production in the Pre-quota Years', in *The British Cinema Book*, edited by Robert Murphy, 2nd edn (London: BFI, 2001), pp. 20–7 (p. 25). For press reports on the crisis see, for instance, *Kinematograph Weekly*, 13 November 1924, p. 66 and 'British Film "Slump" – New Move Against U.S. Invasion – European Co-operation', *Daily Mail*, 19 November 1924, p. 7.

4 The term refers to inexpensive British films commonly financed by American renters to meet the required numbers of domestic British films without affecting the number of American films they handled.

5 See Street, 'British Film and the National Interest, 1927–39', p. 29.

6 Bergfelder, 'The Production Designer and the *Gesamtkunstwerk*', p. 21. See also Thomas Elsaesser, 'Heavy Traffic: Perspektive Hollywood: Emigranten

oder Vagabunden?', in *London Calling: Deutsche im britischen Film der dreißiger Jahre*, edited by Jörg Schöning (Munich: text+kritik, 1993), pp. 21–41.

7 See, for instance, Kevin Gough-Yates, 'The British Feature Film as a European Concern: Britain and the Emigré Filmmaker, 1933–45', in *Theatre and Film in Exile: German Artists in Britain, 1933–1945*, edited by Günther Berghaus (Oxford and New York: Berg, 1989), pp. 135–66; and Hilchenbach, pp. 57–62.

8 Tom Ryall, 'A British Studio System: The Associated British Picture Corporation and the Gaumont-British Picture Corporation in the 1930s', in *The British Cinema Book*, edited by Robert Murphy, 2nd edn (London: BFI, 2001), pp. 35–41 (p. 37).

9 John Sedgwick, 'The Market for Feature Films in Britain, 1934: a viable national cinema', *Historical Journal of Film, Radio and Television*, 14.1 (1994), 15–36 (pp. 28–9).

10 See Andrew Higson, 'FILM-EUROPA: Kulturpolitik und industrielle Praxis', in *Hallo? Berlin? Ici Paris!*, edited by Sibylle M. Sturm and Arthur Wohlgemuth (Munich: text+kritik, 1996), pp. 63–76.

11 *Film-Kurier*, 7 August 1928. Cited in Higson, 'FILM-EUROPA: Kulturpolitik und industrielle Praxis', p. 63. If not stated otherwise translations are by the author.

12 *Bioscope*, 25 October 1923. Cited in Higson, 'FILM-EUROPA: Kulturpolitik und industrielle Praxis', p. 65.

13 See Jeanpaul Goergen, 'Entente und Stabilisierung: Deutsch-französische Filmkontakte 1925–1933', in *Hallo? Berlin? Ici Paris!*, edited by Sibylle M. Sturm and Arthur Wohlgemuth (Munich: text+kritik, 1996), pp. 51–62 (p. 58).

14 See Andrew Higson, 'Polyglot Films for an International Market: E.A. Dupont, the British Film Industry, and the Idea of a European Cinema, 1926–1930', in *'Film Europe' and 'Film America': Cinema, Commerce and Cultural Exchange 1920–1939*, edited by Andrew Higson and Richard Maltby (Exeter: Exeter UP, 1999), pp. 274–301 (p. 286).

15 See Low, *Film Making in 1930s Britain*, p. 35.

16 See Gledhill; and Low, *The History of the British Film 1918–29*.

17 For general information on multi-language versions see Christoph Wahl, 'Das Sprechen der Filme: Über verbale Sprache im Spielfilm. Versionsfilme und andere Sprachübertragungsmethoden – Tonfilm und Standardisierung – Die Diskussion um den Sprechfilm – Der polyglotte Film – Nationaler Film und internationales Kino' (unpublished doctoral thesis, Ruhr University, Bochum, Germany, 2003).

18 See Higson, 'Polyglot Films for an International Market', p. 286.

19 Cited in Gough-Yates, 'The European Filmmaker in Exile in Britain, 1933–1945', p. 93.

20 See Dudley Andrew, 'Sound in France: The Origins of a Native School', in *Rediscovering French Film*, edited by Mary Lea Bandy (New York: Museum of Modern Film, 1983), pp. 57–65; and Alastair Phillips *City of Darkness, City of Light: Émigré Filmmakers in Paris 1929–1939* (Amsterdam: Amsterdam UP, 2004), especially pp. 29–33.

21 See Goergen, p. 60.
22 See Sabine Hake, *German National Cinema* (London and New York: Routledge, 2002), p. 52.
23 See Higson, 'Polyglot Films for an International Market', p. 289.
24 See ibid., p. 290.
25 Erich Pommer, 'The International Talking Film', *Universal Filmlexikon 1932: Europa*, edited by Frank Arnau, 2 vols (Berlin: Universal Filmlexikon, 1932), pp. 13–16 (pp. 14–15), reprinted in *'Film Europe' and 'Film America': Cinema, Commerce and Cultural Exchange 1920–1939*, edited by Andrew Higson and Richard Maltby, Exeter Studies in Film History (Exeter: Exeter University Press, 1999), pp. 394–96.
26 See Bergfelder, 'The Production Designer and the *Gesamtkunstwerk*', p. 21.
27 Cited in *London Calling: Deutsche im britischen Film der dreißiger Jahre*, edited by Jörg Schöning (Munich: text+kritik, 1993) p. 6.
28 See Michael Balcon, *Michael Balcon Presents . . . a Lifetime of Films* (London: Hutchison, 1969), p. 62.
29 'German Talkie Classic: Eric Charell's "Congress Dances" Revives past Glories of Vienna – Success of London Girl', *Daily Mirror*, 26 November 1931, film review, p. 7.
30 See Andrew Higson, '"A Film League of Nations": Gainsborough, Gaumont-British and "Film Europe"', in *Gainsborough Pictures*, edited by Pam Cook, Rethinking British Cinema Series (London and Washington, DC: Cassell, 1997), pp. 60–79 (p. 72).
31 Lawrence Napper, 'Geza von Bolvary, Arnold Ripley and "Film Europe"', in *Destination London*, pp. 36–46.
32 *Film-Kurier*, 7 June 1930, repr. in *London Calling*, pp. 7–9 (p. 7). Translated by Ronald Walker.
33 See Tim Bergfelder, 'Negotiating Exoticism: Hollywood, Film Europe and the Cultural Reception of Anna May Wong', in *'Film Europe' and 'Film America': Cinema, Commerce and Cultural Exchange 1920–1939*, edited by Andrew Higson and Richard Maltby, Exeter Studies in Film History (Exeter: Exeter University Press, 1999), pp. 302–24 (p. 311).
34 Lionel Collier, 'Wanted! – A British Spirit', *Picturegoer*, September 1928, pp. 22–3 (p. 22).
35 'Piccadilly', *Close-Up*, July 1929, film review, pp. 45–7 (pp. 45–6).
36 See John K. Newnham, 'Let Them All Come', *Picturegoer Weekly*, 7 September 1931, pp. 7–8.
37 See ibid., p. 7.
38 Michael Balcon to Isidore Osterer, 13 May 1931. BFI Michael Balcon Collection.
39 On the amalgamation of the German company Orplid and Messtro with British and Foreign Films see Horst Claus, 'Commerce, Culture, Continuity: Hans Steinhoff's "Mittelfilm" Production of Stefan Zweig's *Angst* (1928)', *German Life and Letters*, 58.2 (April 2003), 117–31 (pp. 119–22).
40 See Street, 'British Film and the National Interest, 1927–39', pp. 29–30.

41 See Robert Murphy, 'The Coming of Sound to the Cinema in Britain', *Historical Journal of Film, Radio and Television*, 4.2 (March 1984), 143–60. On the attempts of the Tobis Klangfilm conglomerate to compete with the American sound recording systems see *Tonfilmfrieden/ Tonfilmkrieg: Die Geschichte der Tobis vom Technik-Syndikat zum Staatskonzern*, edited by Jan Distelmeyer (Munich: text+kritik, 2003).

42 See Geoff Brown, 'Niederlage in Wembley: Tobis Klangfilm in England', in *Tonfilmfrieden/Tonfilmkrieg: Die Geschichte der Tobis vom Technik-Syndikat zum Staatskonzern*, edited by Jan Distelmeyer (Munich: text+kritik, 2003), pp. 65–72 (p. 67).

43 See ibid., p. 67.

44 On lists of cast and credits, see *Die Tobis 1928–1945: Eine kommentierte Filmografie*, edited by Hans-Michael Bock, Wiebke Annkatrin Mosel and Ingrun Spazier (Munich: text+kritik, 2003), pp. 58–62 and p. 72. The German version of *City of Song* was released as *Die singende Stadt*.

45 'New Films in London: "City of Song"', *The Times*, 23 February 1931, film review, p. 10.

46 *Lichtbild-Bühne*, 30 October 1930, reprinted in *Alliierte für den Film: Arnold Pressburger, Gregor Rabinowitsch und die Cine-Allianz*, conference booklet (Hamburg: Cinegraph, 2003), pp. 25–6. Translated by Ronald Walker.

47 The German version was released as *Das Lied einer Nacht*, the French version as *La chanson d'une nuit*.

48 See Klaus Kreimeier, *The UFA Story: A History of Germany's Greatest Film Company, 1918–1945* (Berkeley/Los Angeles/London: California University Press, 1999), pp. 121–30; Hans-Michael Bock and Michael Töteberg, 'A History of UFA', in *The German Cinema Book*, edited by Tim Bergfelder, Erica Carter and Deniz Göktürk (London: BFI, 2002), pp. 129–38 (pp. 132–3).

49 On the UFA crisis see Bock and Töteberg, pp. 132–3.

50 Claus, p. 120.

51 See Higson, 'Polyglot Films for an International Market', p. 287.

52 See Joseph Garncarz, 'Die Bedrohte Internationalität des Films: Fremdsprachige Versionen deutscher Tonfilme', in *Hallo? Berlin? Ici Paris!*, edited by Sibylle M. Sturm and Arthur Wohlgemuth (Munich: text+kritik, 1996), pp. 127–40.

53 See Low, *The History of the British Film 1918–29*, p. 159.

54 See Gough-Yates, 'The European Filmmaker in Exile in Britain, 1933–1945', p. iii.

55 See Bergfelder, 'The Production Designer and the *Gesamtkunstwerk*', p. 22.

56 Ibid., p. 22.

57 See Bergfelder, 'The Production Designer and the *Gesamtkunstwerk*', pp. 23–4.

58 On Brandes, see Kelly Robinson, 'Flamboyant Realism: Werner Brandes and British International Pictures in the Late 1920s', in *Destination London*, pp. 62–77.

59 On the relationship between the German and the American film industry

see Thomas J. Saunders, *Hollywood in Berlin: American Cinema and Weimar Germany*, Weimar and Now: German Cultural Criticism, 6 (Berkeley, Los Angeles and London: California University Press, 1994).

60 *Der Film*, 7 March 1926, p. 24 (translated by Peter Krämer and Nick Riddle). Cited in Higson, 'Polyglot Films for an International Market: E. A. Dupont, the British Film Industry and the Idea of a European Cinema, 1926–1930', p. 274.

61 E. A. Dupont and Fritz Podehl, *Wie ein Film geschrieben wird und wie man ihn verwertet* (Berlin: Kühn, 1919).

62 See Evelyn Hampicke and Jürgen Bretschneider, 'Biografie', in *Ewald André Dupont: Autor und Regisseur*, edited by Jürgen Bretschneider (Munich: text+kritik, 1992), pp. 111–26 (pp. 116–18).

63 Tim Bergfelder, 'Life is a Variety Theatre: E.A. Dupont's Career in German and British Cinema', in *Destination London*, pp. 24–35.

64 *Kinematograph Weekly*, 18 August 1927, p. 34–5 (p. 34).

65 'British Studios To-Day', *Bioscope*, 23 December 1926, p. 27.

66 See Hampicke and Bretschneider, p. 120.

67 See *Bioscope*, 22 March 1928. Cited in Hampicke and Bretschneider, p. 120.

68 *Berliner Zeitung am Mittag*, 20 March 1928. Cited in Hampicke and Bretschneider, p. 120. Translated by Ronald Walker.

69 See Higson, 'Polyglot Films for an International Market', p. 278.

70 On the opulent sets see Hampicke and Bretschneider, p. 121.

71 With the cameraman Brandes he had previously worked in 1925 on the Berlin-based Terra Film production *Der Demütige und die Sängerin*.

72 Programme booklet for the *Moulin Rouge* premiere at the Tivoli Theatre, 1928 (BFI Library). Cited in Higson, 'Polyglot Films for an International Market', p. 280.

73 See Bergfelder, 'The Production Designer and the *Gesamtkunstwerk*', p. 24.

74 See Robinson, p. 64.

75 Higson, 'Polyglot Films for an International Market', p. 275.

76 See Ryall, p. 39.

77 See Hampicke and Bretschneider, p. 124.

78 Among others, the chairman of United Artists and outspoken critic of the film industry, Joseph Schenck, excoriated British casts in 1925: 'You have no personalities to put on the screen. The stage actors and actresses are no good on the screen.' 'Pertinent and Otherwise', *The Bioscope*, 8 January 1925, pp. 54–5 (p. 54).

79 Michael Balcon to Isidore Osterer, 13 May 1931. BFI Michael Balcon Collection.

80 Newnham, p. 7.

81 Bergfelder, 'The Production Designer and the *Gesamtkunstwerk*', p. 23.

82 See Jones, p. 60.

83 *Kinematograph Weekly*, 3. January 1929. Cited in Gough-Yates, 'The European Filmmaker in Exile in Britain, 1933–1945', pp. 168–9.

84 See Bergfelder, 'The Production Designer and the *Gesamtkunstwerk*', p. 24.
85 Cited in Helbig, p. 13.
86 Robert Stevenson, 'A Year in German Studios', *Proceedings of the British Kinematograph Society*, 20 (1934), 3–12. See Chris Wahl, 'Inside the Robots' Castle: UFA's English-language Versions in Early 1930s', in Destination London, pp. 47–61.
87 *Film-Kurier*, 8 January 1932, reprinted in *London Calling*, pp. 9–11 (p. 10). Translated by Ronald Walker.
88 See Bergfelder, 'The Production Designer and the *Gesamtkunstwerk*', p. 24.
89 See ibid., p. 25.
90 Peter Krämer, 'Hollywood in Germany/Germany in Hollywood', in *The German Cinema Book*, edited by Tim Bergfelder, Erica Carter and Deniz Göktürk (London: BFI, 2002), pp. 227–37 (pp. 230–1).
91 See *The BFI Companion to German Cinema*, edited by Thomas Elsaesser with Michael Wedel, (London: BFI, 1999), p. 218. For early uses of the 'Schüfftan process' in England see *Kinematograph Weekly*, 18 August 1927, p. 34.
92 Michael Powell in an interview with Kevin Gough-Yates on 22 September 1970, in Kevin Gough-Yates, *Michael Powell in Collaboration with Emeric Pressburger* (London: BFI, 1971), unpaginated.
93 Paul Rotha, *The Film Till Now: A Survey of the Cinema* (London: Jonathan Cape, 1930), p. 208.
94 See Robinson, p. 64.
95 See Helbig, p. 13.
96 See Low, *Filmmaking in 1930s Britain*, p. 35.
97 See B. W. *Cinema Quarterly*, Winter 1932. Reproduced in *London Calling*, pp. 153–4.
98 See Ryall, p. 39.
99 Balcon, p. 58.
100 See ibid., p. 58.
101 Powell, *A Life in Movies*, p. 228.
102 *Kinematograph Weekly*, 11 February 1932, p. 33.
103 *Kinematograph Weekly*, 8 October 1928, p. 41.
104 See Andrew Higson and Richard Maltby, '"Film Europe" and "Film America": An Introduction', in *'Film Europe' and 'Film America': Cinema, Commerce and Cultural Exchange 1920–1939*, edited by Andrew Higson and Richard Maltby, Exeter Studies in Film History (Exeter: Exeter University Press, 1999), pp. 1–31 (p. 17).
105 Andrew Higson, 'Transnational Developments in European Cinema in the 1920s', *Transnational Cinemas*, 1.1 (2010), 69–82 (p. 79).
106 '"Moulin Rouge" Miss Tschechowa's Acting Saves Poor Film', *Daily Mail*, 23 March 1928, film review, p. 8, *Daily News and Westminster Gazette*, 23 March 1928, p. 7, and Reginald J. Whitley, 'The Film World Reviewed – Latest Gossip about Pictures and Personalities: "Moulin Rouge" at the Tivoli', *Daily Mirror*, 19 March 1928, film review, p. 4.
107 *Kinematograph Weekly*, 7 February 1929, pp. 56–7.

108 *Film Weekly*, 12 November 1928. Reprinted in Rotha, pp. 40–3 (p. 43).
109 Higson, 'Polyglot Films for and International Market', p. 280.
110 *Kinematograph Weekly*, 7 February 1929, p. 57.
111 Collier, 'Wanted! – A British Spirit', p. 23.
112 *Kinematograph Weekly*, 29 March 1928, p. 49, 'Eight Minutes of Super Thrill: New Film Saved from Boredom', *Daily Express*, 23 March 1928, p. 11 and 'New British Film: *Moulin Rouge* at the Tivoli', *Daily Telegraph*, 23 March 1928, p. 8.
113 'New British Film: *Moulin Rouge* at the Tivoli', p. 8.
114 *Kinematograph Weekly*, 29 March 1928, p. 49.
115 Contemporary review of *Moulin Rouge* (name and date of paper unspecified, press clipping, BFI Library).
116 'Eight Minutes of Super Thrill: New Film Saved from Boredom', p. 11.
117 *Film-Kurier*, 11 April 1929. Cited in Bergfelder, 'Negotiating Exoticism', p. 311.
118 *Film-Kurier*, 27 February 1930. Cited in Bergfelder, 'Negotiating Exoticism', p. 313.
119 Patrick F. Sheeran, *The Informer*, Ireland Into Film Series (Cork: Cork UP, 2002), p. 53.
120 See Laura Mulvey, 'Visual Pleasure and Narrative Cinema', *Screen*, 16.3 (1975), 6–18.
121 See Sheeran, pp. 54–5.
122 See *Women in Film Noir*, edited by E. Ann Kaplan (London: BFI, 1978).
123 On Anna May Wong's cultural reception see Bergfelder, 'Negotiating Exoticism', p. 313.
124 Official newspaper announcements cite reviews by the *Daily Express* ('A World-Beating Film'), *Daily Mail* ('A masterly and most enjoyable picture') and the *Daily Telegraph* ('E. A. Dupont has beaten all his past achievements'), see *Piccadilly* advertisement, *Daily Mirror*, 11 February 1929, p. 24. See also '"Piccadilly" Film', *Daily Mirror*, 1 February 1929, film review, p. 6.
125 'Piccadilly', *Close-Up*, July 1929, film review, pp. 45–7 (p. 46).
126 See Bergfelder, 'Negotiating Exoticism', p. 307. On the trajectory of Josephine Baker, see Nancy Nenno, 'Feminity, The Primitive and Modern Urban Space: Josephine Baker in Berlin', in *Women in the Metropolis: Gender and Modernity in Weimar Culture*, edited by Katharina von Ankum (Berkeley, Los Angeles and London: California University Press, 1997), pp. 145–62.
127 Bergfelder, 'Negotiating Exoticism', p. 307.
128 See Barbara Steinbauer-Grötsch, '"Two shadowy figures framed à la Siodmak ...": Der deutsche Stummfilm, die Filmexilanten und der amerikanische Film Noir', *FilmExil*, 6 (1995), 53–71; ibid., *Die Lange Nacht der Schatten: Film noir und Filmexil*, 2nd rev. edn (Berlin: Bertz, 2000); and Thomas Elsaesser, 'A German Ancestry to Film Noir? Film History and its Imaginery', *Iris* 21 (Spring 1996), 129–44.
129 Sheeran, p. 57.
130 Bock and Töteberg, p. 131.

131 John Gillett, programme leaflet 'Archive Treasures', Los Angeles International Film Exposition, March 16 – April 1, 1982 (press clipping, BFI Library).
132 Rotha, p. 229.
133 Sheeran, p. 51.

2 *Little Friend*, 1934. Courtesy of Deutsche Kinemathek, Berlin

3

Refugees from the Third Reich, 1933–1939

The year 1933 stands out as a decisive moment in cinema history. After no more than a few weeks in power, the National Socialist German Workers' Party (Nationalsozialistische Deutsche Arbeiterpartei, NSDAP) established the Reich Ministry of Enlightenment and Propaganda (Reichsministerium für Volksaufklärung und Propaganda, RMVP) under the leadership of Joseph Goebbels in order to regulate all aspects of cultural affairs through *Gleichschaltung* ('co-ordination' or 'forced integration'). The term refers to a National Socialist principle aimed at the synchronising of all German institutions in accordance with NSDAP policies. For the film industry this meant fundamental changes, as it implied the eradication of all political opponents and groups seen as racially inferior – above all German Jewry.[1] The developments in the German film business after the takeover by the NSDAP and its reconstruction of the industry alongside its political policies eventually caused the migration of some 2,000 film workers; about 20 to 30 per cent of the whole industry fled to neighbouring countries or the US. This heterogeneous group of political refugees is an exceptional one amongst all exiles insofar as virtually everyone who stood for the achievements of Weimar cinema sought refuge outside Germany. Internationally acclaimed exiles include Fritz Lang, Robert Wiene, Billy Wilder, Conrad Veidt, Eugen Schüfftan, Karl Freund, Robert and Curt Siodmak, Anton Walbrook, Seymour Nebenzahl and Erich Pommer.

This chapter deals with those film workers who came to Britain after the NSDAP came to power and those who had already come and were turned into refugees due to the events in Germany and later in Austria. This chapter first pays attention to the general situation in the German film industry after the NSDAP seized power in 1933 and the subsequent exile of hundreds of film workers. It then focuses on specific aspects of England as a country of domicile for film professionals from 1933 to the beginning of the Second World War. Particular areas of interest are the ways in which German-speaking personnel influenced the British cinema and the continuities and discontinuities of their work under the condition of exile.

57

Undoubtedly, many film émigrés experienced severe problems in exile through temporary or complete loss of social status and income. Unlike other occupational groups of exiles such as writers, publishers and politicians, which comprised a higher percentage of political refugees, the vast majority of exiled film practitioners were Jewish. The general lack of opposition against their expulsion can be read as evidence that anti-Semitism had been part of the industry – despite the diverse character of Weimar cinema and the many Jews who were working within the film business.[2] This view is also supported by the fact that only about 5 per cent of those film professionals who would be classified as 'Aryans' and did not need to fear politically-motivated reprisals chose exile.[3] This also helps to explain why Weimar cinema may have textually prefigured and anticipated Nazi policies and world-views as Siegfried Kracauer suggests in *From Caligari to Hitler*.[4]

As a highly esteemed cog of the Nazi-propaganda machinery, the film industry was one of the first cultural spheres to feel the full impact of Nazi ideology. Together with radio, which after its introduction in the early 1920s advanced to the predominant medium of mass communication in the Third Reich, Nazi officials regarded cinema as an appropriate modern medium to convey the new zeitgeist. The fundamentally changed political climate, however, was less obvious in films themselves since Goebbels, unlike Hitler, rejected direct propaganda. He wanted films that 'were more than a dramatisation of the Party's programme' and that there was 'no particular value in having . . . stormtroopers march about on stage or screen. Their place is on the street.'[5] Despite propaganda films ranging from *Hitlerjunge Quex* (Hans Steinhoff, Germany 1933) to *Kolberg* (Veit Harlan, Germany 1945), the vast majority of films were made to entertain and, although very affirmative and in favour of the *status quo ante*, they were far from open Nazi indoctrination and a long way from dealing with contemporary political issues.[6] The effect of NSDAP ideology, however, was less subtle regarding the employment pattern of German production companies. Only one day after Goebbels' first address to leading film officials on 28 March 1933, the industry, that is the executives of the predominant national film corporation UFA, concurred with the ending of all contracts with Jewish employees as soon as possible. Given the arguably fairly open-minded, liberal and multi-cultural environment of Weimar cinema, it comes as a surprise that virtually no one within or outside the film industry expressed disapproval or protested against the policy of segregation.

Only in certain exceptional cases were Jewish film workers offered a future within the film industry under NSDAP control, and only as long as they pledged allegiance to the fascist regime. This contradictory policy can be explained by the serious dilemma of the RMVP. The plans to eradicate all Jews and other 'un-German' elements from the industry resulted in an exodus of key film workers and thus posed a serious threat to German film production and its international competitiveness. This is especially true if one keeps in mind Goebbels' intention to transform German cinema into a second Hollywood.[7]

As a first measure towards reorganising the film industry, the RMVP banned all trade unions and founded first a temporary Film Guild (*Filmkammer*) on 14 July 1933 and then a permanent one on 1 November 1933. Membership was mandatory and all candidates had to prove their Aryan ancestry in order to be permitted to join. After the elimination of Jewish staff in so-called Aryan production companies, the NSDAP's complete control of the *Filmkammer* also prevented Jewish-owned production companies from employing Jewish personnel although some exceptions were permitted in the early phases of the Guild.[8] After the exclusion of Jewish filmmakers, the '*Arisierung*' of Jewish film capital commenced.[9]

Austria, for reasons of cultural and linguistic commonalities, could theoretically have offered employment for exiles from the Third Reich. This is particularly true for the Austro-Hungarian film professionals among them. However, the close ties between the German and the Austrian cinema implied that the Austrian film industry was highly dependent on the bigger German film market under Nazi control. Constant pressure from NSDAP officials and economic difficulties as a result of films being banned in Germany meant that Austria was a safe country of domicile for Jewish and anti-Nazi film professionals for a limited time only. Moreover, protests against films made with Jewish personnel underline the anti-Semitic resentment that ran deep in Austrian society. In addition to independent films made by mainly Jewish filmmakers in Austria, Nazi sympathisers and conservative voices also ran campaigns against the release of critical foreign films. They attacked the release of the British émigré production *Jew Süss* (Lothar Mendes, 1934), for instance, which criticised pogroms and contained some exceptionally clear attacks on Nazi policies.[10] As Susan Tegel's research has shown, Austrian newspapers described the costume drama as a Jewish *Tendenzfilm* and an insult to Catholics.[11] Disillusioned about Austria as a safe place to live and work, many film professionals left the country for England before its formal annexation by the Third Reich. Examples include the composer Nicholas Brodsky (Miklós Brodszky, Nikolaus Brodszky), the author and director Rudolph Cartier (Rudolf Kacser, Katscher), and the actors Gitta Alpar and Oscar Homolka.

The remaining Jewish and anti-Nazi film practitioners fled after the *Anschluss* in 1938 – again many of them to England. Members of this group had either previously worked with British film companies or had friends or good contacts among the refugees who had already found work in Britain. Richard Tauber, for instance, had already featured as a leading actor in four English music films before he finally left his beloved Austria in 1938. Other examples of film personnel who fled to Britain after 1938 are the actors Sybilla Binder, Ludwig Stössel, Hans Wengraf, the authors Anton Kuh and Friedrich Porges, the publisher of the Viennese film journal *Der Film*. Before his departure, Porges wrote an article about the growing Austrian community of film expatriates. Under the heading 'Austrian Film in London', he accentuated the contributions of Austrians and Hungarians which made possible the recent critical acclaim of British productions and reports their successful efforts to learn English and establish themselves in the British film industry. What Porges omits, however, is that most émigrés did not leave the continent for England voluntarily. His final résumé sounds therefore perhaps a bit too euphoric (especially in view of those émigrés who were not able to continue their careers in exile):

> Austrian film is represented in London by the best it has to offer. An influential colony within the vast empire dominated by film and theatre, in a world that is as interesting as it is tasteful and in which only the most outstanding prevail. And the fact that the Austrians can already be counted amongst these is both an honour and a triumph that one cannot praise highly enough![12]

Given the numerous links between the Austrian and German film industries, it is not possible to differentiate clearly between Austrian-Hungarian and German filmmakers. Attracted by the vibrant culture and the film scene in Berlin, many Austrians, on the one hand, learned their craft in Germany; in particular in the UFA studios – one of the biggest and most modern production facilities outside Hollywood. Calling them Austrian filmmakers seems problematic given that many of them had never worked in their home country. On the other hand, many Germans came to Austria as part of co-operation agreements to work for a period of time in Vienna. The great number of German-speaking Hungarians, Czechs, and other filmmakers who worked for the German/Austrian film industry make simplistic national distinctions even more difficult. Alexander Korda's career path serves as a good example. Born in Hungary, he started to work in the film business in Budapest before he became a producer in Vienna from 1919–1923. From 1927–1930 he worked in Berlin before he eventually came to Britain in 1932 after some time in Paris and Hollywood. The itinerary of Korda's fellow countryman Josef Somlo also illustrates the mobile and global character of the film business. Born in Papá, Hungary, Somlo studied law in Budapest. After his graduation, he began to work as the managing director of Viennese-based film companies in 1908. From 1919–1922 he then acted as head of UFA's foreign department in Berlin before founding his own production company with Hermann Fellner. In

1933 he came to Britain as a refugee, where he was involved in numerous film productions until 1958.

After having fled, émigrés were expatriated and their assets were confiscated on the basis of an emigration tax (*Reichsfluchtsteuer*). As many refugees initially headed for France, the French trade press cited the German Minister for the Interior, Hermann Göring, who threatened those who left the Reich: 'Most of their names are known and they figure on a blacklist. If they do not reply to the letter of reintegration, that they can obtain from the Ministry of the Interior, they will lose their nationality and their possessions.'[13] Because of this practice, exile meant a significant downturn in the economic situation for most refugees as they more often than not arrived in their new country of domicile without any money. As Horak notes, for many film professionals from Germany or Austria 'who enjoyed an upper middle-class standard of living in their native country, life without a home, a passport, residency papers or the prospect of a steady job, was a major shock'.[14]

British immigration policies

In the aftermath of the First World War, British liberal immigration and asylum policies of Victorian times were changed fundamentally. The 1919 'Aliens Restrictions Act' and the 1920 'Aliens Order' ruled that immigration officers were entitled to refuse people entry to the UK without the right to object. The implementation of these laws greatly affected political exiles from Germany and Austria after the NSDAP seized power.[15] Anxious about the consequences of a possible influx of mainly Jewish refugees, immigration officers were ordered to make sure that newly arrived immigrants would neither rely on public funding nor enter the highly strained labour market in professions other than those agreed by the government.[16] As recent comprehensive studies of the British response to the plight of European Jewry under Nazism have found, the refugee problem ranked low among other political issues in Westminster.[17] The complex stance of Britain is arguably best illustrated by the stark contrast between great private efforts to relieve the victims of National Socialist oppression and official government policies. Louise London, for instance, makes it clear that only a lucky few were granted entry to Britain whereas the majority were left to their fate. Given the disparity between actual historical policies and the collective memory, she concludes that the still prevalent view that Britain had done everything possible to save the Jews is a persistent modern day myth: the 'touching photographs and newsreel footage of unaccompanied Jewish children arriving on the Kindertransports' are still remembered while images of their 'Jewish parents left behind in Nazi Europe' are not part of the 'British experience, because Britain never saw them'.[18]

Westminster maintained its restrictive measures concerning the refugee problems, among other reasons because of economic concerns and its appeasement policy. British attempts to avoid any conflict with the German Reich in order to prevent another World War also meant that Westminster investigated exile activities in the UK. The at times unyielding immigration and asylum policies, however, can only partially explain the overall low numbers of refugees in the initial years of Nazi rule in Germany. According to current data, approximately 21,000 people were emigrating each year whereas the refugee figure for Britain was at first relatively small with 2,274 people in 1933 and 1,836 in 1934.[19] In fact, the Netherlands, France and Czechoslovakia were countries of first choice in the initial years of the Third Reich. J. M. Richie explains this with reference to personal connections to these countries (family, friends or colleagues) and cultural affinities as 'many Germans knew a great deal of French but little English [and] preferred the continental café culture of Prague to the unknown hazards of English beer and English cooking'.[20] With regard to the German and Austrian film industry such considerations are very likely keeping in mind the number of film personnel who spoke Hungarian or Czech as a native language.

The overall situation, however, changed drastically between 1937–1939 when the numbers of people seeking refuge in Britain exploded from 1,836 in 1934 to 11,000 in 1937, 20,000 in 1938 and 27,000 plus 9,354 children in 1939.[21] This was the outcome of the shattered belief in a quick collapse of Hitler's government, the Austrian *Anschluss* and later that year the pogrom of the *Kristallnacht* on 9 November 1938. Whereas the US as a traditional immigration country introduced a quota system in order to deal with the ever-increasing number of European refugees by stating exactly how many refugees from a single country were allowed entry, Westminster refrained from such measures. In order to deal with the ever-increasing number of immigrants, the British government rather introduced a visa system that decided each case individually. This practice, however, was still very restrictive despite British promises at an international refugee conference held in summer 1938 in Evian that the UK would undertake 'on the ground of humanity to adopt an even more liberal policy in the matter of admission and employment'.[22] Not until the pogroms and the German annexation of Austria and the eastern territory Sudetenland did the UK finally ease its restrictive immigration policy and become a refuge for a significant number of exiles, 70 per cent of whom came to Britain between November 1938 – September 1939.[23] Estimates of refugees from Nazi persecution in the UK vary greatly between approximately 50,000 and 90,000, of whom 85 to 90 per cent were Jewish.[24]

As émigrés had their share in the consolidation and expansion of the British cinema in the 1930s, the boom period of film production from 1932–1937 in turn created a positive economic environment for the

German-speaking film personnel who came to Britain immediately after Hitler seized power in 1933. As can be inferred from the cast and credits of films made during that time-span, they could by and large still find a job within the film business easily[25] – notwithstanding strict immigration control and fierce opposition on the part of the trade union Association of Cinematograph Technicians (ACT).

The film debacle of 1936–37 and the mass purge of filmmakers from Austria after the *Anschluss* in 1938, however, exacerbated the situation as more and more personnel competed for fewer jobs. Without the help of organisations like the German Film Fund in the US, the peak of immigration after 1938 thus coincided with a very unfavourable economic climate and hardly any vacancies for German-speaking film exiles. This explains why those émigrés who came in the 1920s or early 1930s were far more successful in establishing themselves in the British film business. Although a number of help organisations such as the German Emergency Committee or the Arden Society tried to support exiles, for most unemployed film workers the only prospect was to obtain one of the visa documents for the US. Consequently, a significant number of émigrés, among them Friedrich Feher, Erich Pommer, Eugen Schüfftan and Berthold Viertel, eventually moved from Britain to Hollywood because of better employment opportunities.[26]

Anti-Semitic resentment in European countries meant that émigré film practitioners were constantly in danger of being deported to the Third Reich because of passport, labour or residence misdemeanours throughout the 1930s. Britain was no exception. As Jan-Christopher Horak reminds us, Curt Siodmak, for instance, spent several weeks on the Calais-Dover ferry because he was not allowed to enter either Britain or France without a valid residency permit.[27] When refugees were granted leave to land at Dover this was usually done under the condition that they did not remain in the UK longer than one month. Exceptions were often only made if the émigré had important business obligations in the UK. Following a letter from the British subsidiary of Twentieth Century, the Home Office, after consultation with the Minister of Labour, for example twice postponed the date on which Otto Kanturek and his wife were originally required to leave the country by a few months.[28] Without such backing, Rudolph Cartier's passport, for instance, meticulously documents his monthly day trips to France in order to apply for a renewal of his residence permit.[29] Although Siodmak and Cartier eventually found refuge in the US and the UK respectively, other film practitioners – denied entry by British authorities in an attempt to contain the size of the refugee problem – were caught by the Nazis and most certainly murdered in one of the many concentration camps.

The main reason for the great difficulty in giving an exact number of exile films is that many of the émigrés who were not in possession of a valid visa or work permit are not mentioned in the cast and credits of films. Accordingly it is very difficult to reconstruct the uncredited film personnel. The film *Pagliacci* (Karl Grune, 1936) that was produced with the help of numerous German-speaking émigrés serves as a good example. Whereas director Karl Grune, producer Max Schach, composer Hanns Eisler, cinematographer Otto Kanturek, set designer Oscar Werndorff, singer Richard Tauber and production manager Fritz Brunn are mentioned, neither Bertolt Brecht nor Fritz Kortner who wrote the script are named in the credits because they were not in possession of a valid work permit for Great Britain.[30] Further examples are the Austrian authors John Hans Kahan and the director Carl Mayer. Like so many of their fellow exiles, Kahan's participation in the script of the Basil Dean production *I See Ice* (Anthony Kimmins, 1938) remains unnamed just as are Carl Mayer's contributions to the George Bernard Shaw adaptations *Pygmalion* (Anthony Asquith and Leslie Howard, 1938) and *Major Barbara* (Gabriel Pascal, 1941).

For both the large-scale purge of exiles after 1933 and migration processes that took place from the mid-1920s, one can make out different phases in terms of direction and intensity. The migration of film personnel from the mid-1920s to the Second World War was never a one-way phenomenon as is wrongly suggested by an exhibition at the Max Kade Institute at the University of Southern California of film artists of Austrian and German origin in Los Angeles.[31] The career paths of German-speaking film practitioners like Conrad Veidt, Curt Courant and Dupont clearly reveal that in the late 1920s and early 1930s we have to assume a lively to-and-fro rather than one-way movements. Conrad Veidt's stays in various European countries and the US, for instance, are representative of many of the predominant figures of Weimar cinema. After having established himself as the best-known actor of German expressionism due to his performance as the lead in *Der Student von Prag* (Henrik Galeen, Germany 1926) and, above all, his role as the somnambulist Cesare in *Das Cabinet des Dr. Caligari* (Robert Wiene, Germany 1920), Veidt was employed by Hollywood. He then returned to Germany after the introduction of sound before going to Britain for Dupont's multi-language productions, then to Germany to play Fürst Metternich alongside Lilian Harvey and Willy Fritsch in *Der Kongreß tanzt/The Congress Dances* (Eric Charell, Germany 1931) and then back to Britain where he produced a number of films as the most successful German actor in Britain of the 1930s. After his last German film at the end of 1933, *Wilhelm Tell*, he first went to England where he became naturalised and in 1940 he eventually emigrated to the US where he is best remembered for his role of Major Strasser in *Casablanca* (Michael Curtiz, USA 1942).

The high number of film professionals who could not continue their career in Germany does not imply, however, that the widespread mobility of film workers ceased to exist after 1933. Besides the politically-motivated expulsion of film professionals, economic reasons remained an incentive to work in another country for a limited period of time. The professional mobility on economic grounds thus persisted throughout the 1930s. In fact, the German film industry after 1933 was not nearly as isolated as often presented. Although Bergfelder's conclusion that '[e]ven after 1933 the major incentive and motivation for a film technician to move seems to have been economic, not political'[32] might go too far given the reality of Jewish film workers who were simply not able to continue working for German productions, one has to acknowledge his judgement that the professional mobility between the national film industries as well as pan-European co-operations did well exist under the different political situation. This is particularly true for Anglo-German relations and joint ventures that continued well up to 1938.[33]

Despite the exodus of ethnically or politically ostracised film workers, examples to prove that the German film industry was far from isolated can be found for every profession within the film business. The actress Charlotte Ander, for instance, returned to Germany after having worked for British productions after the inauguration of Hitler as chancellor, as did actor Karl Ludwig Diehl. Although some film practitioners were granted only limited work permits after their return as in the case of Ander, others had their most successful years after their return. The composer Werner Bochmann, for example, wrote the music for the English feature *The Amazing Quest of Ernest Bliss* (Alfred Zeisler, 1936) before becoming one of the most active composers in the German film industry. And actor Gerhard Dammann, who participated in *Maid Happy* (Mansfield Markham, 1933), eventually became one of the busiest supporting actors in Germany up to 1945.[34]

As the case of the polyglot actor Andrews Engelmann shows, not even the events of the war ended professional mobility. Engelmann, who had been making films in France since 1923 and had participated in his first German production in 1929 (*Tagebuch einer Verlorenen*, Georg Wilhelm Pabst), was able to establish himself as a villain in British films (*The Three Passions*, 1928, and *Baroud*, 1933, by Rex Ingram, or *Atlantic*, 1929, and *Two Worlds*, 1930, by Dupont). In 1939 he returned to Germany before going back to France after the war. The German-speaking art director Andrej Andrejew, who made his first films in the Weimar Republic in the 1920s and worked frequently in both England and France throughout the 1930s, serves as another example for migration processes during the Second World War as he continued designing sets for French productions despite the Nazi occupation before going back to Britain in 1946 for Alexander Korda's production of *Anna Karenina* (Julien Duvivier, 1948).

Because film professionals continued travelling back and forth between European countries including the Third Reich, it is not possible to categorise all German-speaking personnel working in the British film industry after 1933 as political refugees.[35] This also implies that German-speaking filmmakers who worked for British production companies were not always critical of the Nazi regime. Here the cases of cinematographers Hans Schneeberger, who shot three films for Korda's London Film Productions in 1936 and 1937 (*Conquest of the Air*, released in 1940, *Forget Me Not*, 1936, and *Farewell Again*, 1937) before becoming an acclaimed cameramen within the cinema of the Third Reich, and Franz Weihmayr, who shot *Calling the Tune* (Reginald Denham, 1936) in Britain before returning to work successfully for the UFA in Germany, serve as examples.

Until the late 1930s, furthermore, a fairly indifferent attitude towards political preferences or affiliations can be observed in the English film industry as firms also employed German film personnel who had previously participated in obviously propagandistic NS productions. Sepp Allgeier, the leading cameraman of the propaganda documentary film *Triumph des Willens* (Leni Riefenstahl, Germany 1935), was repeatedly employed for English productions (*The Queen's Affair*, Herbert Wilcox, 1934, *Escape Me Never*, Paul Czinner, 1935, and *The Great Barrier*, Milton Rosmer, 1937). Although his works may have been resented on ideological grounds, UK-based producers as well as their German colleagues valued his expertise as a specialist in on-location filming.

In the same way that we cannot assume all German-speaking film workers in the 1930s and early 1940s in Britain to be political refugees critical of Nazi ideology we cannot conclude that those who travelled back or remained in Germany always supported NSDAP interests. This holds true for cinematographer Günther Krampf, who returned to the UFA studios in 1935 for the production of what was to be his last German film (*Das Mädchen Johanna,* Gustav Ucicky, Germany 1935). Remarkably, Krampf, who was in possession of a permanent contract with Gaumont-British since 1931 and had established himself as a successful cinematographer in the UK, was allowed to work in Nazi Germany despite his participation in the communist picture *Kuhle Wampe* (Slatan Dudow, Germany 1932). This again can only be explained by his artistic reputation and NSDAP attempts to maintain an air of internationality, openness and normality.

London's émigré community and exile film genres

Soon after the refugees left Germany it became apparent that there was no hope of a quick return. Those who were able to stay in Britain in spite of the restrictions imposed by the British government had become exiles – many of them stateless. Owing to the concentration of British studios in the metropolitan area of London, almost all film exiles headed for the English capital. Despite the help of refugee aid agencies such as the Jewish Refugee Committee (until 1938 the German Jewish Aid Committee) many film exiles were among those who experienced severe problems in exile through temporary or complete loss of social status and income. Some film personnel such as script writer Carl Mayer and director/producer Max Mack never gained a foothold in exile. Others such as Leo Lasko, the long-time silent film director and script writer, stopped making films altogether. Yet not all refugees experienced long-term obstacles. While the less fortunate exiles stayed in basic lodgings such as the émigré boarding house at 13 Cleveland Square, which was run by the German refugee and former silent film star Lo Hardy,[36] or Paul Marcus' accommodation at 43 Norfolk Square, London W2, where he published his émigré newsletter *Pem's Privat Berichte*,[37] others like Adolf Wohlbrück (69 Frognal, NW3), Alexander Korda (81 Radlett Place, NW8), or Elisabeth Bergner (Admiral's House, Admiral's Walk, NW3 and 3 The Grove, N6) resided in rather luxurious accommodation.[38] Far from being a homogeneous entity, the London community of German-speaking film personnel was clearly a two-class society. Here, the situation of refugees in England was similar to those who fled to Paris. Referring to Fritz Lang's expensive accommodation at the Hotel George V, which clearly signified his status as an internationally respected filmmaker, Curt Riess called him 'an emigrant deluxe'.[39] In fact, as Kevin Gough-Yates observes, '[f]or every Elisabeth Bergner and Conrad Veidt, who found it easy to establish themselves, there were half a dozen actors and actresses who did not; for every Korda there were two or three producers and directors who found it less than easy'.[40]

In their endeavour to be granted a work permit and, in many cases, to acquire British nationality, émigrés were primarily subject to two governmental bodies: the Ministry of Labour and the Aliens Department of the Home Office. While both ministries were equally important, their agendas differed substantially. The Ministry of Labour was under constant pressure from lobby groups. British unions such as ACT or the Musical Conductors' Association, on the one hand, strongly opposed the employment of foreign nationals – sometimes with admittedly xenophobic undertones. Production companies in Britain, on the other hand, repeatedly stressed their importance for keeping up the international appeal of domestic films and improving production standards. Whilst the producers were able to make the case for the employment of émigré experts, those personnel who were not deemed 'ace' technicians or outstanding filmmakers, as called for by the trade unions, were not allowed to work within the industry. Gough-Yates reports that the animator Peter Sachs, who was not granted a work permit for the film industry when he entered the country in July 1939, regarded it as 'a joke' that he and his wife first had to work as a servant for two elderly women only to be interned thereafter.[41]

The case of Paul Czinner, moreover, shows that the speculative nature of the film business repeatedly worked against the expectations of recognised émigrés. An unusually extensive report that was compiled following his application for naturalisation lays out Czinner's and his wife Elisabeth Bergner's precarious financial situation, giving sums owed, the names of their creditors and their attempts to avoid paying income tax. Justifiably and tragically given the unsteady nature of the film business, the report argues that the future prospects of the well-known married refugees

> cannot be regarded as even "fair", because Elisabeth BERGNER is approaching forty years of age and this makes it particularly difficult to caste [sic] her for star parts; added to which is the fact that her last three efforts have been financial failures and she is regarded as one of the most difficult and temperamental women associated with the present day theatre or film business.[42]

According to the report, Czinner's prospects were equally unpromising: 'In the film trade he [Czinner] is regarded as a most extravagant producer and not completely efficient in regard to modern technical developments and trade conditions.'[43]

The careful screening of applicants' assets and income was a decisive factor for naturalisation as Czinner's and many other cases illustrate. The confiscation of refugees' personal assets by Nazi Germany and the subsequent inability of some émigrés to support themselves and dependents (especially if they were subject to working permit restrictions), so thwarted or significantly delayed expectations of acquiring British citizenship in a number of cases. This practice was in place from the 1930s until well after the war. Having scrutinised Rudolph Cartier's finances in 1947, for instance, an unfavourable police report to the Home Office notes: 'His future financial situation appears to be precarious.'[44]

The financial assessment criteria of the Home Office, however, could also work in favour of émigrés. Stable economic circumstances was viewed as a strong argument for naturalisation when it came to the application process. This is particularly true in the case of those German-speaking émigrés for whom exile opened up new opportunities. As the confidant and close friend of Alexander Korda, Lajos Biró, for instance, made an exceptional career as a scenario writer in the British cinema. Being the author of internationally successful films such as *The Private Life of Henry VIII*, he was well established within the industry and earned a good salary plus royalties. The police report on Biró, dated 16 December 1938, lists his various assets in America and Britain (including shares, stocks and life insurance endowment policies) and concludes that '[a]s far as can be ascertained [he] is not owing money and appears to live within his means'.[45]

In order to collect information on émigrés, police and MI5 reports in some cases also relied on hearsay and gossip as a source of information. The police file on Cartier, for example, states that 'he is not well regarded in film circles' and that he 'lacks ability to prepare satisfactory scenarios and is considered not intelligent enough for the work' without mentioning any sources or proof for these damaging allegations. The personal files that were put together by the Home Office were not limited to the émigrés' profes- sional lives, though. In particular when individuals had applied for British citizenship their knowledge of English, previous convictions, their political orientation as well as financial and personal circumstances were thoroughly screened. Driving convictions were as meticulously listed as rather curious youthful misdeeds such as Lajos Biró's 17-day prison sentence for duelling.[46]

In spite of the differences between the Home Office and the Ministry of Labour and their particular way of handling the émigré issue, some similari- ties are nevertheless evident. It was generally advantageous in dealing with the ministries if German-speaking foreigners could rely on professional help – some of the wealthier refugees such as Conrad Veidt were advised and represented by solicitors[47] – or good personal contacts. Émigrés who could rely on members of the British public deemed important by the class-aware and conservative Home Office to speak on their behalf had a huge advantage over those who could not. While such vital support some- times came from British family members (as in the case of Cartier whose application was backed by a second cousin, a professor at the London School of Economics)[48] or fellow émigrés who had already been naturalised (Alexander Korda, for example, wrote letters in support of Biró's applica- tion),[49] the most promising supporters were influential British decision makers and upper-class politicians. Among the few émigrés who had such links was Veidt. In a letter sent from the prestigious St Stephen's Club in Westminster on 30 December 1938, Commander Locker-Lampson, MP, writes to the Home Office: 'Very many thanks for having seen me respecting Mr. Conrad Veidt. I should be most grateful if you could help speed things up.'[50] The request was fulfilled promptly. Addressing Locker- Lampson by his first name, Oliver, the Home Secretary himself, Samuel Hoare, informs him on 26 January 1939 that he had decided to grant a certificate of naturalisation to Conrad Veidt.[51]

Repeatedly émigrés tried to help their fellow refugees either through their involvement in one of the many aid organisations (as in the case of Bergner for example) or by assisting fellow countrymen in finding employ- ment. While Alexander Korda made it no secret that he preferred first class foreigners over second rate Englishmen, his decisions were often also influenced by social considerations. Full of admiration, Paul Marcus noted in his newsletter after the war: 'We don't have to tell you how helpful [Korda] always was to everybody who knocked at his door – he even bought a script by the late Alfred Kerr before the war.'[52] To a point the same can be said about other producers like Max Schach or Erich Pommer, who also employed a significant number of German-speaking personnel. Some of the wealthier émigrés also offered financial help, such as Emeric Pressburger who financially supported the hapless Carl Mayer.[53]

The economic difficulties of some émigrés, however, must not suggest that film exiles were unsuccessful. Although the new situation was not easy for the numerous German-speaking foreigners in the British film industry, their contributions to the cinema was certainly one of the success stories of exile. In fact, the new political climate in Europe with the rise of Nazism changed the British film industry insofar as an increasing and steady quota of talented film personnel was available to the film studios. In particular those who could already rely on contacts made while working on the various remakes, multi-language films or pan-European joint ventures prior to 1933 were likely to find a permanent job in the British film industry. Thus as a rule the most successful exiles were the professional travellers who participated in co-productions and who were consequently used to working in an international team. Multi-language productions, moreover, continued well into the 1930s and continued to offer valuable employment opportunities for political refugees. *Unfinished Symphony* (Anthony Asquith and Willi Forst, UK/Austria 1934) and the Max Schach production *Koenigsmark* (Maurice Tourneur, UK/France 1935) are among the multi-language production made after 1933. As invaluable experts, émigrés participated in all German versions that were produced in 1930s Britain. In point of fact, many refugees launched their careers outside Germany through their participation in such films. Anton Walbrook's leading role in all the German, English and French versions of *Michel Strogoff/Der Kurier des Zaren* (Jacques de Baroncelli and Richard Eichberg, UK/France 1935), for instance, helped him to gain international recognition and to launch his successful English career.

Among the most significant general achievements of British cinema of the 1930s, one has to mention its assimilative power. In a similar way to Hollywood, which owed much of its success to the ability to assimilate foreign talent for its own purposes, the cosmopolitan atmosphere of studios like Elstree and Denham contributed to a thriving industry. When the international success of films aimed at an international market allowed production companies to increasingly attract investors from outside the film business, this again meant good employment opportunities. In this positive economic situation new studios mushroomed, increasing the total

number of stages from 19 in 1928 to 70 in 1938,[54] and production companies were increasingly looking for new personnel. Thus Britain became,
besides Hollywood, the main centre for refugee film personnel from the
Third Reich. The programme listings of London's prestigious West End
cinemas published in *The Times* give evidence of the tremendous émigré
screen presence. On Saturday, 23 November 1935, German-speaking
émigrés featured in all six British films on release. *Heart's Desire* (1935) was
directed by Paul L. Stein, co-written by Bruno Frank and its cast includes
Richard Tauber and Paul Graetz; Lucie Mannheim played Miss Annabella
Smith in *The Thirty-Nine Steps* (Alfred Hitchcock, 1935) for which Oscar
Werndorff designed the sets; *Sunshine Susie* (Victor Saville, 1931) featured
actress Renate Müller and was shot by Max Greene (Mutz Greenbaum);
Curt Siodmak's script for *The Tunnel* was based on a novel by Bernhard
Kellermann, Günther Krampf was cinematographer, Ernö Metzner was art
director and Joe Strassner designed the costumes; *Moscow Nights* (Anthony
Asquith, 1935) featured music by Walter Jurmann and set designs by
Vincent Korda and *First a Girl* (Victor Saville, 1935), a remake of a
German film by Reinhold Schünzel, was made by Joe Strassner who was
responsible for the costumes and with Oscar Werndorff as the set designer.

Benefiting from the cross-fertilisation between the British industry and
its continental workforce, British feature film production rose from 164
feature films in 1932 to 224 in 1937.[55] These numbers are further proof of
the influence of continental filmmakers from Germany and Austria. Indeed
the simultaneous ascent of British films and the international failure of Nazi
productions are by no means coincidental developments. On the contrary,
the migration processes and their political intensification after 1933 suggest
that the two developments are directly linked.

Given the commercial intentions behind productions made by émigrés in
Britain and the fact that they were primarily directed at an English-speaking
audience, exile films by and large reflect the genre preferences of the new
country of domicile. Horak gives an overview of the preferred genres. His
list reads as follows: 'comedies (23 per cent), musicals (20 per cent), melodramas (16 per cent), costume dramas (14 per cent), crime dramas (8 per
cent), literary adaptations (6 per cent) and fantasy films (5 per cent).'[56]
What can be inferred here is that to write about German-speaking émigrés
means, to a large extent, to write about popular commercial genre cinema.

What proved helpful for German-speaking film exiles was the fact that
the commercial imperatives and genre predilections in Britain were on
the whole fairly similar to the well-known diversity of the émigrés' home
market. Their contributions to the British cinema include popular musicals
such as *Blossom Time* (Paul L. Stein, 1934), suspense thrillers like *The Spy
in Black* (Michael Powell, 1939), fantasy films such as *The Man Who Could*

Work Miracles (Lothar Mendes, 1936), costume dramas (*Jew Süss*, Lothar Mendes, 1934), science fiction (*The Tunnel*, Maurice Elvey, 1935), musical comedies (*First a Girl*, Victor Saville, 1935) and avant-garde productions such as *Pagliacci* (Karl Grune, 1936). They were also responsible for some of the oddities of British cinema such as the silhouette films of Lotte Reiniger (such as *Daughter*, 1937)[57] or the experimental, abstract short films by Bauhaus artist László Moholy-Nagy (for example *Life of a Lobster*, 1935, and the science fiction film *Things to Come*, 1936). Friedrich Feher's experimental film *The Robber Symphony* (1936) further illustrates the fact that the émigrés' oeuvre is not limited to popular genre cinema. Made with only about 300 spoken words as a fairytale-like '"composed" film in which music is the "star"',[58] it clearly stands out as one of the extravagant curiosities of British exile cinema. The use of sound is praised by *The Times* as 'clever' because it 'heightens the excitement, adds point to the jokes, and, most happily of all, dispenses with all but the most essential dialogue',[59] while *Sight & Sound* admires the fact that it 'completely breaks away from routine methods and develops a new technique' while acknowledging its German roots:

> The film has a further interest on account of the associations of the leading people concerned in its production. Friedrich Feher, the composer and director, played a leading role in the silent classic *The Cabinet of Dr. Caligari*, and was prominently associated with Dr. Robert Wiene in the production of that film. In *Hunted People* he introduced for the first time his technique of music and sound instead of dialogue. The chief camera-man is Eugen Schufftan [sic] who photographed *Metropolis*, inventor of the famous process which bears his name. Erno [sic] Metzner, the art director, is well known for his work on *The White Hell of Piz Palu*, *Westfront 1918*, and *Kameradschaft*.[60]

In a similar way, the review of Berthold Viertel's *Little Friend* (1934) in the exile newspaper *Pariser Tageblatt* emphasises the positive effects of a cross-fertilisation between British cinema and its German-speaking professionals: '[The Film] should be seen as a product of British-German cooperation, almost as a classic proof of the benefits and fruitful influence of this German input into a British film industry that is gratifyingly receptive to it'.[61] Writing for the same exile paper, Erich Kaiser praises Karl Grune's *Abdul the Damned* (1935) for its psychological depth and Fritz Kortner's superb performance, and argues: '[The film] is yet another argument for how much international films have gained from giving work to those artists who are no longer able to live and work in Germany'.[62]

Besides innovative techniques and original film projects, experimental filmmakers such as Moholy-Nagy brought to British cinema notions of avant-garde filmmaking and theoretical discussions about the nature of cinematography, non-narrative film forms and the role of cinema between artistic creativity and economic imperatives.[63]

In addition to a few filmic extravaganzas and avant-gardist meta-narratives, experienced German-speaking film professionals were on the whole employed for large-scale productions like the BIP films *Jew Süss* (1934), *Rhodes of Africa* (1936) or *The Tunnel* (1936), which had budgets of £100,000 or more.[64] In fact, only major film producers were willing and able to pay the high wages of the German-speaking experts. This explains why almost all major British production companies of the late 1920s and throughout the 1930s that were making films with a high-cost bracket for international consumption – including Gaumont-British, BIP, Powell and Pressburger's The Archers and Korda's London Film Production – employed a noticeable contingent of German-speaking personnel. Apart from the critically acclaimed technicians of Weimar Cinema, these émigrés drew upon their educated middle-class intellectual background to produce storylines that often dealt with ancient mythology, works of European literature or other cultural texts such as operas and European history. Émigrés thus chose, as Horak puts it, 'film genres that were under-represented in the film industries of host countries, and in which they could demonstrate their special talents'.[65] Despite such appropriate generalisations, however, the overall diversity of émigrés means that their influence cannot be strictly limited to specific genres or indeed non-realist traditions. As Tim Bergfelder notes, 'a distinction between realist and non-realist strands in British cinema, at least as far as émigré involvement is concerned, is rarely clear-cut'.[66] Wofgang Suschitzky's important contributions to British documentary filmmaking and photography are a case in point.[67]

When many multi-language projects did not qualify for British registration (e.g. *Happy Ever After*, Paul Marin and Robert Stevenson, 1932; *F.P.1*, Karl Hartl, 1933; *The Only Girl*, Frederick Hollander, 1933, and *Early to Bed*, Ludwig Berger, 1933), this decreased the prospective earnings by British production companies which more often than not relied on the home market to break even despite their international aspirations.[68] As a consequence Max Schach, Alexander Korda, Michael Balcon and others increasingly turned towards the production of remakes of popular films,[69] many of them German musical comedies of the early 1930s (*My Song Goes Round the World*, Richard Oswald, 1934; *City of Song*, Carmine Gallone, 1931; *The Divine Spark*, Carmine Gallone, 1935; *Let's Love and Laugh*, Richard Eichberg, 1931; *Happy*, Frederick Zelnik, 1933, etc.).[70] Other remakes of German films made with numerous émigrés include: *The Tunnel* (participating émigrés: Günther Krampf, Ernö Metzner and Joe Strassner), *Emil and the Detectives* (Milton Rosmer, 1935; participating émigrés: Allan Gray and Mutz Greenbaum), *The Challenge* (Milton Rosmer and Luis Trenker, 1938; participating émigrés: Emeric Pressburger, Allan Gray, Günther Stapenhorst, Alexaner Korda and ent Korda), *Storm in a Teacup* (Ian Dalrymple and Victor Saville, 1937; participating émigrés: Andrej Andrejew, Alexander Korda and Mutz Greenbaum) and *Dreaming Lips* (Paul Czinner, 1937; participating émigrés: Paul Czinner, Elisabeth Bergner, Carl Mayer, Max Schach and Joe Strassner). At one stage there was even a plan to make sound remakes of classics of Weimar Cinema such as *The Cabinet of Dr. Caligari*.[71] However, as these plans never materialised, it was first and foremost popular genre cinema that was filmed anew.

With the benefit of films now being generally registered as British, remakes continued to appeal through their escapist nature, especially their notable cosmopolitan feel and light-hearted storylines. An advantage over multi-language films was that only one production company was in charge of making a film. Rather than shooting a British version strictly according to one model film, remakes offered more scope for alterations and artistic freedom. Indeed they allowed for an effective and careful adaptation able to harmonise perfectly with the cultural milieu of the particular country of release.[72] The British remake *First a Girl* (Victor Saville, 1935) of the German comedy *Viktor und Viktoria* (Reinhold Schünzel, 1933), for example, owes much of its success to several alterations as a means of cultural adaptation. The setting, for example, has been convincingly changed from the Berlin Variété to the British music hall.

The amalgamation of British and continental European cultural characteristics, symbols and traditions in films suggests that the many German-speaking film experts had an effect on themes and aesthetics. Directors (such as Berthold Viertel, Paul L. Stein, Wilhelm Thiele, Paul Czinner and Karl Grune), and script-writers (including Walter Reisch, Robert Neumann, Ernest Bornemann, Fritz Gottfurcht [Frederick Gotfurt], Carl Mayer, Wolfgang Wilhelm, Carl Zuckmayer and Lajos Biró) had a major impact on narratives and styles while actors (such as Anton Walbrook, Richard Tauber, Elisabeth Bergner, Lilli Palmer, Oscar Homolka, Conrad Veidt and Frederick Valk) were pivotal for the representation of foreigners in British films that more often than not deal with themes of displacement and carried an anti-fascist message. Indeed, as Gerd Gemünden, Michael Williams and Barbara Ziereis have shown in connection with Conrad Veidt, Anton Walbrook and Lilli Palmer respectively, their exile status had an impact on their performances and ultimately on their star personae.[73]

Among the large group of German-speaking filmmakers in Britain it was especially the strong presence of émigré producers such as Schach or Korda that helped many refugees to find employment. Korda among others surrounded himself with numerous other polyglot continentals and in some instances enabled their flight as in the case of Alfred Kerr or Carl Zuckmayer.[74] While both Schach and Korda were central figures within the London exile community and among the most important independent producers at that time in England, other German-speaking producers also played an important role. The list includes Erich Pommer, Hermann Fellner, Isadore Goldschmidt [Goldsmith], Marcel Hellmann, George Hoellering, Otto Klement, Max Mack, Gabriel Pascal, Arnold Pressburger, Josef Somlo, Sam Spiegel, Günther Stapenhorst, Eugen Tuscherer and Friedrich Zelnik. In many cases, émigré producers continued their collaboration with film personnel they worked with in Austria and London. Over the years several partnerships developed: Schach, for example, frequently worked together with Rudolf Bernauer and Karl Grune while Korda often collaborated with Oscar Werndorff and Lajos Biró. The latter collaboration between Korda and Biró soon developed into a strong and deep friendship as C. A. Lejeune noted in 1936.[75]

Arguably one secret of the success of Korda and of other émigrés was their willingness to embrace English culture and, while maintaining an enigmatic continental flair, turn into quintessential Anglophile gentlemen. By contrast Max Schach never left his home country emotionally and refused to assimilate to British society; in fact, as Kevin Gough-Yates notes, 'his interest in British life and culture was minimal'.[76] His press officer Monja Danischewsky recalls an episode in which Schach was reluctant to play the customary national anthem at the premiere of *Dreaming Lips* (Paul Czinner 1937; remake of *Der träumende Mund*, Paul Czinner and Lee Garmes 1932) despite the presence of Queen Mary in what was her first public appearance since the death of King George V.[77] It seems hardly surprising that émigrés who showed evidence of rapid cultural assimilation were in the long term generally more successful than fellow countrymen who mentally never left Germany or Austria. The behaviour of Ferdinand Bellan, who was described as being 'more English than the English'[78] or Conrad Veidt and Emeric Pressburger, who very rarely spoke German when British colleagues were around,[79] certainly helped them integrate into otherwise British production teams.

Apart from the language, a main difficulty for German-speaking actors in Britain was the significantly different acting style. While theatres and film studios in Germany and Austria expected expressive performances that often over-emphasised feelings and actions, British audiences were used to a more realistic style of acting. Speaking for many of his fellow émigrés, Fritz Kortner stressed the importance of toning down his German style and adjusting it to the practice of British actors. In his memoirs he claimed that his British colleagues had a tendency to 'underplay' and that he, in turn, was expected to renounce his efforts 'to achieve the utmost in expressiveness'.[80] Such was the disparity between British and continental performances that many an émigré actress and actor struggled to show their acting skills. *Film Weekly* critic Frank Jennings, in this vein, claimed that Lilli Palmer was never able to show her many talents in Britain:

> Lilli was unfortunate in never playing in a Continental film. Only a Continental writer, producer and director can fully understand her and bring her quality out on the screen. Her features, manner, way of speaking, and style of acting, are as individual as the American or English girl's. None of them can be altered or transformed.[81]

Besides different styles of performance, many foreign production companies were unfamiliar with the second and third rank of émigré actors – and this in a business where names and reputation were paramount assets in finding employment. Apart from a few stars among the refugees or those who appeared in foreign productions before, the majority of émigrés had to start from scratch as the foreign production companies, with few exceptions, were indifferent to the big names of German cinema. Whereas some actors fostered their careers by adjusting themselves to the different production conditions of the British studio system, others were not as fortunate. Given the dependence on language in sound films and a general expectation that film English ought to be that of a 'pure' received pronunciation, it comes as no surprise that of all German-speaking refugees, actors (besides perhaps script writers) experienced the greatest loss of income and status. The only chance of success was the acquisition of the necessary language skills. In her autobiography, Salka Viertel later comments that London was filled with refugees: 'Elisabeth Bergner had a sensational success. . . . Fritz Kortner and Johanna Hoofer, Oscar Homolka, and many others were furiously learning English.'[82] However, despite all their effort for most actors the end of silent films fatally coincided with the Third Reich. Often the only roles for native speakers of German were silent bystanders, mysterious strangers or foreign antagonists. Having said this, the success of actors like Anton Walbrook and Conrad Veidt seems to suggest that British cinema allowed for linguistic permutation and otherness in character roles (see Chapter four).

Composers such as Nikolas Brodszky, Walter Goehr, Allan Gray, Mátyás Seiber and Mischa Spoliansky also left their mark on musical scores by mixing continental European and Anglo-American traditions or by attempting to use the modernist ideas and forms of expression associated with Arnold Schönberg and Hanns Eisler.[83] However, it was especially the work of German-speaking technicians and art directors who revolutionised the modes of studio production. The cinematographers Otto Kanturek, Günther Krampf, Mutz Greenbaum and the set-designers Oskar Werndorff, Alfred Junge, Vincent Korda, Ernö Metzner, who all worked in Austria or Germany, introduced pioneering camera techniques, rationalised production processes, and increased the importance of mise-en-scène. In so doing, their contributions are a continuation of the early émigrés' legacy. While Karl Freund had already used his celebrated 'unchained camera' and Günther Krampf had likewise introduced back projection to British cinema with *Rome Express* (Walter Forde, 1932) at Shepherd's Bush,[84] the technical ingenuity of Erwin Hillier's work for the Powell and Pressburger film *I Know Where I'm Going* (1945) illustrates the innovative creativity of German-speaking cinematographers at the end of the Second World War. Using a variety of telescopic lenses Hillier achieved sophisticated deep-focus effects in exterior location shots and rear projection filming at the Denham studios.[85] His achievement, as Pam Cook notes, 'is even more unusual when it is considered that there were no light meters, and exposure had to be judged by eye'.[86] British and émigré producers and directors equally admired such expertise and innovation. Berthold Viertel, for example, told a *Film Weekly* interviewer that he desired the camera in his new film *The Passing of the Third Floor Back* starring Conrad Veidt to play an active role by creating 'the correct atmosphere' and 'laying symbolic emphasis on the right people at the right time'. In view of the difficult film project in which the action is restricted to a London house, he furthermore expressed his contentment that he was assigned a German cinematographer: 'I must say how fortunate I am in having as a chief cameraman, young Curt Courant, who is certainly one of the most brilliant creative photographers to graduate from the famous UFA studios.'[87]

One main reason for the popularity of German-speaking cinema-tographers, besides technical and artistic capability, was arguably their understanding of what the job of cinematographer entails. Since the 1920s cameramen had commonly understood their own role as members of a cooperative rather than as individual technical and creative experts.[88] In an address at the first meeting of the Klub der Kameraleute Deutschlands, Karl Freund expressed his opinion that filmmaking requires the teamwork of several creative filmmakers as early as 1926:

> a film has to be the product of the work of many artistically creative people. . . . [Film requires] a positive distillation of team spirit through the honest cooperation of close groups of artists.[89]

What seems a commonplace in today's production was still a novelty in Britain some four years later when Paul Rotha called for film as a truly collaborative medium in *Close-Up*.[90] It was not until German-speaking professionals entered British studios that notions of the filmmaking process changed in line with international developments. Indeed, the widespread cooperative culture of German production crews, as Pam Cook argues, had a deep impact on the organisation of labour in British studios: 'The col-laborative methods in operation at the German studio must have provided invaluable experience in the context of Rank's IPL (Independent Producers Limited, the production company of Powell's and Pressburger's The Archers) experiment, and The Archers' working ethos in general.'[91]

Moreover, Karl Freund also underlines the importance of training the new generation of film experts ('after all, even the great masters of cinematography need to have successors').[92] The willingness and determination of German-speaking émigrés to teach young professionals, which had begun in the 1920s and continued in the 1930s and 1940s, made them ever more valuable to the major British studios such as BIP or Gaumont-British with their international, long-term aspirations. In fact, by promoting training schemes, it may well be argued that they imported the successful German/Austrian apprenticeship system. Michael Balcon, among others, presented the foreign experts he employed 'to his homegrown force as teachers as well as studio colleagues, partly, perhaps, to justify the superior income his émigrés enjoyed; their lessons at any rate, were readily absorbed'.[93]

When émigré art directors and cinematographers came to Britain in increasing numbers during the 1930s, following early émigrés such as Alfred Junge or Mutz Greenbaum, they introduced new schemes of work. This represented a pivotal change in the studio environment. While the sets had previously been constructed by carpenters and painters without a coherent approach,[94] all designing processes were now supervised and managed by one person. So art directors such as Alfred Junge, as supervising director at Gaumont-British, soon exercised unprecedented levels of creative control. Among other things this led to an improved consistency between set design and cinematography through an anticipation of camera movement in his designs.[95] In the tradition of Weimar Cinema, German-speaking art directors often infused British films with a style that originated in German productions in which, according to Paul Rotha, 'the decorative environment was the binding element of the realisation, against which the thematic narrative moved with a slow, psychological deliberation'.[96] And indeed, productions such as The Ghoul (T. Hayes Hunter, 1933), shot by Günther Krampf and designed by Alfred Junge, are visibly more design-motivated than narrative-motivated. In the tradition of German expressionism, Hunter's film expresses meaning through symbolism and atmosphere rather than dialogue. Instead of changing the style of individual films only, however, Junge and also Vincent Korda brought continental sophistication, order and flair to British cinema.[97] Acknowledging the pivotal role of émigré designers such as Alfred Junge, Ernö Metzner, Oscar Werndorff and Zoltan Korda, a critic pointed out in 1935 that the 'ritualistic sumptuousness [of contemporary British films] seems to derive more from the continental than the American schools'.[98] This noticeable artistic expertise of German-speaking art directors was much admired throughout British studios and offered individual 'aces' easy employment opportunities – a privilege that was by no means universal as the employment patterns for the film business in the 1930s and 1940s demonstrate.

Émigrés and politics: Censorship and anti-Nazi messages

With the increasing prominence of émigrés in British studios in both number and seniority, their contributions exceeded technical or industrial innovation in that they also had an impact on the characterisation of roles and the storylines themselves. This, perhaps above all, can be observed with regard to the many films containing more or less explicit political plots or sub plots that were made with the help of émigrés. The costume drama *Abdul the Damned* (1935), which raises questions about totalitarian regimes, for instance, was directed by Karl Grune, produced by Max Schach, the script was co-written by Fritz Kortner and based on a story by Robert Neumann. Otto Kanturek was in charge of the cinematography, Joe Strassner designed the costumes, the friend and colleague of Bertolt Brecht, Hanns Eisler, composed the music and two of the leading actors were Fritz Kortner and Walter Rilla.

Looking back on the situation in Hollywood during the pre-war years in 1949, Siegfried Kracauer stated that Hitler was news everywhere during the 1930s except on the silver screen.[99] Britain was not so different in this respect as Michael Balcon observed retrospectively: 'Now that events can be seen in their historical perspective, one cannot escape the conclusion that in our own work, we could have been more profitably engaged. Hardly a single film of the period reflects the agony of those times.'[100] And indeed, at first glance, the vast majority of British films produced in the 1930s seem to support such a judgement. A closer examination, however, reveals that by no means all British films were devoid of political statements and critique. In order to circumvent the rigid censorship by the British Board of Film Censorship (BBFC), which acted in concert with Westminster's appeasement policy by banning all films it saw as controversial (including all films referring to contemporary politics), pre-war films such as *Abdul the Damned* recurrently dealt with themes that were deemed controversial in the veiled form of historically and geographically displaced settings. This, in other words, actually meant that criticism was inscribed into films by émigrés often in the concealed forms of allegories or symbolism that could be deciphered by examining production files, scripts, contemporaneous reviews and casting decisions.

Although numerous countries opposed the racist and expansionist policies of the Third Reich, the first anti-Nazi film, *Borzy* (Gustav von Wangenheim), was produced in 1935 in the Soviet Union with the approval of the government. In Britain, the situation was considerably different. As in other western European countries before the war, all demonstratively anti-fascist films were subject to political censorship. This rule was applied to British productions as well as to imported films. Film production in the UK was not directly controlled by the government, but the industry itself had set up the BBFC in 1912. The censors' policy was to avoid sensitive, i.e. contemporary issues. When the BBFC was given the right to vet scripts in the early 1930s, this proved to be a powerful control instrument. In 1937 the President of the BBFC, Lord Tyrell, assured the public that there was not 'a single film shown today in the public cinemas of this country which dealt with any of the burning questions of the day'.[101] Although the Home Office always emphasised the independence of the BBFC, which was supposedly free of governmental interference, this was not quite the case as can be inferred from the appointment of BBFC presidents after consultation with the Home Secretary and from their ties to Westminster.[102] For instance, the Board's president from 1929–1935, Edward Shortt, had been Home Secretary from 1919–1922 and several other Board members were Members of Parliament.[103] Moreover, the BBFC often operated through official policy-making channels through meetings with MPs or senior administrators and viewed critical films together with Foreign Office staff.

In the light of the official government policy of appeasement, the BBFC was careful to review all proposed scripts dealing with Nazi Germany and rejected all films denouncing the persecution of Jews or openly opposing fascism. Berthold Viertel, who prepared a biopic of the life of Byron under the title *Chained Eagle* – a proposed film that was to place emphasis on his love of freedom and rejection of totalitarianism –, soon learned that Michael Balcon abandoned the project after the Foreign Office expressed its disapproval on the grounds that the film alluded to Hitler.[104] The censors' report on another rejected script, *The Mad Dogs of Europe*, reads as follows: 'This is pure anti-Hitler propaganda and as such I think unsuitable for production as a film.'[105] Speaking in the Commons in 1938, MP Geoffrey Mander stated that '[n]othing anti-government, nothing anti-fascist is permitted . . .'.[106] British film-makers nevertheless tried to address issues such as anti-Semitism, racism and Nazism in films – although their attempts were not always successful.

Here, the two Gaumont-British exile film projects 'City Without Jews' and 'A German Tragedy' serve as good examples. When they were presented to the BBFC as synopses in 1933, producer Michael Balcon was told to refrain from pursuing both projects. The script review, which was identical for both film projects, argued that the proposed films were undesirable because of their direct connection with actual events in Nazi Germany. The report states:

The story is pathetic and would probably in itself be quite free from any objectionable feature, but with the recent political agitation which has just taken place in Germany in connection with the Jewish population, it undoubtedly comes definitely under the head of political propaganda.

Feeling still runs very strongly in London on this subject and a film based on this story might easily provoke a disturbance (vide *Times* May 9th 1933). On these grounds we do not consider the subject a desirable one at the present juncture.[107]

Although the projects were abandoned and the actual scripts lost – perhaps they were among the BBFC records that were destroyed by German bombings in 1940 – the remaining scenario reports prepared by the BBFC illustrate their importance in the context of émigré attempts to address issues such as anti-Semitism and Nazism.

Written by German-speaking émigré Franz Schulz, who started as a scriptwriter in Berlin and was responsible, among other films, for the Erich Pommer UFA productions *Die Drei von der Tankstelle* (Wilhelm . Thiele, Germany 1930) and *Bomben auf Monte Carlo* (Hanns Schwarz, Germany 1931), 'A German Tragedy' is a drama about the tragic life of a secular Jewish doctor in Germany. Although he had a distinguished career in a flying squad in the First World War, and became one of Germany's foremost doctors in a major Berlin hospital, he loses his family and job as a result of anti-Jewish persecution.

'City Without Jews', which had already been made into a silent film in Austria in 1923–1924 by Hans Karl Breslauer,[108] is an adaptation of the controversial novel by Austrian writer Hugo Bettauer published in 1922. The proposed British remake is a unique film project insofar as it not only deals with the issue of anti-Semitism but also addresses the role of Jewish exiles. The script tells the story of how Christian Socialist and German Nationalist parties in Austria pass a law that expels all Jews from the country, including converted Jews and children of 'mixed marriages'. After a brief period of enthusiasm and prosperity, the country experiences a severe crisis leaving half its people on the verge of starvation because all the experts in science, finance, art and commerce were Jewish.

It was no coincidence that the script of 'City Without Jews', which is set in contemporary Vienna, was submitted to the BBFC in June 1933. After having eliminated the Austrian parliament in March 1933, Chancellor Engelbert Dollfuß sought to install an authoritarian Catholic corporatist state (*Austrofaschismus*) with the backing of fascist Italy. His Christian Social party was not only deeply conservative but also anti-liberal and anti-Semitic. Within this context, the script reads as a representation of these events. It also includes a warning about the real strength of anti-Semitism in Austria prior to the *Anschluss*. In contrast to the myth of Austria as the first victim of German aggression, which was intentionally forged by Austrian officials preceding the Moscow Declaration of 1943,[109] the script shows great willingness on the part of Austrians to follow a racist ideology. In fact the cheering crowds in the proposed film anticipate the thunderous applause that welcomed German troops marching into Austria in 1938.[110]

By drawing a dystopian picture of the downfall of a society and economy as the result of anti-Semitism and the expulsion of Jews, 'City Without Jews' is a comment not only on Nazism and events on the European continent, but also on a growing anti-Semitism in Britain. *The Times'* article of 9 May 1933 which is mentioned in the censor's report, shows that there were indeed reasons for concern. It refers to clashes involving about 300 Jews and fascists around Leicester Square in London. Alerted by such incidents, which culminated in the battle of Cable Street in 1936, the BBFC felt obliged to ban all anti-fascist films so as to preserve the public order.[111] One can hardly avoid the conclusion that the street violence and threats of British fascists were able to hinder the production of feature films that were critical of racist ideology. Thus film production in 1930s Britain shied away from cinematic realism and was to a large extent restricted both by domestic concerns and foreign policy, that is the government's appeasement policy. In a similar way to Chamberlain's government the BBFC may thus be accused of having unintentionally supported the rise of fascism and anti-Semitism.

The successful co-operation between the government and the BBFC not only hindered the release or the making of British films but also led to a ban on several foreign productions. One such example is the Soviet production *Professor Mamlock* (Adolf Minkkin/Herbert Rappaport, 1938), an adaptation of Friedrich Wolf's play about a Jewish doctor who is persecuted in Nazi Germany although he saved the life of a Nazi official. In spite of good reviews by film journals like *Kinematograph Weekly* in April 1939 after the feature was screened at the Film Society in London and its approval in the US where it had already been released, *Professor Mamlock* was refused a certificate by the BBFC on the grounds that it was 'not in the public interest'.[112] In addition to feature films, the BBFC also banned a number of anti-Nazi documentaries such as *Hitler's Reign of Terror* (Michael Mindlin, USA 1934) in September 1934 and *Free Thälmann* (Ivor Montagu, 1935) in February 1935.[113] As can be seen elsewhere, script vetting and strict censorial enforcement led to the establishment of a very effective self-censorship by the industry. The BBFC banned 21 films in 1933, but only six in 1936.[114]

Westminster's cautious and restrictive stance was fostered by the fact that the Third Reich regarded all cinematic criticism as provocation.[115] Since motion pictures were generally thought crucial by NSDAP officials, German film publications like the party-controlled *Film-Kurier* meticulously observed foreign productions, film projects and censorship decisions.[116] Moreover, Nazi stormtroopers violently demonstrated against screenings of British productions featuring German-Jewish and anti-fascist actors. The émigré costume drama *Catherine the Great* (Alexander Korda, 1934) with Elisabeth Bergner as leading actress, for instance, caused great indignation in the Reich and was eventually taken off after distributors met with Goebbels. In Britain, where Elisabeth Bergner's acting was heralded as a great achievement,[117] the press repeatedly ran articles about the film's reception in Germany; thereby telling the public about the plight of Jews under the Nazis.[118] For some émigré actors, however, the often-successful attempts by the Nazis to prohibit the screening of films featuring émigrés in continental Europe were an increasing problem. Among others, the outspoken anti-fascist actor Fritz Kortner was not cast in any British film from 1936 to the beginning of war because such films could not be released in the Third Reich and the neighbouring countries under its leaverage.[119]

The strict control over the production of motion pictures, which only allowed for subliminal and veiled political criticism, was responsible for the fact that many émigré filmmakers sought alternative ways of addressing politically sensitive issues in the years before the war. Owing to the fact that the control over theatre was generally speaking quite liberal compared to the intervention of the BBFC, many German-speaking film exiles took part in stage performances of refugee theatre groups such as Four and Twenty Black Sheep, Laterndl or Kleine Bühne.[120] Often, these groups were organised by or with the help of larger influential refugee organisations such as the Freie Deutsche Kulturbund. Among its members were not only exiled authors such as Alfred Kerr, Oskar Kokoschka or Stefan Zweig, important British members like author J. B. Priestley, the former head of *The Times* Henry Wickham Steed and the Lord Bishop of Chichester, George Bell, but also a number of film émigrés such as director Berthold Viertel.[121]

Contrary to their engagements in the film industry, film exiles who were involved in refugee theatre performances such as scriptwriter Rudolf Bernauer, composer Mischa Spoliansky and actress Agnes Bernelle were able to address a mainly German-speaking audience with politically critical theatre performances. Groups like the *Kleine Bühne* were famous for their political cabaret in a so-called 'refugee speak', a combination of German and English with a French accent.[122] The theatre performances often engaged with issues such as political criticism of the Third Reich or the refugee situation and thus offered émigrés a compensation for their less-critical film work.[123]

Content control by the BBFC, however, was only one reason for the differences between theatre and cinema. Besides the intervention of censors, another cause for the subtle treatment of political issues in films lay in the

capitalist nature of the industry. In the course of the increasing industri-
alisation of film production, British cinema developed a Hollywood-like
genre structure. In order to make profits, producers in Britain as elsewhere
especially favoured popular genre cinema such as musical films or comedies
because of their overwhelming popularity at the box-office where light-
hearted comedies and musicals made up something over 40 per cent of
all productions.[124] By and large, then, the majority of British films from
1933–1939 tended to be escapist and followed a general tendency towards
depicting a harmonious society. Because film exiles had to assimilate to the
respective markets of their host country, films made with émigré participation generally followed this trend. Moreover, the international aspirations
of major British production companies forbade controversial films and
critical depictions of foreign affairs in a way that would jeopardise their
overseas revenues.[125] However, this does not mean that all films were apo-
litical. In fact, some scholars even point out that British films were more
critical of the Third Reich than, for instance, their French counterparts.[126]
Neither the BBFC nor self-imposed control mechanisms could prevent a
number of films from evading censorship.

While all film genres potentially offered the possibility of critiquing the
Third Reich, costume dramas and spy thrillers seemed to be particularly
well suited to warning against the perils of Nazism. They did this either by
creating analogies or by evoking scenarios based on existing fears, international tensions and political conflicts.[127] Or, as James C. Robertson puts
it, 'subtle tactics provid[ed] a better way of circumventing the BBFC than
direct challenges'.[128]

The most prolific period for spy thrillers in British cinema was the mid-
and late 1930s when there were adaptations of stories by Buchan (*The
Thirty-Nine Steps*, Alfred Hitchcock 1935), Sapper's Bulldog Drummond
adventures (*The Return of Bulldog Drummond*, Walter Summers 1934;
Bulldog Drummond at Bay, Norman Lee 1937), W. Somerset Maugham
(*Secret Agent*, Alfred Hitchcock 1936) and Edgar Wallace (*The Four Just
Men*, Walter Forde 1939).[129] Between 1930 and 1939, some 350 thrillers
were produced in Britain – about one-fifth of all feature films made.[130]
Alongside comedies, the thriller was thus one of the main genres of the
British cinema at that time.

The formulaic structure of spy thrillers only offered limited opportunities to German-speaking émigrés. As a rule, the protagonist in such films
is an English gentleman, preferably with a public school background, who
represents the traditional values of chivalry and sportsmanship whereas the
antagonist, by contrast, is usually a cunning, unscrupulous foreigner who
seeks to harm Britain and her interests. It follows that continental émigrés
were commonly cast in the part of villains. As can be seen in the later US

anti-Nazi films, German-speaking actors in spy thrillers were constrained to play so-called accent roles. Conrad Veidt, who repeatedly played foreigners in British films, serves as a good case in point. After having been corrected for his pronunciation, he is reported to have said: 'But it's not my fault, my scriptwriter writes with an accent!'.[131] However, although he was predominantly bound to portray strangers, the example of Veidt also demonstrates that with the few better-known émigrés the distinction between good and evil, black and white, was not always clear-cut. Veidt, who played a leading role in more British spy films than any other émigré, often played grey characters who challenged the binary oppositions of friend and foe. His cool, elegant performances made him popular with British audiences despite the fact that he often played the part of the enemy.

On account of the genre's specific aesthetics, spy thrillers occupy an exceptional place within the broader context of British national and exile cinema. Whereas the vast majority of 1930s British films presented a harmonious, peaceful and idealised society with close-knit communities and a romanticised countryside, a Britain that is characterised by national integration, spy and crime thrillers depicted dark back streets of big cities as they drew upon dangerous threats, violence, conflicts and foreign infiltration. In this way, thrillers go against the grain of 1930s British cinema, as James Chapman observes.[132] Like their literary models, which represent the hostile political climate between the great powers of Europe before and during the First World War, the growing geopolitical tensions caused by Nazi Germany in the 1930s are also inscribed into the genre.[133] Indeed, spy thrillers were inextricably linked to their historical contexts and, as Chapman notes, became 'a vehicle for urging military preparedness and criticising the foreign policy of appeasement'.[134] The more political tension between the European powers intensified, the more stories of espionage were made into films. This also helps to explain why the relatively small number of British spy and crime thrillers that were produced in the first half of the decade gradually increased during the second half of the 1930s with a growing uncertainty over the government's appeasement policy.[135]

Despite the rigid BBFC censorship, thrillers were able to address contemporary political issues. Two common strategies to get around censorship were applied in spy thrillers: first, the First World War was used as a matrix for contemporary political events; and, second, secret agents in Britain fought unspecified foreign powers because the BBFC forbade all direct contemporary references to actual names or countries. Feelings of alienation and paranoia, which were commonly created by the dark and gloomy atmosphere increased the general sense of uneasiness and anxiety depicted in the films. The German-speaking cinematographers' and set designers' expertise in the creation of symbolically expressive sets, costumes, lighting and camera angles made them first choice experts for the production of British thrillers. Indeed, whereas the storylines were commonly based on novels by British authors, a continental influence can clearly be spotted in the very specific cinematography and mise-en-scène of 1930s thrillers which, more often than not, bear great resemblance to the later American *film noir*. Émigrés in Britain, as in America, transformed the look of spy and crime thrillers made in Britain including *The Wrecker* (Géza von Bolváry, 1929; cinematography: Otto Kanturek), *Non-Stop New York* (Robert Stevenson, 1937; cinematography: Mutz Greenbaum) and *Seven Sinners* (Albert de Courville, 1936; cinematography: Mutz Greenbaum; art direction: Ernö Metzner). Especially Hitchcock preferred to engage German-speaking personnel to create suspense and the sinister atmosphere that characterises his thrillers: Alfred Junge was art director and Curt Courant cinematographer of *The Man Who Knew Too Much* (1934), Oscar Werndorff designed the sets of *The Thirty-Nine Steps* (1935) and, with Joe Strassner as costume designer, also of *Secret Agent* (1936) and *Sabotage* (1936), Alfred Junge was art director of *Young and Innocent* (1937). In particular the dark alleyways so prominent in Weimar cinema (for example Lang's *M*, 1931, Murnau's *Der letzte Mann*, 1924, and Grune's *Die Straße*, 1923) were recreated and formed an important element of the films' suspense. Hitchcock, furthermore, also had a preference for German-speaking actors (for example Peter Lorre in *The Man Who Knew Too Much*, Lucie Mannheim in *The Thirty-Nine Steps* or Oscar Homolka in *Sabotage*). Often cast in the role of villains, they constituted a warning against renascent militarism in Germany.

The full extent of German/Austrian participation and the allusion to contemporary politics by way of geographically or temporally displaced settings, however, can also be seen in thrillers made by other filmmakers. The film *I Was a Spy* (Victor Saville, 1933) starring the anti-Nazi actor Conrad Veidt, for instance, is set during the First World War. Its release was approved by the BBFC on 24 September after only superficial cuts. Besides Veidt, another German émigré, Alfred Junge, was part of the cast and crew. He constructed the enormous sets that give the production its particular look emphasising the dire scenario laid out by the film. Under the heading 'War Theme Drama as Super-Sensation', *Kinematograph Weekly* praised the 'stark realism' of the settings that had been created with 'great care'.[136] Produced the same year Hitler seized power, the film implies the use of poison gas by the German military by way of repeatedly depicting choking British POWs as they arrive at a Belgian infirmary. Consequently, the motion picture brought into play British fears of a revival of Prussian militarism and German aggression. Such fears are also evoked in a scene where German soldiers inappropriately sing the infamous national anthem '*Deutschland über alles*' ('Germany above all') during an open-air church

service. Especially the mise-en-scène, which shows German soldiers marching ominously through an occupied city, offered powerful images that
could well be read as an admonishment against German rearmament at
the time. The journal *Picturegoer* observed '[a] recrudescence of the war
atmosphere in films which may or may not be a sign of the perturbed time
through which we are passing'.[137] Like so many other exiles, Veidt was
accused of treason by the Nazi regime for his appearance in the film.[138]
Fortunately the success of the film secured him a long-term contract with
Gaumont-British.

The theme of a threat posed by Germany also features in another movie
with Veidt, *Dark Journey*. Produced and directed by Victor Saville in 1937,
the 'good fast-moving film of the adventurous type' (*Daily Mirror*) was
made with participation of further film practitioners from Germany or
Austria.[139] Andrej Andrejew and Ferdinand Bellan were responsible for the
production design, Lajos Biró wrote the play on which the film was based
and, in co-operation with Arthur Wimperis, the script; although uncredited, Korda co-produced the film. Set in 1918 Norway, the First World
War, again, served as a matrix for a rather general warning against German
state bellicosity. Among other things, the screenplay includes the lines 'Is it
a crime to be a German? It's worse – it's a vulgarity.'[140]

Another common threat that is inscribed into British spy thrillers of the
1930s is sabotage carried out by foreign powers on British soil. Commonly
such fears are represented within the formulaic structure of spy thrillers by
means of oppositions such as good and evil, gentleman and villain, British
and foreign. By casting a British actor as hero and a German-speaking
émigré as antagonist, the accent hints at Germany as the country behind
the plot of foreign infiltration. Although the British authorities in Alfred
Hitchcock's 1936 film *Sabotage*, the filmic adaptation of Joseph Conrad's
novel *The Secret Agent*, are fighting unnamed foreign powers, the casting of
Austrian émigré Oscar Homolka changed the perspective of the original
story. Whereas the book suggests Russia as the foreign power behind acts of
terrorism and sabotage in England, Homolka's heavy German accent hints
at the Third Reich, although his employer remains unnamed throughout
the film for reasons of censorship. In fact, Hitchcock intentionally and
systematically cast German-speaking émigrés in order to warn against Nazi
aggression and the possible threat posed by a revived Third Reich under
Hitler. As early as 1934, for example, when the Nazi government intentionally and increasingly violated the levels of rearmament set out by the Allies
in the Versailles treaty, one of the criminals in Hitchcock's thriller *The Man
Who Knew Too Much* is German-speaking exile Peter Lorre.[141] Moreover,
in *The Thirty-Nine Steps* a mysterious woman played by Austrian-born
exile Lucie Mannheim is stabbed to death in hero Richard Hannay's flat.

Her death may well be interpreted as symbolising and anticipating Hitler's intentions to annex Austria. Whether one follows such an interpretation or not, the timing of the release of *The Thirty-Nine Steps* corresponds strikingly with Hitler's stated intention to rearm beyond the limits imposed on Germany at Versailles.[142] Anti-Nazi criticism is even more pronounced in Hitchcock's thriller *Secret Agent* (1936). Made after the Third Reich had sent troops into the officially demilitarised Rhineland zone on 7 March 1936, the film set during the First World War openly names Germany as the enemy. The First World War context, however, is relegated to the background as it only appears at the opening of the film and in late combat sequences. Most of the time the fight between British and German agents 'might easily be taken as contemporary', as Robertson points out.[143]

Thus directors and producers repeatedly cast German-speaking actors like Oscar Homolka or Peter Lorre as 'Germanic' villains. German actor Conrad Veidt, for instance, was never to play a British person despite his outstanding reputation following his acclaimed performances in German films. Yet, Veidt's roles as the mysterious stranger in *The Passing of the Third Floor Back* (Berthold Viertel, 1935) or 'the other' as in *The Spy in Black* (Michael Powell, 1939) did not necessarily carry negative connotations. Set on the Orkneys during the First World War, *The Spy in Black* tells the story of German attempts to gather top-secret information about the British fleet. Although Veidt starred as German U-boat captain and spy Ernst Hardt, the highly ambiguous thriller dealing with the theme of national security apparently called upon the viewers to sympathise with Hardt regardless of his foreign descent, as reviews suggest.[144] Whereas on the surface the script suggests clear animosities ("'You are English! I am German! We are enemies!" "I like that better!" "So do I! It simplifies everything!"'), a second look reveals a rather equivocal situation.[145] Scriptwriter Emeric Pressburger included subtleties in the script that suggest a more balanced view of the enemy. *The Spy in Black* is another example of a motion picture set during the First World War that at the same time includes numerous allusions to Nazi Germany. It is, however, exceptional because of its nuanced depiction of its German protagonist. For the film script, Pressburger altered the character of the U-boat captain in the novel, originally published by J. Storer Clouston in 1917, into a more sympathetic character. The charismatic Prussian officer Hardt in the film was thus not to equal Nazi villains. His secret German code phrase taken from Heinrich Heine's 'Lorelei', which remains untranslated in the film, ('*Ich weiß nicht, was soll es bedeuten, daß ich so traurig bin – ein Märchen aus alten Zeiten, das geht mir nicht aus dem Sinn*' – 'I search in vain for the meaning, the reason I'm so full of woe – a tale of old times haunts me, and will not let me go')[146] clearly distances him from the official Nazi ideology that ousted writers like Heine as 'degenerate artists' and burnt their works. In his book on Pressburger, Kevin Macdonald speculates that the character of Hardt might have been modelled on émigré producer Günther Stapenhorst, who was a flagship commander in the *Reichsmarine* during the First World War.[147]

The claustrophobic atmosphere prevailing throughout the film can well be seen as a reflection of the international tensions just before the war. Unlike the American émigré production *Confessions of a Nazi Spy* (Anatole Litvak, USA 1939) which opened in Britain at the same time as *The Spy in Black*, the British picture deals with war-related issues and Nazism in a far more ambiguous way, representing innate British fears of war through the tropes of *film noir*.[148] In particular Pressburger's alterations regarding the role of Captain Hardt and Veidt's ambiguous performance, which had become the actor's trademark, turns a simplistic story into a complex thriller that opens up many uncertainties. In this regard, Andrew Moor points out that 'simple national loyalties are confused for the audience by identification with the charismatic German anti-hero'.[149]

It is no coincidence that the production of spy thrillers peaked in the aftermath of the Munich agreement of September 1938 when developments clearly revealed the failure of the appeasement policy to contain the aggression of the Third Reich. A Mass-Observation report in December 1939 emphasised the relationship of public fears to the abundance of British and US spy films:

> [Numerous films with a spy theme] were ready or released just before the outbreak of war. To a psychologist this simple fact would give a good picture of the mentality of the sort of people producing films at that time and of the general atmosphere of inferiority which the American democracies were unconsciously feeling towards aggressive Germany. This inferiority so accentuated by Munich was released by the fact of war and we at last showed ourselves able and ready to stand up to this sinister enemy with his humanity-eliminating Gestapo.[150]

Referring to the obvious parallels between the plot of *The Spy in Black* and the political situation in Europe at the eve of war, Graham Greene pointed out that *The Spy in Black* marks a decisive turn away from the BBFC's former policy of objecting to any films that were not in line with Westminster's appeasement policy.[151]

The film's release in America was overshadowed by the acts which opened the Second World War. The distributor Columbia used the sinking of the passenger ship 'Athenia' by a German submarine on 3 September 1939 for promotion in the US. Not only was the picture renamed *U-Boat 29* but also the whole marketing campaign followed the new political climate. Whereas the focus of advertisement for the film in Britain was on the female lead Valerie Robson and her role as a Mata Hari-like *femme fatale*, on posters in the US use was made of the powerful image of a sinking cruise liner. This image was accompanied by sensationalist headings proclaiming 'War in Europe – U-boats turn the sea red!'.[152]

Apart from actors, script writers, directors and producers, German-speaking cameramen and art directors were pivotal in the making of British spy thrillers. Their influence was seismic insofar as the thriller genre – like the American *film noir* – often portrayed the dark, tense atmosphere of the time by relying heavily on the same elements of mise-en-scène that had formerly contributed to the success of Weimar Expressionist Cinema. Indeed, the combination of claustrophobic sets and the villains' SS or Gestapo-like leather coats and uniforms, created by German-speaking designers became an inherent part of the iconography of 1930s British spy thrillers. In addition to the German accent of émigré actors, it was especially such costumes and props that hinted in the direction of the Third Reich as the foreign power behind the sinister plots of spies and saboteurs. On one level this is further proof for the thesis that émigré spy thrillers represent the fears and the plight of their makers before their escape from Germany or Austria. On another level, such characteristics stand for an inter-mingling of two cinematic traditions. As Andrew Moor points out films like *The Spy in Black* 'demonstrate a generic wedding, vamping up British territorial anxieties of the late 1930s into a gothic mode by intertwining the genealogies of the spy genre with some of Expressionism's uncanny motifs'.[153]

After the overwhelming international success of Alexander Korda's *The Private Life of Henry VIII* (1933), German technicians also became vital for the production of costume dramas with their often lavish sets. Besides spy thrillers, it was especially this genre that was used as a vehicle for political critique. The films commonly used the method of political analogy in order to convey their messages. Often, however, allegories are kept in the background as costume melodramas focussed more on personal relationships and tragically terminated love as can be seen in films such as the French émigré production *Mayerling* (Anatole Litvak, France 1936). While Prussia had been central to Weimar's costume film production, émigré films rather referred to the Austro-Hungarian dual monarchy and imperial Russia as historical subjects.[154] Horak infers that 'foreign audiences were . . . possibly more comfortable with Viennese *Gemütlichkeit* than with Prussian coldness. . . . [The] Prussians also brought on a new world war, while the Austrians were thought of as benign victims of Nazism.'[155] Especially émigré musical and opera films such as the British *The Robber Symphony* (Berthold Viertel, 1936), *Land without Music* (Walter Forde, 1936) or *Pagliacci* (Karl Grune, 1936), which could often be regarded as a sub-genre of the costume picture on the basis of their opulent production values, cinematographically resurrected the Austrian-Hungarian monarchy with ample Viennese charm and music. Among others, the films featured popular émigré opera stars such as Richard Tauber or Matha Eggerth.

As in Hollywood, British émigré films often diluted their anti-fascist message within existing genre conventions and stereotypes, calling attention to moral rather than political issues.[156] However, the two are closely connected. This can be seen in biographical films that constitute yet another sub-genre of the costume drama. Alexander Korda's exile film *Rembrandt* (1936), for instance, depicts the famous Dutch painter as a fragile character who refuses to put his talent to the service of the ruling classes and subsequently loses his reputation and social status. In this way, the film differs significantly from popular Third Reich productions which hero-worshipped public characters as in *Robert Koch*, *Rembrandt* (both Hans Steinhoff, Germany 1939 and 1942) and *Paracelsus* (Georg Wilhelm Pabst, Germany 1943). Accordingly, Horak's general thesis holds true for British productions such as *Rembrandt*: 'While exile film biographies presupposed democratic assumptions about politics and the world, the biographical films of the Third Reich underscored heroic legends which metaphorically supported the cult of the Führer.'[157] Apart from the characterisation of the protagonist, the difference between the exile film *Rembrandt* and Third Reich biopics is obvious in the way the former deals with Jewish issues. When Rembrandt loses his house and possessions after having refused to glamorise Dutch officers in one of his commissioned paintings it is a Jew who stands by the stricken genius. Whilst most people regard him as a fool, he reminds the others: 'He was a good man, a just man – he didn't deserve this.'

Jewish themes were central to many British costume dramas produced by émigrés. The high-budget Gaumont-British production *Jew Süss* (Lothar Mendes, 1934), which should not be mistaken with the notorious later Nazi production *Jud Süss* (Veit Harlan, Germany 1938), offers a particularly interesting case of a pre-war film that addresses sensitive political issues. Within the context of British cinema the controversial film demonstrates the determination of Gaumont-British to produce feature films with a political message. *Jew Süss* was the third proposal by Gaumont-British dealing with an anti-Nazi message after the aforementioned 'A German Tragedy' and 'City Without Jews' were rejected by the BBFC. Perhaps their determination to look into a project that disapproves of anti-Semitism and fascism can partly be explained by the prominence of the Jewish Osterer family on the company's Board of Directors.[158] Besides the Osterers the actual realisation of the film owes much to Michael Balcon, who produced it despite numerous obstacles. Not only did the film well exceed its budget of £85,000 by but he also had to 'fight much resistance on the ground that it was a "dangerous" subject', as he later claimed in his memoirs.[159] The film was finally passed for release by the BBFC despite its controversial story on 14 June 1934 after minor modifications concerning language, sexual aspects, nudity and some depictions of violence.[160] 'Once again', according to historian Jeffrey Richards, 'a historical setting made the message palatable'.[161]

Despite a probable personal interest on the part of Balcon and the Osterers in a film that positioned itself against anti-Semitic resentment, they were also convinced of the financial opportunities of such a project. In line with Fleet Street journalists who claimed 'Jews is News', Gaumont-British certainly financed the opulent production *Jew Süss* in the belief that it was 'unlikely to fail, because Jews were never so much news as they are to-day',[162] as a contemporary critic argued. While this belief proved to be right for Britain where the high-budget production was the sixth most successful film at the box office in 1934,[163] this was not the case everywhere, as Susan Tegel shows by comparing its release in London, New York, Vienna and Berlin. Not surprisingly prohibited in the Third Reich, the film was also banned by the Austrian police, despite its official approval by the censor. Moreover, Austrian newspapers rejected the costume drama as a Jewish *Tendenzfilm* which affronted the feelings of Catholic people.[164] After fascists prevented the film from being shown in Germany and Austria, negotiations for the film to be shown in Hungary and Poland were also cut off, limiting its international release.[165]

Unlike other films of the era that criticise Nazism in a rather subtle way, *Jew Süss,* which was produced with numerous émigrés such as Lothar Mendes, Conrad Veidt, Paul Graetz, Alfred Junge and Günther Krampf, included the unprecedented direct statement '1730, 1830, 1930 – they will always persecute us'.[166] It is surprising that the otherwise meticulous censors overlooked this reference to the 1930s in a film that is supposed to be set in the eighteenth century. Whilst contemporary reviews did not quote this line itself, some acknowledged that a national and international audience 'will interpret this film in the light of German events' as the film had 'the air of being a luridly antedated comment on some aspects of the Hitler regime'.[167] In a similar way, a critic in *Monthly Film Bulletin* thought that '[t]he theme of the film, toleration for Jewry, is one which most people will sympathetically accept to-day, particularly in the face of contemporary events in Germany and elsewhere'.[168] That said, a number of reviews also missed the allusions to Nazi Germany. The *Observer* film critic C. A. Lejeune, for instance, thought that the large sum 'spent so generously on a film about a little German municipality of two hundred years ago' should rather be used for documentaries on shipbuilding, English farming and the 'epic story of unemployment'.[169] Given the numerous references to the Third Reich, this seems surprising, if not ignorant. Apart from the above-mentioned line, the opening titles of the film directly point at Nazi

Germany: 'Württemberg in the eighteenth century – A time of brutal and universal intolerance and the Jews above all suffered oppression and boycott.' The latter form of harassment was not so much a form of eighteenth century anti-Semitism but rather a method of persecution the Nazis used against Jewish businesses once they seized power in early 1933.[170]

The similarities of the eighteenth century duchy of Württemberg, as represented in the film, to the Third Reich are particularly evident in the sequence leading to the protagonist's execution. In the fictional *Jew Süss*, an old forgotten law, which states that sexual intercourse between Jews and Gentiles is to be punished by death, is utilised to justify the execution of Süss. The actual execution scene in the film, then, seems like an act of anti-Semitic hysteria. The justification of Süss' execution, indeed, bears striking similarities to the allegations of Julius Streicher's racist propaganda paper *Der Stürmer* as one critic in the exile paper *Pariser Tageblatt* notes: 'One sees that "Stürmer" Streicher can look back over a long tradition of worthy predecessors who, just like him, knew how to whet the people's appetite for the execution of Jews'. And he adds cynically: 'Today the same "offence," according to the latest proposal from the National Socialist doctors, is to be punished by a five-year prison sentence. At least there is a discernible amount of progress. There is no reason to despair for humanity quite yet.'[171]

Not surprisingly the release of *Jew Süss* prompted hostility among Nazis. In this respect, the film can be regarded as the beginning of a war of information between Western democracies and the Third Reich. The Nazis, as Susan Tegel points out, 'chose to interpret the significance of the British film'[172] by banning it in Germany and by urging other countries to follow suit. Moreover, the fact that the German Propaganda Ministry ordered an anti-Semitic remake of the film to be produced by Veit Harlan further indicates the importance of the British production and its propaganda value in the eyes of Nazi officials. When Harlan's feature film was about to be completed in 1940, Goebbels viewed the original British version with Veidt once again, noting in his diary that the new film may correct what he believes to be a distorted image of Jewish propaganda that had made a saint out of a financial hyena.[173] As the Nazis had monitored the international reception of *Jew Süss* ever since its premiere, Harlan's version can, in many respects, be seen as a direct filmic reply to the British exile film production.[174]

Although *Jew Süss* and the other notable costume drama of 1930s British cinema dealing with the iniquities suffered by Jews, *The Wandering Jew* (Maurice Elvey, 1933), primarily allowed for readings that exposed German atrocities against Jews, these films did not limit their criticism to the Third Reich. At a time when Oswald Mosley's British Union of Fascists, known as the Blackshirts, was responsible for numerous outbreaks against Jews in London and beyond, they can also be read as a moral statement against anti-Jewish resentment in England. And indeed, as their reception illustrates, a form of 'genteel' anti-Semitism was very much acceptable in British film criticism at the time.[175] Many comments that were perhaps meant to be satirically flippant turned sour in view of their historical context. Linking the three English language films dealing with Jewish issues that were released shortly after Hitler came to power, the magazine *Punch*, for instance, warned the Tivoli theatre in London, where *Jew Süss* premiered, that it:

> must begin to Aryanise itself or it will be too much thought of as the abode of Hebraic eminence and idiosyncrasy. First we had Conrad Veidt as *The Wandering Jew*, the victim of destiny; then George Arliss as the urbane successful Jew in high finance in *The House of Rothschild* and now here is Conrad Veidt again, this time as the inexorable hero of Feuchtwanger's novel, *Jew Süss*, with the downtrodden virtuous ghetto all about him. A little Gentile leaven in the Tivoli pogroms – I mean programme – would not be unwelcome.[176]

Besides films like *Jew Süss* or *The Wandering Jew*, the exile film *Abdul the Damned* (1935), which was directed and produced by the refugees Karl Grune and Max Schach respectively, also sought to avoid censorship by using fictitious or historically and geographically displaced settings. The Viennese-born actor Fritz Kortner not only played the lead but also contributed to the script, although the latter is omitted in the credits. His critically acclaimed personification of sultan Abdul Hamid[177] – whose initials A. H. were not coincidentally those of Adolf Hitler – was a harsh condemnation of totalitarian dictators in general and of Hitler and Mussolini in particular. Although analogies to the *Führer* or *duce* were veiled in a plot that on the surface deals with historical events in the Turkish empire leading to the 1908 Young Turk revolution and the deposition of sultan Abdul Hamid II, they were nevertheless identifiable as contemporary reviews show. A *Sunday Times* review of 3 March 1935 notes that although *Abdul the Damned* was '[b]ased on historical events belonging to the Gladstone era, it nevertheless has some relationship to present-day affairs'.[178] Likewise, émigré Erich Kaiser views the film as a general statement against contemporary totalitarian regimes by comparing Abdul Hamid implicitly with dictators such as Stalin, Mussolini and Hitler in the exile paper *Pariser Tageblatt*.[179] While the film turns into a study of paranoia as a precondition and mental basis for political dictatorship, its plot furthermore bears striking parallels to the power struggles within the Nazi movement that culminated in the 'Night of the Long Knives' in 1934.[180]

After *Abdul the Damned* was viewed by BBFC president Edward Shortt and members of the Foreign Office it was cut by almost seven minutes.[181] Whether the omissions were made because of concerns over Anglo-Turkish relations, which had already led to the ban on a film based on Jewish émigré Franz Werfel's novel *Die vierzig Tage des Musa Dagh* (1934) on the 1915 Armenian genocide in Turkey, or because of Anglo-German relations cannot be ascertained since the film held by the National Film and Television Archive is not the original uncensored version. It is likely that both concerns informed the decision, as the BBFC generally banned all scenes dealing with 'subjects which are calculated to wound the susceptibilities of foreign people'.[182]

A further example of how exile films tried to get around censorship is *The Lilac Domino* (Fred Zelnik, 1937) starring the Hungarian actor Szöke Szakall.[183] Émigré scriptwriter Rudolf Bernauer included obvious asides to Hitler's Germany and racist ideology by including a ballroom scene featuring 'shadows of men dressed in Ku Klux Klan costume'.[184] It can be inferred that Max Schach also intended contemporaneous political associations when he acquired the rights to Morris Collis' novel *Siamese White* about a 'fantastically cruel monarch'[185] (*Kinematograph Weekly*) of the seventeenth century.

As this and other examples show, political criticism in exile films was not limited to National Socialism. Many émigrés opposed totalitarianism in all its forms – whether from the political right or left. Inscribed into the lavish costume drama *Knight without Armour* (1937), for instance, are the fears of a disorder caused by a Communist revolution. Despite an otherwise rigid vetting process, the BBFC had no objections to the film that was co-written by Lajos Biró and produced by Alexander Korda. Starring Hollywood star and émigré Marlene Dietrich, *Knight without Armour* tells the story of a widowed aristocratic daughter of a Tsarist minister whom a British secret agent rescues after the outbreak of the Russian revolution in 1917. Although the plot focuses on action and romance rather than politics, the setting of the film makes it almost impossible, as Jeffrey Richards underlines, 'to come away seeing [the film] without thinking that the Russian revolutionaries were a thoroughly beastly crew'.[186]

Émigrés and displacement: Representations of the diaspora and recollections of the *Heimat*

Closely linked to political messages in many films made by or with émigré were representations of their own diasporic existence as a sine qua non circumstance following the rise of totalitarian regimes in Europe. So Whitehall's restrictive measures increased the forced mobility of exiles making it harder to settle. Work permits were frequently refused or the duration of residency permits not extended. As such, the nomadic lives of German-speaking film personnel in Britain – which were characterised as much by intercultural exchange and mobility as by instability and exclusion

– found their way into many British films of the period thereby underlining the fact that all films are inseperable from their specific contexts of production and consumption.

Leaving one's home country was influenced by a variety of factors including 'the material and intellectual capacity to abandon Germany in an attempt to construct a new existence abroad', as Jean-Michel Palmier notes.[187] Wherever German-speaking exiles found refuge, they created texts about their own diasporic situation. The exile situation, indeed, stylistically and thematically influenced films made by or with émigrés in Britain, often in the veiled form of narratives or filmic representations dealing with travelling or loneliness. A reading of films thus cannot be limited to explicit statements or references to refugees and exile. It also needs to take into account the identification of subtle and allegorical references to displacement and alienation. The sheer number of such allusions in films made by German-speaking filmmakers is significant. Through them, the various experiences of mobility and border-crossings inscribed into films form part of a general characteristic of exilic and diasporic filmmaking. Many émigrés were involved in the production process, and they had an impact on both film aesthetics and storylines to create what Hamid Naficy refers to as the 'accented style'. Although it seems inappropriate to apply all aspects of Naficy's work to the situation of German-speaking émigrés in Britain – not least because many if not the majority of them worked within dominant means of film production rather than alternative cinema – his general argument still holds true. The constant presence – both in terms of quantity and quality – of such themes in films made by or with émigrés from Germany or Austria can hardly be interpreted as coincidental. On the contrary, the many statements and references that can be identified justify the method of reading films against the background of the émigrés' own situation. Whilst themes of exile and displacement have formed the basis of many fictional plots ever since Homer's *Odyssey* and a presence of travelling, dislocation, foreignness, etc. also form the basis of many films without an émigré input, the 'accented cinema' is more than a mere matter of plot device or narrative: it is a response to a particular social experience. At odds with the dictum of the 'death of the author', Naficy therefore insists on a general presence of émigré filmmakers within their creative works.

In addition to compulsory journeys abroad so that émigrés could renew their temporary residence permits and business trips (Rudolf Bernauer, for instance, paid eight work-related visits to Holland, Switzerland and France from April 1936 to August 1939),[188] German-speaking émigrés remained on the move even in the UK. Owing to the unsteady nature of the film business and to residency restrictions during the war, they repeatedly changed – or had to change – their accommodation. The various changes of address were meticulously listed by émigrés in their naturalisation applications or in the reports compiled by the Metropolitan police for the subsequent review process. The police report for the scriptwriter and journalist Heinrich Fraenkel, for example, states that he moved eight times in the war alone. Excluding his time in an internment camp from 21 August 1940 to 15 January 1941, all of his addresses were situated within London (mainly NW3).[189] The situation of Rudolph Cartier offers a similar picture. Between January 1936 and August 1945 he moved 16 times mainly within London but also to addresses in Glasgow and Chalford.[190]

As with all political content, censorship and above all the commercial nature of the film business as popular entertainment influenced the way in which foreign film personnel were able to represent their life as strangers. It soon becomes apparent that émigré film professionals on both sides of the Atlantic used the topics of exile or diaspora as a central motif far less than their literary colleagues – although films made during the war such as *Casablanca* (Michael Curtiz, USA 1942) or *Voice in the Wind* (Arthur Ripley, USA 1944) count as prominent exceptions. Refugee director Billy Wilder explains this notable difference between exile literature and exile films with a lack of interest within the émigrés' new country of domicile: 'The tale of refugees was a sensation when Alexandre Dumas and Victor Hugo told it, but now, when I tell my tale, everybody just yawns.'[191]

Within the commercial imperatives of the film business on both sides of the Atlantic, this meant that many film projects centring explicitly on refugees from the Third Reich were shelved. Films that were announced but never materialised include titles such as *Port of Hope* and *Refugees*.[192] While a possible lack of interest was one reason for this, censorship was another. The fact that the topic of enforced exile was linked with events in Germany prevented the development of such films in the British arena as a result of the content control exercised by the BBFC. Even if films were not banned, they were subject to certain conditions. Submitted by United Artists in 1938, the proposed film *The Exiles*, which tells the story of a prominent scientist fleeing from an unspecified country to America, where he initially faces deportation but is ultimately granted permission to stay because his case receives great public support, was carefully monitored by the censors. The script examiner in charge, Miss Nora Shortt, plainly expressed her opinion that the film project could only be allowed to proceed on condition that 'the producers carry out their intention of not making the country identifiable in any way and [only if] the exiles themselves are not made to look unmistakable Jews'.[193]

Within the variety of émigré films, transitional and transnational places and spaces reappear in various forms. The diversity of films made by German-speaking filmmakers in the UK thus reflects the diversity of

London's émigrés who by no means formed a uniform entity. Some films are euphorically optimistic in dealing with the new host country or the lost homeland, whereas others are bleak stories of failure and trauma. While some praise the new freedom of the host country, others offer nostalgic views of the land they must leave behind.[194] Notwithstanding this filmic diversity, Naficy offers a useful set of universal tropes that can be found in many an émigré film, including displacement, claustrophobia, assimilation processes, 'imprisonment, imagined homelands, borders, journeys and symbolic locations and objects of itinerancy such as trains, buses, airports, hotels, suitcases'.[195] So the circumstances of the émigrés' situation are repeatedly inscribed into their films metaphorically by analogy. The number of transnational train journeys (as in *Heart's Desire*, Paul L. Stein 1935, and *The Lilac Domino*, Frederic Zelnik 1937), ship passages (e.g. in the remake of Griffith's *Broken Blossoms*, John Brahm 1936 and *Victoria the Great*, Herbert Wilcox 1937), plane travel (*The Tunnel*, Maurice Elvey 1935) or border crossings (*Land Without Music*, Walter Forde 1936 and *The Rake's Progress*, Sidney Gilliat, 1945) strongly supports such a reading.

Since the pressure of assimilation was high, films made by émigrés depict many performative strategies of camouflage resembling their own situation. As a result many films are characterised by a masquerade of national identity and feature characters who appear as 'ethnic go-betweens', that is to say people who live at the intersection of two or more cultures. Whatever the preliminary message of individual films, the fictional protagonists allude to the life of émigré filmmakers to a certain degree. Apart from the storylines, the performances of exile actors play a pivotal role. Repeatedly cast as foreigners, their performances underline that a display of heterogeneous national identities, conflicting recollections of one's home country, disorientation, assimilation and failed cultural adaptation are a common phenomenon of exile cinema. Thus, the findings of Gemünden's analysis of Peter Lorre's performances in American films are applicable to German-speaking émigrés in Britain. He argues that the performances of émigré actors 'are not so much about mimicking as about mimicry – not a simple imitation of a dominant acting style but a blurred copy that always retains the traces of forced assimilation while at the same time mocking the coerciveness of acculturation'.[196]

As wanderers or travellers émigrés visually perceive their new, unfamiliar environment as outsiders or through the eyes of what Walter Benjamin referring to Baudelaire calls *flâneurs*.[197] This key spectator of the modern urban environment, who can be portrayed as an uninvolved, yet highly perceptive bourgeois wanderer, seems an ideal fictional character to illustrate the life of refugees in films. Coming to an unknown country, refugees as well as *flâneurs* explore their new environment first and foremost as strollers ambling through unknown cities. Benjamin's fellow refugee, the critic Siegfried Kracauer describes this type of distant observer appropriately as an 'aimless saunterer', someone who seeks 'to conceal the gaping void around him and within him by imbibing a thousand casual impressions. Shop windows, . . . elegant equipages, newspaper sellers – he indiscriminately absorbed the spectacle of life that went on around him.'[198]

A number of émigré films of in the 1930s and more so – as outlined in the next chapter – in the 1940s capture issues of estrangement, exile and life in the diaspora through the gaze of the *flâneur* and the character of the foreigner. The authentic feel of these films, as will be argued here, owe much to the personal experiences of the foreign personnel involved in their production. In a similar way to the filmmakers' own situation as exiles the fictional characters correspond to the new situation of being a refugee by going through the same processes of assimilation and estrangement. So filmmakers and dramatis personae share a variety of initial responses to their new home, ranging from the desire to keep a low profile to curiosity, desolation, hope and contentment. The following analyses of films show how German-speaking émigrés as strangers in Britain, unfamiliar with their new habitat, felt more at ease with fictional films set in transnational or foreign places rather than narratives dealing with contemporary English subject matter. They thus particularly often participated in Empire Films (e.g *Rhodes of Africa*, 1936), historical costume pictures (e.g. *The Private Life of Henry VIII*, 1933 and *Victoria the Great*, 1937) and fantasy films (e.g. *Chu Chin Chow*, 1934 and *The Thief of Bagdad*, 1940). As Greg Walker has demonstrated relating to Korda's foreign roots, émigrés' cultural chameleonism and as a consequence of their role as outsiders impacted on their ideas on filmmaking.[199]

One of the main characteristics of exile films is that they not only offer new insights into the new country of residence but also convey many ideas of the old homeland. Although this phenomenon can be identified in émigré films across all genres, recollections of romanticised homelands can perhaps best be identified in the many popular melodramas and musicals set in idyllic Austrian-Hungarian or southern German landscapes.[200] Following Ernst Lubitsch's international success with *Old Heidelberg* (1927), many German-speaking émigrés exploited pre-existing romanticised views of their *Heimat*. The escapist films offered a refuge from the everyday by depicting picturesque Alpine rural Bavarian and Austrian landscapes untouched by the industrial revolution and international political tensions. Apart from Empire Films, costume dramas and spy thrillers it was especially these films that offered employment opportunities to many German-speaking émigrés who could demonstrate their special talents in the romantic musical comedies that these productions tended to be. Having been a chief representative of the production of light-hearted German musicals, Wilhelm Thiele, for example, was contracted to direct *Waltz Time* (1933), an adaptation of the operetta *Die Fledermaus*. Other projects included multi-language productions filmed in Germany such as *The Empress and I* (*Ich und die Kaiserin*, Frederick Hollander, 1933), English-German or English-Austrian co-productions such as *Unfinished Symphony* (Anthony Asquith and Willi Forst, UK/Austria 1934), a Martha Eggerth star vehicle that tells the life-story of Franz Schubert, or remakes of previous Austrian or German films such as *Prince of Arcadia* (Hanns Schwarz, 1934; based on *Der Prinz von Arkadien*, Karl Hartl, Germany/Austria 1932). In addition to providing work for set designers and the numerous actors cast in minor parts, who added 'genuine' flavour to the central European settings, these melodramas and musicals were an ideal star vehicle for continental émigrés. Besides Walter Reisch, who wrote many scripts of continental musicals (*Prince of Arcadia, The Song You Gave Me, Two Hearts in Waltz Time*, etc.) two names in particular are inseparably connected with the production of musical films set in Vienna: the director Paul L. Stein and the actor Richard Tauber.[201]

The latter was a successful opera singer in Dresden, Berlin, and Vienna as well as an actor before he featured in the British film *Heart's Desire* (Paul L. Stein, 1935) as the down-to-earth Austrian street musician Josef Steidler. The role, which was described by a critic of *The Times* as a most human 'peasant, cramming beer and liver-sausage into his mouth before he sings',[202] was similar to the characters he played in earlier light-hearted musical films in German with evocative titles such as *Land des Lächelns* (*The Land of Smiles*, Max Reichmann, 1930) or *Melodie der Liebe* (*Melody of Love/Right to Happiness*, Georg Jacoby, 1932) and thus permitted the singer an easy transition. The film's Austrian director Paul L. Stein had also gained much experience in popular theatre and musical films before he came to Britain in 1932. Among other things, he worked at the *Volksbühne* in Berlin and the *Deutsche Volkstheater* in Vienna and became a sought-after director from the early 1920s with titles such as *Es leuchtet meine Liebe* (1922) and *Liebesfeuer* (1925).

Thus Stein's British film *Heart's Desire* with Richard Tauber in the lead seems to be nothing if not a continuation of their work within the preferred genre of musical films and light-hearted romantic comedies depicting idealised and nostalgic views of Austria as a country of grandeur, music, and Viennese *Gemütlichkeit*.[203] In the film, which relies heavily on music as a carrier of atmosphere and therefore meaning, this is for instance expressed through songs such as 'Vienna, City of My Dreams'. However, what appears at first glance to be no more than a conventional, idyllic representation of Vienna is a pivotal film in the context of border crossing, homesickness, transnationality and the diaspora. The narrative focuses on Steidler who together with his manager Florian leaves his beloved home

Vienna with its scenic beer gardens and endearing people to seek 'fame and fortune as a singer on the London stage'. Played by the émigrés Richard Tauber and Paul Graetz, the decision by the Austrian street musician and his manager to leave their Viennese environment gains political actuality because the two actors also had to leave their home for London. One of the many parallels between the filmic roles and the lives of the actors that the film deals with are the problems that such a move from continental Europe to Britain implies. First there is the language. After Josef Steidler reluctantly takes the decision to go to England he forces himself to learn English. Far from being an enthusiastic student of the foreign idiom he appears annoyed and slightly piqued throughout. Depicting Steidler's struggle, the short and comic, yet very significant dialogue in the assessment of German-speaking émigré actors in Britain, is almost identical with the accounts of émigré actors themselves. Fritz Kortner, to name one example, noted in his memoirs: 'My reputation as an actor was sufficient to bring me my first film part, but between my profession and me stood the English language.'[204] Kortner later transformed his experiences into the play 'Spell Your Name' about the destiny of an exiled Jewish refugee.[205] As Salka Viertel notes in her recollections of the time as a refugee in England 'Fritz Kortner and Johanna Hofer, Oscar Homolka, and many others were furiously learning English'.[206] Many other German-speaking actors, despite their efforts, had difficulties adapting to the English language and many had to laboriously learn their lines phonetically. Walbrook, too, struggled with English and took lessons from a native speaker – just like his diegetic fellow émigré in *Heart's Desire* Josef Steidler, who repeatedly relapses into German expressions.[207]

Unlike Walbrook, however, who developed into a popular screen personality and in the judgement of *The Times* had been notably successful in solving the problem of re-establishing himself in an English-speaking environment,[208] Steidler finds less of a home in England. When he leaves his treasured Vienna for London, less because he wants to than to earn the money to marry the woman he loves, he sings a melancholic romantic song by Robert Schumann about his beloved *Heimat* while the picture-perfect mountains of Austria – reconstructed at the Elstree studios – pass by his train window. His knowledge of England, its idiom and people, includes little more than the information in a phrase book he used for language learning. The significance of the train-travel sequence is stressed in formal terms by its duration of approximately seven minutes and its central position within the narrative, dividing as it does the scenes set in Vienna and London into two roughly-equal parts lasting about half an hour. This both formally and qualitatively central sequence underlines the main conflict. Within the diegesis of the film, the sequence signifies the alienation of Steidler and emphasises that his departure was a mistake. However, the trope of travelling also has resonance in relation to the situation and experiences of émigré filmmakers and their nomadic life once they were forced out of the Third Reich.

The overall 'cobbler, stick to your last' message of the film is visualised by the contrasting representations of Vienna and London. While the former's inhabitants are depicted as happy salt-of-the-earth people who always seem to have a song on their lips, London and the Londoners are characterised by a general lack of *joie de vivre*. They are cold, taciturn and stiff. When Steidler is asked by his English companions to refrain from smoking in the train compartment – a clear sign of lacking *Gemütlichkeit* – he joins his seemingly joyful fellow countrymen. While the situation before was characterised by misunderstanding as a result of the language barrier, he appears at ease among his compatriots. Together they joke and laugh and sing the emotional German folksong 'Muss i denn' written in a southern German dialect. While the popular romantic song about the temporary parting of two lovers comments on the separation of travellers and their loved ones, it also anticipates the eventual return equally desired by the fictional Josef Steidler and many of the actual émigrés.

Upon arrival, London appears in stark contrast to the peaceful tranquillity of Austria. The English capital is introduced as a modern urban landscape. The first image captures the façades of Piccadilly – it is loud, there are no plants or trees, and neon-signs dominate the scene. The two expatriates are clearly marked out as strangers. Apart from the struggle with the language, Steidler appears out of place among the many businessmen in bespoke Savile Row suits wearing a traditional Bavarian/Tyrol *Gamsbart* hat with a tuft of hair from a chamois. The talented Austrian singer immediately realises his alienation: 'Florian, it is all so strange here; we go back to Austria!'. And later, when he performs in the chic environment of London bourgeois society, he utters concerns shared by fellow émigrés, fictional or actual, that 'these people here are so different, I'm afraid they'll not like me because I am not like them'. His impression is not totally unfounded. When a producer reluctantly agrees to meet the Austrian tenor he simply orders him to 'Sing!' without indulging in the usual small talk, greeting the foreign musician or even introducing himself. Stunned by such impudence, Steidler utters in German '*In Wien sand's freundlicher*' ('People in Vienna are more amicable') only to be told with more than a hint of snobbishness 'In London we like to call a spade a shovel and we like it!'.

Although Steidler eventually achieves critical acclaim and is celebrated by an English audience, his homesickness and love for Anna, whom he had almost forgotten in the meantime, are stronger than his success in London. In the end neither his desired relationship with an English lady nor the mountain paintings in his theatre changing room can adequately replace his true love and his *Heimat*. On his return to Austria both Steidler and Florian are happy to get home. Once again Steidler euphorically notes Austria's charm ('I never realised that Austria was so beautiful!'). When Florian then remarks 'Isn't it great to be home', Steidler contentedly replies 'Back in our own world!'.

Arguing that human beings only have one real home where they belong and where they feel at ease, *Heart's Desire* – notwithstanding its comic, cheerful nature – paints a bleak picture of the diaspora. If the fictional character of Josef Steidler is understood as a symbolic figure who stands for all German-speaking émigrés, the film's narrative implies that their life in analogy to Steidler's experience in London is first and foremost characterised by isolation and trauma. Indeed, such a reading suggests that no matter how much émigrés try to assimilate themselves their effort will inevitably fail to be rewarded as the new environment remains unfamiliar and their real desire is to return to the place they had once left. In this regard, the Austrian roué Josef Steidler with his zest for life becomes the tragic figure of the homeless individual. His failed integration into British society in *Heart's Desire* thus represents the painful experience of being a refugee. Yet the moral ('stay where you belong') propagated by the film can only be partially applied to the situation of refugees from Nazi Germany because a homecoming – which is possible for the fictional characters in the film – was not an option during the 12 years of Nazi rule. *Heart's Desire*, in line with its fictional escapist quality, neglects the political actualities of the time when it was made.

A potential relationship between the Austrian star singer Josef Steidler and the English Frances Wilson in *Heart's Desire* comes to an end before it really started because she announces her engagement with an Englishman. Steidler and Wilson are depicted as being fundamentally dissimilar from the start as the film constantly underlines their cultural differences. Whereas Steidler is depicted as a traditional, down-to-earth street musician from Austria who loves the countryside, she is an upper-class London city girl wearing elegant robes, exquisite jewellery and handsome fur shawls. Like a number of other films representing themes of the diaspora or exile, *Heart's Desire* thereby negates cultural permutation in that none of the characters permanently transcends or overcomes national differences.

Apart from allusions to a Viennese *Gemütlichkeit* that is central to Steidler's character and the film, the Austrian capital is commonly associated with romance and a zest for life while its inhabitants are seen as charming roués. In many cases, this image rubbed off on Austrian émigré actors and production companies used it for their publicity campaigns. Anton Walbrook, for example, was intentionally displayed as a gentleman playboy, or in the words of *Film Weekly* critic Tom Dysart a 'tough romantic',[209] not least to cover up his homosexuality. In fact, in order to retain his appeal to female audiences, the mysterious press reports of his engagement to the 18-year-old actress Maud Courtney can be interpreted as a sophisticated PR campaign as the proposed marriage was eventually 'indefinitely postponed';[210] officially because of the future bride's age and Walbrook's Austrian nationality. When the engagement was ended, Walbrook once again could be described as a 'bachelor' – an attribute he never lost throughout his successful career in British cinema. Although he had a long-time partner his obituary in *The Times* describes his private life simply by stating that 'he was unmarried'.[211]

The general fad for films drawing on the myth of 'Old Vienna' was not only beneficial for Austrian actors but also for scriptwriters, composers and directors. Paul L. Stein's *Waltz Time* (1945), which featured the tenor Richard Tauber, was based on an idea by Karl Rossler, and its music was composed by Hans May. Vienna is portrayed by means of recurrent tropes such as welcoming wine gardens with sets of antlers on the walls, dancing the waltz and peaceful street life. In one scene before Richard Tauber sings, an Alpine landscape is rolled onto the stage, which also features hanging lanterns and lavish floral arrangements. The positive picture of Vienna is augmented by universal cheerfulness and laughter throughout the film. Even when the council discusses important state business a jokey atmosphere prevails. As can be seen in other émigré films set in Vienna, the popular escapist formula comprises a variety of waltz music, nostalgic nineteenth-century Austrian settings and a romantic love story.

This mythical perception of 'old Vienna' was both a blessing and a curse for the émigrés from Austria. On the one hand the light-hearted musicals set in their country of origin provided jobs at difficult times, on the other it meant that Austrian actors were increasingly typecast in clichéd roles and limited in their artistic self-expression. What is perhaps more significant still about these films, however, was that they also seem to play down Austria's active role in the pogroms against Jews and other minority groups. Although some expatriates believed in the nostalgic recollections of their homeland anti-Semitism in Austria was severely criticised by some refugees. In a feature column on representations of Austria in motion pictures, the London exile publication *Die Zeitung*, for example, underlines the absurdity of the idealised filmic Austria in the Hollywood production in the light of actual events:

> The year 1938, when Austria sank beneath a sea of brown, has changed nothing [with regard to the idealised film images]. The [filmic] Vienna of March 1938 looks more like the city of around 1890: it seems that the First World War has not yet begun and, of course, there has been no 1918. . . . Poor Austria; it is bitter to be tortured by one's enemies, but it is certainly not sweet, to be misunderstood by one's friends.[212]

Likewise, the absurd discrepancy between actual events in Vienna and the romanticised image of the Austrian capital in British films is captured well in Christopher Isherwood's colourful *roman-à-clef Prater Violet* (1945) about the British film industry of the 1930s, which is loosely based on his work with Berthold Viertel on the film *Little Friend* (1934). In an outburst of anger the fictional German director Dr. Bergmann curses the lavish production *Prater Violet*, which he was contracted to produce in London while his own family in Austria was in danger: 'The picture! I shit upon the picture! This heartless filth! This wretched, lying charade! To make such a picture at such a moment is definitely heartless. It is a crime.' And he continues by explaining his anger that the film which depicts a nostalgic and romanticised Vienna 'covers up the dirty syphilitic sore with rose leaves, with the petals of this hypocritical reactionary violet. It lies and declares that the pretty Danube is blue, when the water is red with blood.'[213]

Taking on a similar critical perspective as their fictional *alter ego*, some Austrian filmmakers even sought to deconstruct both the myth of Austria as the first victim of Nazi aggression and the idealised romantic images of Austria in general and of Vienna in particular. The 1936 British production *Land Without Music* (Walter Forde), for instance, counteracts the myth of a peaceful and liberal Austria that was the first victim of the Nazi war of conquest. Interestingly, many of the participating filmmakers were from Austria: the script was written by the Viennese author Rudolf Bernauer, Max Schach produced the film, Oscar Straus composed the music, and Richard Tauber played the main protagonist. The film tells the story of a star singer who returns to his beloved home country, the fictional land of music of the title, only to find out that any form of musical activity is prohibited because Austria threatens the little country and its music-loving harmonious people with war if the country does not immediately repay debts resulting from the idleness of its people. What seems to be a rather fantastic plot is in fact a sophisticated filmic experiment that ironically mocks popular notions of the Danubian monarchy. In fact, the Austria in *Land Without Music* threatens to invade its own myth, the country of music and a harmonious, peaceful society.

The flight from Nazi-controlled Germany or Austria was *the* most significant event in most émigrés' life. Its drastic and far-reaching implications changed many career paths as exile commonly meant the complete loss of status and income. As a tragic figure the 'penniless exile'[214] became a fictional plot device – not only in Isherwood's literary account of *Prater Violet* but also many actual film scripts that more or less explicitly included the themes of the struggling artist. One of those individuals who suffered much under the condition of exile was the prominent German theatre critic and author, Alfred Kerr. Even if he ultimately failed to establish himself in Britain working for the cinema industry, he is exemplary of many German-speaking exiles who sought new ways of employment after their often rushed flight from the Third Reich. His desperate situation becomes clear in a letter he wrote in 1934 explaining that he would even attempt to work as an actor in order to make a living.[215] Although he was able neither to realise his acting ambitions nor to turn his scripts, which were only discovered recently, into successful motion pictures, the screenplays offer insights into how German-speaking refugees tried to incorporate their own situation into films.[216]

His first film script 'Letizia', for instance, was based in large part on articles Kerr wrote for the *Berliner Tageblatt* in 1932 and which he turned into the travel book *Eine Insel heißt Korsika* (*An Island Called Corsica*) published in the following year.[217] In addition to the material that can be found in his book, Kerr's exile experience had an impact on the script, which centres on Napoleon's mother Letizia.[218] As a comment on his own financial needs and changed status in exile, the proposed film reflects the transitory nature of affluence and reputation in the diaspora. In Kerr's words, the script serves as 'a tremendous symbol of rise, climax, storm. Highs and lows. A wonderful allegory of earthly transitoriness'.[219] Against the backdrop of the author's *curriculum vitae* in which he went from being an important, if not the predominant, theatre critic of the Weimar Republic to his desperate situation in poverty and alienation after he was forced into exile, the script is an astoundingly candid recollection of his own life.

Although written in France, Kerr's first stage of exile, he sold the film rights for 'Letizia' to Alexander Korda in London – a deal which temporarily helped to ease Kerr's financial situation. Before he reached this agreement, however, Kerr experienced the way in which his displacement fundamentally affected interpersonal relationships. It is one of the tragic episodes of exile that Viertel, whom Kerr initially approached about his film project asking for support in the unfamiliar British film scene, did not reply to his letters. While it might be argued that Viertel's neglect of Kerr reveals the former's indifference towards fellow émigrés, the situation was more complex than that. Although Viertel, who was contracted for three films by Gaumont-British following his adaptation of *Kleine Freundin* (*Little Friend*, 1934), certainly could have helped Kerr to get in touch with producers, he himself increasingly faced constraints that might explain why he did not write an answer. Early in 1935, following the general release of the costly production *Jew Süss* in January, Gaumont-British sought to cut costs and as a result imposed restrictions on its directors and production crews. Viertel's inability to direct in limited time frames and within budget put his own position at risk. This was particularly the case as Viertel's personality, which was widely regarded as difficult, further increased the pressure on him. Having quarrelled with Viertel about the starting date of *The Passing of the Third Floor Back*, the film's associate producer Ivor Montagu expresses his opinion in a letter to Michael Balcon's brother Chandos

that, having regard to his [Viertel's] character, better practical results could
be obtained from placing before him a schedule which he thought practicable
or attainable, than [by] putting him under the shadow of a schedule he knew
quite well to be – for him at least – impracticable.[220]

Given his own problematic position as director, it is plausible that Berthold
Viertel was not in an ideal position to supply Kerr with a contract in
Britain. Under the conditions of exile there was a tendency to look after
oneself first. However, the fact that he did not answer his letter at all seems
a different matter. Viertel's disregard of one of the Weimar Republic's most
important critics illustrates in a surprisingly harsh manner how positions
and social status changed under the conditions of exile. Moreover, this
episode also demonstrates that the exile community was not without its
own problems – despite the common experiences of its members and its
universal condemnation of Nazism. Thus disappointment and bitterness
dominates the tone of Kerr's blunt follow-up letter to Viertel, which ends
with the postscript 'What I find intriguing in all this (perhaps you do also)
is the question: whether you would have left a letter from me unanswered
ten or twelve years ago.'[221]

Other émigrés were more successful than Kerr in earning a living as regular workers for British film studios. While Kerr did not manage to transform
any of his film scripts written in exile into a motion picture, it was especially
those émigrés who came to England early, who had good contacts within
the film business, and who were experienced film practitioners who were
given long-term contracts with production companies. As an example of
how the authorial control of émigrés extended beyond the work of producers, directors and script writers, a number of films dealt with themes of travelling, otherness, alienation and diasporic lives as per émigré actors featuring
in them. Produced and directed by Herbert Wilcox, the feature film classic
Victoria the Great (1937), for instance, serves as a good example of a film
that negotiates the problems of migration at a time when the film crisis of
1936/37 made it increasingly difficult for exiled film professionals to find
work. The film articulates the difficulties of life in the diaspora through the
person of Prince Albert, who is played by the Viennese Anton Walbrook.
The role of the Prince Consort seemed ideal for refugee actors as it allowed
them to use their otherness as a reason for employment. Thus Albert, whose
native language was German and who came to Britain as a foreigner, was
a popular character among refugee artists; for months Paul von Herrenried
and Albert Lieven, for instance, toured through England as Albert in the
play "Victoria Regina".[222] Not least in consequence of the many émigrés
who played the popular Prince Consort on stage, the historical character
was repeatedly seen in connection with the situation of foreigners in 1930s
Britain. For Walbrook, at least, the role marked the beginning of a successful

émigré career, prompting *Film Weekly* to praise him as 'the most interesting Continental player to have been introduced to English and American filmgoers since Charles Boyer'.[223] By 1938, the same publication predicted an exceptionally prospering career for the 'first truly cosmopolitan star'.[224]

Right from the beginning of *Victoria the Great*, England appears as an unfriendly environment. When Prince Albert arrives in England after an unpleasant ship passage, it is raining, stormy and grey. Moreover, his question 'how can one live happily in a country that is so difficult to get to?' acquires actual significance in the context of the 1930s when British authorities implemented a number of restrictive measures to limit the number of refugees from central Europe.[225] The fact that Albert and his companion prince Ernest (played by the German émigré Walter Rilla) lose all their belongings during their journey across the English Channel is another indication of the immediacy of the refugees' situation. Forced to leave their possessions behind, many exiles arrived in England just like the filmic Albert with little more than the clothes they were wearing.

Given the inhospitable conditions of his arrival, Albert initially wants to go straight back home to Germany – a wish he repeats upon arrival in London. The fact that he still speaks German with a servant foregrounds his otherness and his problems adapting to his new surrounding. Then again, once he dances with Victoria, he rapidly and radically changes his mind. In an important scene before Victoria and Albert get married, they talk about Albert leaving his beloved Germany for England:

Victoria: Do you think there is a great difference between England and Germany?
Albert: Yes, there is!
Victoria: You are very fond of your country, Albert.
Albert: Of course I am.
Victoria: You like England, too?
Albert: Very much!
Victoria: Do you think you could ever feel at home here?
Albert: I hope I will!

While incorporating concerns of émigrés in Britain, this conversation anticipates the problems Albert has assimilating into British society. Although he quite successfully acts according to the court's protocol and finds temporary relief in the English countryside that resembles that of his German homeland, he remains uprooted.[226] He becomes increasingly melancholic as he has almost no one to talk to, and expresses his regret that although he is the husband of a Queen he remains an outsider without recognition: 'Peel cuts down my income, Wellington refuses my rank and the royal family cry out against the foreign interloper.' Talking about his alienation he continues by saying that he cannot tell anyone that he misses his German home because 'the English wouldn't understand – sentiment is a plant that will not grow in England. If an Englishman finds himself growing sentimental, he goes out and shoots himself.'

Among Albert's fiercest critics are snobbish Members of Parliament who despise both his foreign descent and his interest in British politics. When Albert tries to prevent war with the US at the time of the American Civil War by changing the wording of a note to Washington, the Prime Minister Lord Palmerston clearly displays his antipathy. His argument exhibits many parallels to the growing xenophobia towards foreign immigrants over fears of espionage and acts of sabotage in the late 1930s. Holding his foreign descent against Albert, Palmerston expresses concerns that the throne is influenced by a man 'brought up in a foreign court, full of foreign ideas' and with 'many ties both of blood and sympathy with foreign governments'. Even Albert's wife, the Queen of England, initially wants to exclude him from all political decision-making stating that the English are very suspicious about any foreigner interfering in their government. Although she changes her mind in the course of the film and finds in Albert both a loving husband and a valuable advisor in political, economical and social questions, he never fully assimilates. As a consequence, British society as represented in *Victoria the Great* does not allow for the same exoticism that characterises many of Alexander Korda's films or other roles played by Walbrook. Otherness is quickly overwritten by 'British' character traits while foreigners are expected to turn themselves into perfect English gentlemen – only to learn that they are never fully accepted in spite of their efforts. What seems true for the film also applies to the many German-speaking actors. While Anton Walbrook as Albert might learn English quickly and eventually becomes accustomed to English habits, neither Walbrook nor the filmic character he plays will be able to speak English perfectly or fully blend in with his new surroundings.

As a result of the unfriendly environment in *Victoria the Great* and the loss of his beloved home country, Albert dies a fearful and estranged man. His last words on the deathbed once again underline his alienation: 'Don't leave me. They are waiting for me at the Tower. I've done my best.' Whilst *Victoria the Great* was made in full awareness of the quarrels between British fascists and the London Jewry which culminated in the battle of Cable Street on 4 October 1936, roughly half a year before filming started in April 1937,[227] the paranoia of the filmic Albert can be seen as a critical comment on British racism. Albert's dystopian vision of being incarcerated thus calls into question the belief that British liberalism and tolerance would resist the persecution of minorities.

However, this bleak outlook does not prevent the film from presenting a positive, patriotic ethos. Rather than holding English society as such responsible for his unsuccessful attempts to feel at home in the new country, several individuals such as Lord Palmerston are responsible for Albert's homesickness. Thus the box-office hit *Victoria the Great* is able to negotiate issues such as xenophobia without sacrificing the positive image of Britain that is commonly conveyed in historical epics of the time. In fact, both of Wilcox's successful 'Victoria films' *Victoria the Great* and *Sixty Glorious Years* (1938), as Sarah Street observes, 'represent a reverent depiction of monarchy [and] a celebration of consensus politics'.[228] Yet, her claim that Wilcox's films offer a nationalistic notion of Britishness may at least be partially questioned considering the central role of Prince Albert in *Victoria the Great* and the Queen's own German heritage. Repeatedly, the royal couple sing in German and in a scene in which he praises her pronunciation of the German word for honeymoon, 'Flitterwochen', she reveals that until the age of nine she spoke German regularly. Moreover, despite the problems he faces integrating into English society and his apparent foreign status, the audience is clearly directed to sympathise with Albert throughout the film. Although the title might suggest a focus on Victoria as the sole protagonist, it rather concentrates on both Victoria *and* Albert. The prince consort is central inasmuch as his persona allows for a closer personal look at the monarch – which was especially interesting bearing in mind that Wilcox's film is the first to portray Victoria after the ban on representing her was lifted. It is in the scenes with Albert that Victoria is talking about her own feelings. This intimacy is furthermore underlined by the many eye-level close-up or medium-close-up shots when the couple is together. In fact, while Anna Neagle's personification of Victoria remains, with the exception of the scenes when she is alone with Albert, distant – a sublime leader to be worshipped rather than identified with – the humanised representation of Albert calls for strong empathy. Walbrook's sensitive performance ensures that Albert's sorrows and worry as well as his dedication and decency turn him into a more advanced and challenging character than Victoria. His swift and noble decision to shield his wife with his own body against an assassination attempt and his devotion to England regardless of his own health gains him the audience's approval. In order to convey a positive image of the monarchy, the film even alters in his favour the events surrounding British foreign policy during the American Civil War. According to Wilcox's film the royal couple prevent a disastrous conflict with the Union troops by redrafting a harsh British note formulated by Parliament and so defusing a looming war. Indeed, it is Albert who explicitly claims that his foreignness enables him to examine the situation from different angles: 'Perhaps *because* I am a foreigner I can see clearly the sheer madness of [waging war].' Although Albert's positive intervention helps to defuse the looming British-American conflict, he remains an outsider. Wilcox's version of the regal court proves an unreceptive surrounding for the uprooted

German prince consort who misses his home country. As a consequence Albert remains isolated and alienated. While his body lives within the palace walls, his thoughts roam over the past and his beloved German countryside.

Repeatedly, diasporic themes are part of émigré films by way of multi-national settings and foreign meeting points. Resembling the twilight atmosphere of Rick's Café Américain in the 1942 émigré film *Casablanca*, many British films of the 1930s and 1940s also featured settings that added an element of coercion as they often echo the lives of those who were forced to live a nomadic life as exiles from continently Europe. Central to such filmic representations is the dual deficit of artistic expression and social relations as the result of an intensified diasporic experience of loneliness and loss. As isolation and solitude forms part of many narratives in various ways it is often the travelling artist who serves as a general metaphor for the diaspora in British films. In addition to Steidler in *Heart's Desire* and the group of travelling musicians in *The Robber Symphony* (Friedrich Feher, 1936), this can clearly be seen in *Pagliacci* (1936). Based on Leoncavallo's opera, the film tells the tragic story of jealousy and murder in the milieu of a small comic-opera company touring through the Italian provinces. While the leader of the travelling troupe of players, Canio (Richard Tauber), appears as a clown to offer comic relief for the audience, his own life disintegrates when he finds out about the affair between his beautiful wife (Steffi Duna) and a young soldier (Arthur Margetson). He kills his wife and her lover on stage during a symbolic play which reflects their real-life situation. Though his actions are triggered by his wife's infidelity, the reasons for the tragic murder lie, as often, deeper and can be partially explained by Canio's displaced identity. As Horak argues, '[t]he husband, wounded in his pride, homeless, constantly on the move, his emotional life lacking all fixed points, cannot come to terms with the pain of rejection'.[229]

Although the film, which was partially filmed in colour, failed to gain much international recognition, it prompted favourable reviews and achieved reasonable revenues in England. The *Daily Mirror*, for example, makes special mention of Richard Tauber's voice and the colour shots used in the prologue and during the dramatic climax.[230] In addition to its aesthetic qualities, however, *Pagliacci* occupies an exceptional position within the corpus of British émigré cinema and constitutes a central text in any assessment of the influence of foreign émigrés because its cast and credits almost entirely comprise German-speaking staff. Having secured the screen rights for the (at the time) considerable sum of £18,000,[231] the producer Max Schach filled most positions with fellow émigrés. The film's director (Karl Grune), cinematographer (Otto Kanturek), set designer (Oscar Werndorff), costume designer (Ernst Stern), production manager (Fritz Brunn), and leading actor (Richard Tauber) were film professionals from

Germany or Austria. Together with the chief laboratory technician, both the director Karl Grune and the cinematographer Otto Kanturek were also the innovators behind British Chemicolour Ltd. Above all Schach's decision to approach no less creative a trio than Bertolt Brecht, Fritz Kortner and Hanns Eisler to adapt Leoncavallo's opera to the screen made *Pagliacci* a bona fide exiles' picture. Owing to their strong presence it is not surprising at all that the film touches upon issues of displacement and loss. It was in particular the contribution of Brecht that was pivotal.[232] Whilst he remained uncredited alongside Fritz Kortner because they were not in possession of valid work permits for Great Britain,[233] his alterations to the original, including his recognised *Verfremdungseffekt* (alienation effect) and *Grundgestus* theory (i.e. the view that the overall storyline, or *Fabel*, is broken down into scenes with one essential meaning that should be captured by the actors)[234] turned *Pagliacci* into a sophisticated screen version. Through constant retellings of the story (in the prologue, the main storyline and the stage play) and elements of anti-realist acting, he achieves a critical detachment from the film and infuses the narrative with a level of self-reflexivity. Contrary to the common use of the alienation effect, however, the actors do not always seem to keep a distance from the part they were interpreting. Several scenes at least imply a constant awareness of the foreign identity of the actor as well as the character. The film consequently suggests a direct connection between the German-speaking actors' lives and experiences and the plot. Consistent with this interpretation, Horak reads a scene with the German opera tenor Richard Tauber as a direct reference to his own refugee status: 'In the prologue [. . .] Tauber sings an aria from a stage, but stares out in the reverse shot onto the real ocean, as if his unfaithful wife were Nazi Germany and he a stateless émigré'.[235] Although Horak has only viewed a black and white print, the original colour version held by the BFI further supports his thesis. Whilst the subjective reverse-angle shot of the actual ocean does not seem to match the other highly stylised and theatrical sets at all, it depicts a romantic yellow and red sunset evoking feelings of homesickness and nostalgic recollections of the lost *Heimat* which seems to lie somewhere behind the horizon.

Apart from musicals set in continental Europe, the so-called Empire Films were predestined to include transnational journeys and borderland themes, as these were an essential part of the conventionalised narratives of the genre. Set at the margins of the British-controlled territory, Empire Films brought together the literary heritage of adventure stories by popular authors such as Henry Rider Haggard and Rudyard Kipling with characteristics of Hollywood Westerns – such as the frontier theme, the clash of industrial modernity and wilderness, and the ideological belief in the supremacy of White Anglo-Saxon culture. Not only did many émigré filmmakers participate in Alexander Korda's cycle of Empire Films *Sanders*

of the River (1935), *The Drum* (1938), *The Four Feathers* (1939); Berthold
Viertel also chose an imperial plot for his last British film as director, *Rhodes
of Africa* (1936). The fact that émigrés often participated in arguably the
most British of all film genres seems, on the face of it, quite odd. However,
these films not only offered great commercial opportunities, they also
permitted émigré film personnel to deal with a number of familiar issues
connected to their own life in a foreign environment, separated from their
homeland, friends and family. Before his successful collaboration with
Michael Powell, Emeric Pressburger, for instance, wrote the script "The
South East Frontier" for Korda in 1938. Although the script was never
turned into a film, it serves as a good example of how closely the storyline
corresponded to the exile situation of its author. Telling the story of how
a group of Europeans flee Kabul during a mullah's uprising, the proposed
film shows many parallels to the expulsion of filmmakers and other occupational groups from the Third Reich.

Resembling the uncanny roles he played in Germany such as Cesare in
Das Cabinet des Dr. Caligari (Robert Wiene, 1919), Balduin in *Der
Student von Prag* (Henrik Galeen, 1926), or Ivan the Terrible in *Das
Wachsfigurenkabinett* (Paul Leni, 1924), Veidt reappears as the mysterious,
yet less eerie, stranger in British films. While his sharp voice, dark appearance, slim body and angular face all contributed to him being cast as a foreigner and outsider in German films, his refugee status seems to ideally fit his
already established star persona. As a consequence, he did not have to change
his image, which was at least known by many British cinema aficionados.
Given the congruence of Veidt's star image and the roles he plays in most of
his British films he seems an almost consummate example of what Richard
Dyer calls a 'perfect fit'.[236] Apart from *The Spy in Black* or *Contraband*, this
is particularly obvious in his acclaimed performance in Berthold Viertel's
The Passing of the Third Floor Back (1935).[237] Although his accent 'is barely
noticeable and only perceptible to one who watches for it', as a contemporary review in *Variety* puts it,[238] he appears as an unfamiliar figure throughout the film as little about his personality is revealed. He does not even have a
name and appears as 'the Stranger' in the cast and credits. When the landlady
asks about what he does for a living he replies that he was a cosmopolitan
traveller without a real home. When he pays in advance he is nevertheless
welcome. Others are not as easily accepted in the course of the film, which
makes visible rigid class distinctions and exhibits a general distrust of outsiders. When an organ grinder asks through a window if he should play a
song, he is quickly told to go away and that foreigners are neither encouraged nor welcome. As a cross-section of society, the lodgers at the London
rooming house of the film are anything but convivial. Curt Courant's bleak
cinematography – including many medium shots and medium close-ups of

facial expressions in the house at night, and chiaroscuro lighting that creates a troubling atmosphere – sets the tone of the film. Playing with audience expectations, however, the sinister, taciturn character played by Veidt turns out to be warm and sympathetic while the allegedly respectable middle-aged Mr Wright turns out to be evil as he tries to seduce young women. Bearing all the usual connotations of danger when he arrives out of nowhere in the middle of the night, the stranger soon helps the other residents whose relationships are characterised by hatred, parsimoniousness and harassment.

Above and beyond Veidt in *The Passing of the Third Floor Back*, roles as nameless strangers were commonly played by émigré actors – in Britain and elsewhere. This is very obvious, amongst other films, in Peter Lorre's American film *Stranger on the Third Floor* (Boris Ingster, 1940). Within the context of British cinema, Veidt's roles thus also enable him to 'comment on his historical, social, and political predicament despite or beyond the narrative motivation of his characters', as Gerd Gemünden observes in connection with Lorre's performances in Hollywood productions.[239] The spy thriller genre enabled émigrés to explore motifs that correlate closely with the German-speaking film professionals' own situation such as double identities or border-crossings. While numerous spy thrillers such as *The Spy in Black* explore how identity is affected either positively or negatively by geographical places, the décor of a twilight setting can be read as visual imprints of the ambivalence and insecurity of exile.

Another obvious example of a failed transnational relationship and unsuccessful assimilation is the British film *Broken Blossoms* (1936). Following the lead of Alexander Korda's big-budget films, Julius Hagen founded the film company J. H. Productions at Twickenham to make ambitious films aimed at an international market. He was initially able to win D. W. Griffith himself to direct the remake of his classic 1919 silent film in Britain.[240] However, when the American director ended his engagement over a disagreement over who would be cast as female lead, Julius Hagen contracted German refugee theatre director John (Hans) Brahm to direct his first film. Like Korda and Schach, Hagen, who was born in Hamburg and came to Britain as a child, provided work for a number of German-speaking émigré filmmakers. Perhaps because he retained an emotional link to his place of birth they were conspicuously often from northern Germany. Apart from the Hamburg-born director he furthermore engaged Brahm's later wife, Dolly Haas (also from Hamburg) to play the female lead and the Berlin-born émigré Curt Courant for the cinematography.

Through this direct émigré involvement the film serves as yet another example of how films echo the past and present experiences and beliefs of those who made them. Kevin Gough-Yates argues that a comparison of the original version and its remake reveals the full extent of this influence.

Referring especially to elements of *mise-en-scéne*, he makes the case that Brahm's *Broken Blossoms* 'has a distinctly European appearance and could have been lit for Fritz Lang. The crowd scenes, with their sense of mob violence . . . suggest the same influence.'[241] Indeed, the London working class neighbourhood with its dark, labyrinthine alleys and backrooms clearly refer to the dystopian underground city in Lang's *Metropolis* (Germany 1927), the working class quarters in *M* (Germany 1931) and the streets and houses in *Spione* (Germany 1928) where the mob rules. The interaction between the highly stylised sets, which were already part of Griffith's 1919 original, and Courant's omnipresent and gloomy cinematography is reminiscent of the uncanny, socially critical twilight world of Weimar cinema. Translated into mid-1930s Britain, the slums of Limehouse in *Broken Blossoms* appear to be an ideal breeding ground for the British Union of Fascists. Indeed, the ferocious working class gathering that attacks the Chinese missionary both verbally (calling him a 'dirty Chink', 'who should go back to where he belongs') and physically (by throwing a brick at his head) resembles the anti-Jewish rallies of Mosley's blackshirts in the mid-1930s. It was especially in East London neighbourhoods where the British fascists kept a high profile and where they were predominantly active in recruiting new members. In contrast to Griffith's version, where the police largely assume law and order, Brahm's film depicts a sphere of crowd violence and arbitrary law. The deep-rooted scepticism of state authorities arguably stems from the refugees' own experiences. The quasi pogrom when hordes of working class people seek to kill the Buddhist missionary and devastate the Chinese shop in an out-burst of racial hatred, for one, clearly anticipates the events of the so-called *Kristallnacht* in Germany in November 1938 and stands for the rallies of both German and British fascists. By stylistically combining the expressionist tendencies that lingered on in many of the German films of the late 1920s and early 1930s alongside elements of social realism, Brahm's adaptation creates a daunting atmosphere that is symptomatic of the unstable political and socio-economic situation in mid-1930s Britain. The interaction between the chiaroscuro lighting, narrow inner-city alleyways, medium close-ups and mass choreography of crowd scenes can thus be read as filmic ciphers representing the various tensions that were later channelled through the notion of 'the people's war'.

Inasmuch as the film is a humanistic statement against racism and for a mutual understanding of different cultures, moreover, it is supplemented by topoi of travelling, alienation and the diaspora. Unlike its original silent version a greater emphasis is put on the diasporic situation of the Chinese Buddhist missionary. In line with other émigré films such as *Victoria the Great*, a heavy shower of rain furthermore accompanies the Chinese protagonist's arrival in Britain. Significantly the first image of Britain is shown from the immigrants' perspective. After a scene framing the Buddhist missionary on the railing with the downpour in the foreground, the audience sees his point of view through a subjective reverse angle shot. In stark contrast to the initial sequence set in a reconstructed Chinese garden, England appears dark and grey. Instead of green hills he sees industrial docklands with smoking chimneys. Although he still appears happy and looks forward to living in this new country, his arrival is accompanied by a bad omen. His clothes, unsuitable for the English climate, are soaked and when he leaves the ocean liner he is pushed off the gangway. A medium shot framing his legs and feet show how he steps into ankle-deep mud and symbolically drops his treasured book of Buddha. Unlike the original, Brahm's remake then narrates his attempts at adjusting himself to living far away from home in a depressing and violent world. The weather proves to be as inhospitable as the people and the authorities. Notwithstanding his peaceful nature and the good English skills he had acquired in China, he finds himself swindled out of his money, repeatedly facing strong xenophobic hatred and violence and is even unfoundedly imprisoned for causing a public disturbance.[242] In the echo of Whitehall's stance towards the refugees from Nazi Germany, the magistrate suggests to him that he returns home after his prison sentence. While the scene captures the constraints on migration such as immigration office procedures, it may also seem to anticipate the alien tribunals and the alien scare at the beginning of war. Such a reading is supported by the remark of a woman who accuses the Chinese missionary and all other foreigners of espionage by claiming: 'That's what they all are: Spies!'. Although barely noticed by critics,[243] the slight Austrian accent of the female lead played by Dolly Haas adds a further nuance to the already complex film. Her (for censorship purposes seemingly platonic) relationship with the Chinese missionary is only short-lived. It only momentarily helps her, on the one hand, to escape the domestic violence she encounters when alone with her father, and the Chinese missionary, on the other, to get a deeper understanding into English culture. Love, once again, does not enable émigrés to surmount cultural difficulties.

Resentment and protectionism: Public opinion and the Association of Cinematograph Technicians

With an increasing number of German-speaking refugees in Britain and their growing presence in film studios, critical voices uttered concerns that the immigrants were a threat to the UK. Trade unions such as the Association of Cinematograph Technicians (ACT) saw the foreign film workers as rivals to its members. as such, the union introduced varios measures aimed at bringing the employment of foreigners to a halt.[244]

Increasingly, refugees from German-speaking lands had to face fierce opposition, anti-Semitic and xenophobic resentment, restrictive immigration policies, and eventually internment as 'enemy aliens'. While it is impossible to overlook the generous help of refugee organisations, government officials and the public, refugees were, as Louise London has shown, by and large not welcomed in Britain with open arms.[245] The hostility towards continental film practitioners is further evidence for the thesis that Britain was not as liberal and tolerant as it claimed to be. Nevertheless, the fact that foreign film practitioners were also defended and supported underscores the overall ambivalent role of Britain as a country of refuge.

The general issue of refugees from the Third Reich in Britain has been the subject of much attention ever since Norman Bentwich first wrote about the topic as early as 1936.[246] Interestingly, many of the early works, such as Norman Angell's and Dorothy Thompson's publication *You and the Refugee* (1939) or François Lafitte's *The Internment of Aliens* (1940) already took a critical stance towards Westminster's immigration and alien policies.[247] With the exception of Bill Rubinstein's disputed study, *The Myth of Rescue* (1997),[248] which claims that Whitehall could not have done more to help those who were persecuted by the Nazis on the continent, the majority of scholars are critical of Britain's role.[249] In addition to works that disapprove of developments such as the internment of aliens or the government's limitation of immigration, Tony Kushner, among others, has argued that anti-Jewish resentment, though it rarely took the form of political extremism, can be identified within British society.[250] He asserts that the UK only accepted Jews as long as they fully assimilated themselves, and when they were not willing to do so, they were seen as problematic. All foreigners were expected to conform to British culture and to minimise their 'otherness'; among other things this implied that they were told to refrain from speaking German in public. Referring to the situation of exile German and Austrian musicians, Marion Berghahn points out that they were normally not allowed to accept engagements and had numerous other problems owing to their otherness 'since anti-alienism pervaded the world of music just as strongly as other British institutions'.[251]

Moreover, abuse against Jews – both verbal and physical – frequently recurred in the 1930s. During 1936, for instance, the British Union of Fascists had increasingly become active in London and maintained a high street presence. According to Berghahn, some anti-Semitism 'took on alarming forms, continuing long after the Second World War'.[252] Such tendencies were not restricted to the streets and could be seen throughout society. Carl Zuckmayer, for example, reports that, while working for Korda in the late 1930s, he was told by an MP that 'Hitler was 'quite a good chap . . . a bulwark against Communism'.[253]

Émigré film personnel were often directly affected by these xenophobic and anti-Semitic tendencies when they applied for British citizenship. As a legal requirement of the naturalisation process they were required to publish a clearly marked advertisement in two issues of local or national newspapers asking those who know any reason why naturalization should not be granted to contact the Aliens' Department of the Home Office.[254] Some British citizens used these public announcements as an opportunity to utter their general dissatisfaction with the government's policies or, in some cases, their outspoken anti-foreign, anti-Jewish attitudes. Although not written immediately after Conrad Veidt's advertisements appeared in *The Times* on 6 April and 7 April 1938 but rather following the publication of a list of foreigners who had been naturalised, the Home Office received a letter from an agitated Londoner who firmly opposed the naturalisation of foreigners: 'As a Briton by descent may I ask for what service to this country Konrad Veidt & A Korda are naturalised? . . . What benefit to this country (already overpopulated, and with a large figure of unemployment) will accrue from the presence of potential revolutionaries (judging by the names in the list)?'.[255] Although the clearly xenophobic letter was added to Conrad Veidt's file, its annotation suggests that Home Office staff remained unconvinced by some allegations at least. So the claim that '[t]he number of aliens now entitled to use a British pasport [sic] means that a corresponding number of Britons by descent are deprived of their rights' is accompanied by the pencilled remark 'Why?'.[256]

British society was divided over the question of émigrés and how they affected British cinema. On the extreme political right, the journal of the Imperial Fascist League, *The Fascist*, repeatedly attacked production companies, trade journals and institutions, such as the newly founded British Film Institute, claiming that they were all 'in the hands of a gang of Socialists and Jews'.[257] Yet hostility towards Jews and aliens could not be limited to extremists. German-speaking émigrés often reacted by not acknowledging their foreign or Jewish roots – especially when publicity and marketing campaigns were at stake. The German journalist and film critic Paul Marcus records in his newsletter for German-speaking refugees that the popular actor Anton Walbrook, among others, did not acknowledge his Jewish heritage until 1938.[258]

Given that anti-Semitism and anti-alienism was common in British society their absence in films is somewhat surprising. Whereas the upper-class heroes in novels by Sapper and Dornford Yates, for instance, 'battled against an assortment of pernicious aliens, including Jewish influences'[259] that sought to destroy Britain, films did not feature stereotyped Jews posing a threat to British society. The same can be said off screen on the production floors where only some isolated occurrences of anti-Jewish resentment and xenophobia were reported. Dolly Haas' encounter with the pro-fascist views of the producer Walter Mycroft during the production of *Girls Will Be Boys* (Marcel Varner, 1934)[260] was clearly an exception. The cosmopolitan character of the film industry with its many Jewish workers and artists prevented explicit forms of anti-Semitism and xenophobia from occurring within production companies and studios or filmic plots. As Kevin Gough-Yates puts it, '[r]esentment rather than racism remained the root cause of hostility towards the foreign worker and producer in Britain'.[261] Still, the overwhelming presence of continental Europeans working for the British film industry particularly prompted a more general hostility. Resentment against German-speaking film workers did not just surface once the war broke out, but had already been growing for some time. An early example can be found in the September 1928 issue of *The Picturegoer* by Lionel Collier entitled 'Wanted! – A British Spirit'.[262] Many contemporary press reports used the metaphor of an invasion in order to describe the presence of émigrés, thereby neglecting the fact that immigration has also been common in previous years and assuming homogeneity amongst the diverse group of expatriates that did simply not exist.[263]

Once émigré film practitioners were granted entry to the UK, one of their main hurdles in finding a job was the opposition of British trade unions. They repeatedly criticised the employment of foreigners because of fears, fuelled by factors ranging from economic reasons to xenophobia or anti-Semitism, that the film industry was dominated by foreign film professionals to the detriment of British workers. In so doing, the unions' actions were duplicitous. Although the labour movement's reaction to Hitler could well be characterised by what Richard Shackelton has described as 'horrified apathy', the trade unions theoretically opposed NSDAP policies.[264] At the 65th Annual Trades Unions Conference held at Brighton in 1933, they condemned 'Hitler's brutal attack on the German Trade Union Movement, the Social Democratic Party and the Co-operative movement' which had made obvious the 'menace of dictatorship'.[265] Moreover, they called for a ban on German goods,[266] and by 1936 the unions had set up a grant for Trade Union refugees and were raising money for the relief of foreign workers.[267] However, the sympathy and support for the victims of Nazi oppression often collided with union members' interests. Given the vast numbers of émigrés in Britain it was especially the unions of the entertainment industry that criticised the employment of foreigners.

Whereas studios employed émigrés so as to enhance production values through professionalism, first-class technical know-how and economic efficiency, the ACT and other interest groups of the entertainment industry regarded them as the rivals of British workers.[268] In a conference organised by unions of the entertainment business in spring 1933, a resolution was agreed which requested the Ministry of Labour to grant fewer work permits to aliens – many of whom were refugees from Nazi oppression.[269] Part of the resolution, which was published in *Kinematograph Weekly* under the heading 'Influx of Aliens: Unions Urge Stricter Supervision', reads as follows:

> Owing to the political situation in Germany the unions are aware that many alien refugees are being offered employment in British film studios. . . . The unions view with alarm this influx of foreign competitive labour which is already displacing British labour and tending further to depress wages and conditions throughout the Industry.[270]

Although Jewish film professionals who were sent back to Germany would be certain to face persecution, the ACT expressed its opinion that '[t]here appears to be a tendency for a foreign technician to remain in the country for an excessive period of time, often long after his usefulness in the film industry has expired'.[271]

Although the situation of émigrés in the film industry was in many ways unique, the hostility towards German-speaking cinema technicians and artists followed a general campaign against the employment of foreigners. In the wake of mass unemployment in the 1930s, trade unions were at the centre of the campaign. They espoused the implementation of protectionist laws aimed at reducing the number of work permits given to aliens. All too often believing that the end justifies the means, they repeatedly exploited a racist and chauvinistic rhetoric for their cause. In doing so, the unions underlined that xenophobia and anti-Semitism were in fact not limited to the political right.[272] Here, the unions of the film industry, in particular the ACT, were no exception. Ralph Bond, for instance, proclaimed: 'The technicians must no longer be the victims of that inverted snobbery which makes a virtue of a foreign name, relegating the native talent to the third rate stuff.'[273] In holding émigrés, and in particular Jewish producers, responsible for the problems of the film industry, the ACT policies, on the face of it, bore some striking similarities to Oswald Mosley's 'Britain First' programme that was designed to fight the alleged Jewish control over media and commerce.[274]

What must be taken into account, however, is that the ACT, despite its xenophobic rhetoric, did not favour Nazism and firmly condemned Hitler and the Nazis.[275] Whereas British fascists and the political right fought Jews and foreigners on the basis of racist ideologies, the ACT and other unions primarily regarded the issue as a crisis of capitalism as such.[276] Their main concern was that German-speaking Jewish producers like Alexander Korda and Max Schach were capitalists who misused their fiscal power by acting in favour of their compatriots. At the time of the British film debacle the ACT claimed that Korda, 'by virtue of his foreign experience and associations, had a decided preference for foreign technicians and held the view that the really expert British technician did not exist. As a result, a very large number of foreigners found employment at Denham Studios.'[277] Therefore, from the perspective of the ACT, Korda and other foreign producers willingly accepted the fact that over 250 British film technicians were out of work.[278] The common argument that was brought forward against the employment of foreign personnel was that British talent was sufficiently available – often even at significantly lower wages – and that foreigners were therefore not needed in most cases. Following this belief, a 1937 article in *Kinematograph Weekly* criticises the studios' preferential treatment of aliens: 'When a foreign cameraman's illness held up a British film last week, frantic telegrams were sent all over Europe for someone to replace him. Why? Are there no good British cameramen disengaged?'.[279]

The ACT was not opposed to 'reasonable numbers' of foreign film practitioners working in Britain provided that:

a) They are ace men.
b) Their crews are British.
c) Their employment does not deprive equally expert British technicians of employment. . . .
d) They are not engaged to work under less favourable conditions and salaries than those of British technicians.
e) The Association is given an opportunity of being consulted when renewals of such permits are applied for.[280]

Especially German-speaking producers, the ACT claimed, employed foreign personnel who were in fact not ace film practitioners – a term that is repeatedly used in the debate by ACT officials in order to underline that just good was not good enough to be granted a work permit.

The accusation that lies at the heart of such criticism was nepotism. Émigré producers such as Max Schach or Alexander Korda but also British-born producers like Michael Balcon were reproached for preferring foreigners to English film practitioners. The ACT claimed that, as a direct result, employment opportunities for British workers were diminishing. And indeed, at first glance the employment structures of Korda's LFP and Schach's Capitol Group seem to support accusations that German-speaking producers employed a significantly high number of compatriots. While Korda contracted many Hungarians such as composer Miklós Rózsa, script writers Lajos Biró or Emeric Pressburger, numerous Austrians were on the payroll of Schach's enterprises, among them director Karl Grune, production manager Fritz Brunn, writer Rudolf Bernauer, cameraman Otto Kanturek, designer Oscar Werndorff, actor Fritz Kortner, actress Elisabeth Bergner and singer Richard Tauber. Nonetheless, it is debatable whether these filmmakers were employed simply because of their nationality.

Keeping in mind that both Schach and Korda relied on box office success, they could simply not afford to employ any second-rate fellow citizen instead of a first-class British worker. What is more, British producers, such as Michael Balcon (Gaumont-British) or Julius Hagen (Twickenham Studios), also had numerous German-speaking film practitioners on their payroll, thereby underlining the fact that émigrés were often better qualified than their British colleagues. LFP manager David Cunynghame also makes this point by stressing the importance of émigrés: 'It must be realised that ... the British film industry needs their support in order to take immediate advantage of the possibility of extending its export trade.'[281] Ironically, the ACT itself implicitly admitted that émigré personnel were far more skilled than many of their British counterparts. In a report on foreign film technicians for the Ministry of Labour in 1937, the union protested against the assignment of Austrian cinematographer Günther Krampf to a light comedy starring Jack Hulbert. The ACT made the case that Krampf's excellent skills – he had previously worked for films such as Robert Wiene's expressionist film *Orlacs Hände* (Germany, 1924) and G. W. Pabst's acclaimed *Die Büchse der Pandora* (Germany, 1929) – were not needed for this kind of 'simple' production and a British cameraman could also shoot the picture.[282]

Since banks and insurance companies, enticed by Korda's success with *The Private Life of Henry VIII* (1933), invested large sums in the film industry expecting quick returns, the insufficient technical and human resources in Britain left no alternative to producers but to employ large numbers of foreign experts as the training of British workers would have taken years. As can be seen in other exile countries such as Holland, the influx of German-speaking émigrés caused an 'astounding boom',[283] rather than harming national production. Besides, without the numerous German-speaking producers many of the most successful British films would simply not exist. Moreover, émigré film professionals also set up new enterprises and created new jobs for émigrés and British workers alike. Schach and Grune jointly founded Capitol Films and Marcel Hellmann established first his company Criterion films, which produced, among other films, Alfred Zeisler's *Crime Over London* (1936), and then Excelsior Films in 1942, which was responsible for popular wartime films such as *They Met in the Dark* (Carl Lamac, 1943). Above all, Korda's Denham studios created some 2,000 jobs in the summer of 1936 alone. Similarly, though in smaller numbers, other émigré producers – including Hermann Fellner, Isadore Goldschmidt, Joseph Than, Josef Somlo and Erich Pommer – also recruited British personnel.

Despite these overall numbers, Whitehall took allegations of nepotism seriously. As a response to the popular claim – propagated by the unions of the entertainment industry – that the employment of émigré film personnel might disadvantage British staff, employment-related considerations were added to the assessment criteria for the naturalisation of foreign nationals. Underlined by a Home Office official, the police report on Paul Czinner, for instance, notes that he

> has steadfastly refused to assist in training any English personnel in connection with his films, and with the exception of Margaret KENNEDY . . . he has always engaged highly paid foreign associates for his productions, a circumstance which has tended to create friction between the studio executives and staffs on the one hand, and applicant's production group on the other.[284]

The police report and the Home Office annotation is but one example that illustrates how, despite the numerous contradictions in the claims made by the ACT, the union was rather successful as a lobby for its mainly British-born members. Its policy, for instance, certainly contributed to a less open labour market which resulted in the number of work permits refused to foreign film workers more than doubling from 1935 to 1936.[285] Although it was far smaller than the biggest union in the entertainment industry, the National Association of Theatrical Employees (NATE), the ACT had the advantage of not being a general union. Unions like the NATE had the disadvantage of having to represent various groups of employees with differing views. Formed in 1933 as a response to the appalling working conditions of film technicians,[286] the ACT membership only covered technical occupations involved in the making of films. Consequently, it was rather a craft union representing a relatively small group with similar interests.

Thanks to its influence in Westminster, the ACT contributed to the fact that the employment of foreign film technicians was the subject of repeated inquiries and debate in the Commons[287] even if the overall number of émigré technicians was negligible in the face of the overall level of mass unemployment.[288] It must be recorded, however, that despite the various actions taken by the ACT to raise the issue of foreign film workers, the Ministry of Labour was somewhat reluctant to stop émigrés from entering the British film business.[289] Thus the Ministry recognised the industry's dependence on certain foreign specialists such as cameramen, a reliance the unions repeatedly and firmly denied.

Yet, it seems noteworthy that the way unions dealt with foreign film workers differed significantly from case to case. As evidence of the ambivalent manner in which the ACT handled the issue, émigrés such as set designer Ferdinand Bellan or producers Isadore Goldschmidt (Goldsmith) and Emeric Pressburger were accepted as members.[290] Moreover, the Viennese émigré Otto Kanturek even contributed to the ACT trade journal *Cine-Technician* (formerly *Journal of the Association of Cine-Technicians*). Although no reference to his status as foreigner or previous work experience in Germany and Austria can be found, his columns ironically, yet implicitly, give a vivid account of foreign achievements in Britain and the US. He refers, for instance, to 'old friends' such as Ted (Theodor) Sparkuhl who have become acclaimed film practitioners in Hollywood and presents in a positive light his innovative company British Chemicolour which he had founded jointly with his fellow émigrés Viktor Gluck and Karl Grune. The Chemicolour technology was used in 1936 by Grune for his aforementioned film *Pagliacci*.[291]

The situation for German-speaking émigrés was exacerbated in the late 1930s following the financial crisis of the British film industry. In an attempt to produce pictures for the international market the Twickenham group was one of the first production corporations that went into bankruptcy. In 1936, Gaumont-British alone had an overdraft of well above one million pounds and Alexander Korda's London Films' deficit reached more than £330,000.[292] As a consequence, British production gradually fell from 246 feature films in 1936 to 117 films in 1939, so offering fewer jobs and less security for domestic and foreign film personnel.[293] As the crisis amplified existing resentment and protectionism on part of the unions, it helps to explain why an increasing number of film professionals such as Berthold Viertel, Eugen Schüfftan, Erich Pommer or Leo Mittler tried to move to Hollywood at the end of the 1930s.

After the first devastating accounts of the scale of the crisis appeared in the *Financial Times* in July 1937, moreover, those who mistrusted the activities of German-speaking and particularly Jewish filmmakers interpreted the financial problems as proof of their concerns. Subsequently, the unions and other public figures were quick to blame producers such as Alexander Korda and Max Schach for the crash.[294] They were so successful in this that until the 1980s scholars and writers accepted that émigrés were responsible for the crisis. Although Rachael Low has much sympathy for Korda's 'picturesque extravagance', she lays the blame on Schach and his fellow directors who did 'much more to discredit British production as an investment'.[295] Korda's biographer Karol Kulik, though, concludes that 'Korda's particular model for making films and the way he had them financed both made and destroyed the British film industry. He gave the British cinema its first taste of international success and then undermined it all by trying to pull himself and the industry up too quickly.'[296]

The grandeur of Korda's British films that were aimed at an international audience can perhaps best be seen in his last great production at Denham, *Knight Without Armour* (Jacques Feyder, 1937). Hoping to repeat the great success of *The Private Life of Henry VIII* in the US, Korda contracted Hollywood star and German émigré Marlene Dietrich. In the face of £1.8 million in liabilities and £350,000 production costs[297] – a sum about six times higher than the budget for *The Private Life of Henry VIII* –, critics accused Korda of megalomania. What proved particularly unfortunate for the production was the contract with Marlene Dietrich who was not only given the enormous sum of $250,000 plus a percentage of the producer's gross receipts but also numerous other privileges. She had the right to veto the story, the director and the leading actor.[298] In particular the last provision had a deep impact on the making of the picture, when male lead Robert Donat became seriously ill and Dietrich ruled out his being replaced. This increased costs and was responsible for the film falling short of making a profit – despite the enormous publicity it received not least on account of Marlene Dietrich's celebrity status and the fact that it met with general acclaim on the part of the public and critics.[299] Subsequently the making of extravaganzas signalled both the indestructible optimism of producers such as Alexander Korda and the attempt to compete with huge Hollywood pictures. Apart from *Knight Without Armour*, this failure could arguably best be seen in the rushes of the unfinished *I Claudius* (Josef von Sternberg, 1937) also made by Korda's London Film Productions.[300] The German director Josef von Sternberg abandoned the movie following the injury suffered by Merle Oberon, the film's co-star, in a car accident. The accident, however, was perhaps a welcome opportunity to suspend the project because of numerous earlier problems which included Charles Laughton's difficulty getting into his role. Both the film's failure and Laughton's problems, which ended his association with Korda,[301] have been interpreted as symptomatic of the state of the British film industry. According to Stephen G. Jones the inability of Korda's enterprise to live up to expectations is 'personified by the fate of Charles Laughton who is to be seen in . . . *I Claudius* repeatedly fluffing his lines and falling apart in front of the camera'.[302]

By blaming primarily German-speaking Jewish émigrés for the crisis, the unions and other public figures often fostered already existing resentment and anti-Semitic conspiracy theories. In August 1938, for instance, the diplomat and writer Robert Bruce Lockhart wrote in his diary:

> Last night Bayliss-Smith, who is a leading chartered accountant and represents the creditors in some of the biggest cinema financial messes in this country, says the cinema industry here has cost the banks and insurance companies about £4,000,000. Most of this is lost by Jews – like Korda and Max Schacht [sic]. Latter already lost a packet for the German Government before Hitler. He has now done the same here. In Bayliss-Smith's opinion and he would not say so lightly, Korda is a much worse man than Schacht. Schacht is just a slick Jew who sees financial moves ahead of the other fellow. Korda is a crook and, according to Bayliss-Smith, an evil man.[303]

Although it was convenient to blame Jewish émigré producers, a few individuals could hardly alone be held responsible for a crisis of such epic scale:

of the 640 production companies that were registered between 1925 and 1936, all but 20 ceased to exist after the production recession.[304] Lockhart's diary entry is but one example of how opponents of émigrés constantly utilised the predicament of the industry for their cause. They willingly ignored the numerous reasons behind the crisis which more recent scholarship has identified: from US protectionism and market dominance, mismanagement, costly prestige productions to the swift withdrawal of necessary support by financiers when films proved to be box-office failures.[305] In essence this means that discourses which simplistically held the influx of foreign personnel responsible for the unemployment of British employees, deflected the discussion from the instability of the industry itself.[306]

Even if xenophobia and anti-Semitism were prevalent throughout the late 1920s, 1930s and during the war, one can detect developments and events that mark an increase in hostility and restrictive measures against foreign film technicians and artists. In this regard, the years 1937 and 1938 mark a decisive moment for Britain as a country of refuge for continental filmmakers. First, the more production companies went into liquidation, the fewer jobs existed in the industry. Second, the explosion of exile numbers after the Austrian *Anschluss* of 1938 increased the number of foreign film practitioners who were looking for jobs in the UK.

When the recession in film production caused unemployment figures that were running at 80 per cent by 1938, an ACT deputation to the Ministry of Labour once again made the case that 'no further permits be given for the employment of foreign technicians for the film industry until unemployment among British technicians has been reduced to a minimum'.[307] Facing fewer jobs as a result of the financial crash and additional competition on the labour market, an increasing number of British film professionals became staunch trade unionists. This again weakened the émigrés' position. The more influential unions such as the ACT became, the higher the pressure on foreign film practitioners was. Finding a job without union membership became increasingly difficult – especially for refugees from the Nazi regime. Therefore, Tim Bergfelder is right in concluding that

> Established immigrants such as Junge certainly felt this pressure occasionally, but were mostly secure in their positions, some of them becoming thoroughly adapted. . . . Subsequent immigrants, however, . . . faced a much more closed industry.[308]

Often the only remaining option for these 'late' German-speaking exiles was Hollywood. And indeed, career paths clearly reveal that more and more foreign film practitioners left Britain for the US – among them producers Korda and Pommer and scriptwriters Franz Schulz and Curt Siodmak. Within months, the British film industry lost its assimilative powers and effectively ended its 'international years'.[309] What proved particularly problematic for foreign film practitioners in Britain was that the ACT every now and then refused membership to émigrés. In practice this meant that the respective individuals could hardly find any job with British production companies. German film-photographer Hans Casparius, for instance, repeatedly tried to join the ACT after he came to London in 1935. When all his attempts remained unsuccessful despite his previous collaboration with prominent filmmakers such as G. W. Pabst, Paul Czinner and Hanns Schwarz, he eventually sought a career outside the industry when he opened a studio for colour photography in 1938.[310] In another case, the ACT successfully prevented Rudolph Cartier from directing *Corridor of Mirrors* (Terence Young, 1948).[311] Although Cartier still produced the picture, Terence Young eventually directed it in 1948. Such news spread fast within London's close-knit refugee community and further aggravated the fears and uncertainty.

Repeatedly other entertainment industry unions joined in the nationalistic rhetoric against foreign staff. At the 1937 Trade Union Congress (TUC), a representative of the National Association of Theatrical and Kine Employees (NATKE), Tom O'Brien, argued that only British nationals could produce such 'British' movies as *Catherine the Great* (Paul Czinner, 1934), *Tudor Rose* (Robert Stevenson, 1936), *Victoria the Great*, and, using these films as examples, he called for the protection of 'British cultural and educational standards from alien disparagement and infiltration'.[312] Absurdly, yet in a manner symptomatic of many contradictions in unions' arguments against foreign workers, every single one of these films was made with immense émigré participation. Cameraman Mutz Greenbaum and designer Joe Strassner were responsible for the stunning cinematography and opulent costumes in *Tudor Rose* and Anton Walbrook gave a memorable performance as Albert in *Victoria the Great*. Above all, émigré participation in the exile film *Catherine the Great* was overwhelming: it was produced by Alexander Korda, and directed by Paul Czinner, Lajos Biró was responsible for the script that was based on a play he had written with Melchior Lengyel. Vincent Korda designed the lavish sets, Ernst Toch composed the music and Elisabeth Bergner played the lead Catherine II.

Although at the centre of the campaign against foreign film workers, the ACT and other unions were not alone in their criticism. From in- and outside the film industry many vehemently opposed the employment of foreign film personnel and the influence of émigré producers and other decision makers. One major form of prejudice was ignorance. Not only was it apparent in the careless misspellings of émigré names that can be found throughout the 1930s and 1940s, it also became manifest in the derogatory expression of 'the Polish Corridor' at Gaumont-British that referred to Michael Balcon's German-speaking production partners Josef

Somlo and Hermann Fellner.[313] The fact that both renowned filmmakers were labelled Polish regardless of their actual nationality – Hungarian and German respectively – clearly shows that ignorance and incomprehension towards the 'other' was common. The celebration of multi-culturalism so prevalent in the US could hardly be found in Britain at that time, indicating why some German-speaking exiles changed their names to anglicised forms. These changes ranged from the abolishment of the *Umlaut* to far-reaching alterations: the composer Josef Zmigrod became Allan Gray, the camera-man and director Mutz Greenbaum changed his name into Max Greene and the producer Isadore Goldschmidt became known as Goldsmith.

The general tendency to perceive continental film personnel as alien and subversive elements also took the form of fierce accusations and overt hostility. This was particularly the case in trade journals of the time. As early as 1932 the following passage appeared in *Film Weekly* under the heading 'The Director':

> I am Monarch of all I survey,
> My right there is none to dispute.
> Give me a good story, good pay,
> Good staff, then (maybe) I'll shoot.
>
> I'll take stars from all round the map.
> A Yank who can't act but who's skittish;
> A German, a Frenchman, a Jap . . .
> And produce you a picture that's British.[314]

What was still meant as a tongue-in-cheek parody of the increasing influence of producers and their preference for foreign personnel soon turned sour. Racist undertones progressively replaced constructive forms of criticism. Examples can be found in articles by prominent film critics such as the *Daily Herald*'s Patrick L. Mannock or *The Spectator*'s Graham Greene. The latter even drew upon the same signs of decadence and otherness that German anti-Semites used in order to describe Jewish filmmakers in a pejorative way,[315] thereby providing evidence for what Richard Griffiths calls the '"parlour anti-Semitism" of much English society'.[316] In Greene's now notorious review of Karl Grune's *The Marriage of Corbal* (1936), he wrote of 'the dark alien executive tipping his cigar ash behind the glass partition in Wardour Street, . . . the German director letting himself down into the canvas chair at Elstree'.[317] In the climate of latent anti-Semitism that prevailed in mid-1930s Britain,[318] as this review illustrates, prejudice and hostility towards émigré filmmakers were common. Against this background, Greene's remarks cannot simply be downplayed as a mere personal attack on Alexander Korda, as has been attempted by some scholars.[319] His remarks should rather be seen as an attack directed against all foreign personnel, as he speaks less about *The Marriage of Corbal* and more about the general issue of émigré filmmakers in Britain. His resentment against the employment of foreigners *per se* becomes obvious in the initial question as to whether *The Marriage of Corbal* should be considered a British film at all since it 'derived from a novel by Rafael Sabatini, [was] directed by Karl Grune and F. Brunn [uncredited], photographed by Otto Kanturek, and edited by E. [sic] Stokvis, with a cast that includes Nils Asther, Ernst Deutsch and the American, Noah Beery'.[320] He then goes on to accuse 'Herr Grune and his international assistants' of causing harm to the British film industry:

> England, of course, has always been the home of the exiled; but one may at least express a wish that *émigrés* would set up trades in which their ignorance of our language and culture was less of a handicap: it would not grieve me to see Mr Alexander Korda seated before a cottage loom in an Eastern country, following an older and better tradition. The Quota Act has played into foreign hands, and as far as I know, there is nothing to prevent an English film unit being completely staffed by technicians of foreign blood. We have saved the English film industry from American competition only to surrender it to a far more alien control.[321]

In a tone similar to the arguments that were uttered in Germany during the great depression claiming that Jewish investors and speculation had infiltrated the industry and caused the high unemployment rates, he continues:

> It is not that there are no English technicians capable of producing films of a high enough standard to take their place in the international markets (an absurd idea when we think of *Song of Ceylon, The Voice of Britain, The Turn of the Tide, Night Mail, Midshipman Easy*). . . . The reason why English technicians are seldom employed is more likely to be financial: it is not English money that calls the tune, and it is only natural that compatriots should find jobs for each other. And so the big film families are founded, a system of nepotism which recalls the less savoury days of the Papacy.[322]

Inserted into its historical context the review stands out as more than the dismissal of a single film. Many of the common prejudices and accusations against émigrés can be spotted in a nutshell. Greene's remarks are exemplary of a growing hostility towards German-speaking filmmakers and other foreign influences.

Moreover, the strikingly aggressive tone of the review illustrates how prominent figures were not immune to xenophobic and anti-Semitic resentment. Although Graham Greene had previously been a great admirer of Weimar Cinema and later became a close friend of émigré Alexander Korda, he, like so many others, joined in the campaign against the employment of foreign film personnel. Despite the international character of the British film industry, Greene, in the words of Andrew Moor 'draws on a tight and authoritarian definition of "Nation" which sees hybridity as monstrous'[323] – a definition that was common within the discourses around British cinema of the era.

Alongside Greene, even a number of people who had formerly called for continental experts and know-how as the only possible way to raise standards in British productions changed their minds in the face of a widespread alien scare. This can also be seen by comparing *Kinematograph Weekly* articles by film critic and author Patrick L. Mannock. While in 1929 he called for the employment of 'a foreign expert rather than a second-rate Englishman',[324] Mannock openly attacked émigré filmmakers in 1936 by asking 'Are so Many Foreigners Necessary?'[325] and, in another article, 'Have we Grown too Cosmopolitan?'.[326] Apart from constructive criticism, articles in the trade press repeatedly display a more or less subliminal anti-German rhetoric. In his regular colloquial *Kinematograph Weekly* feature 'On the British Sets'. E. G. Cousins, for example, continually alludes to the propaganda of the First World War by referring to German-speaking film personnel as 'Teutons' and picks on their accent ('the Teutons on the set pronounce [the word microphone] "mick-rophone" as though it were of Irish origin').[327] It must be stressed, though, that Cousins generally acknowledged the achievements of foreigners working for British studios and was particularly fond of German-speaking singers such as Richard Tauber, Jan Kiepura or Joseph Schmidt, who helped to make a string of successful musical comedies,[328] or Conrad Veidt whom he regarded the best actor in Britain.[329] Cousins' subliminal – perhaps unintentionally – derogatory remarks were not at all uncommon. Even Michael Balcon, himself a great admirer of German-speaking films and the sophistication of their creators, was capable of offensive remarks. Annoyed by the repeated indiscretion of Josef Somlo and Hermann Fellner, he makes it perfectly clear that he will no longer tolerate such behaviour. While part of his argument in a private and confidential letter (which is also classified as 'quite unofficial' in pencil) is comprehensible, he makes an allegation which may well be understood as a prejudiced remark against continental Europeans: 'It may be a quaint mid-European custom to make this sort of comment but I am telling you now that if we are to work together in the future, as I sincerely hope that we are going to do, this kind of thing must cease.'[330]

Writing anonymously in *World Film News*, the founder of the British documentary film movement, John Grierson, also joined the criticism of the employment of foreigners in key positions of the film industry.[331] His forthright, 'almost paranoid article' (Kevin Gough-Yates),[332] 'Aliens Stifle British Talent', claims that '[t]he preponderance of aliens in key positions in the industry not only tends to produce a product lacking national character, but also develops an unhealthy inferiority complex in the rest of the technical staff, who are of local growth'. Furthermore, according to Grierson, the 'alien expert' was constantly worried about losing his job 'bearing in mind the fact that he was not much sought after when he left his own country' and therefore 'tends to watch his own interests . . . rather than train the staff under him'.[333]

Whatever prompted Grierson's remarks, they were inaccurate. The fact of the matter was that foreign technicians both were in great demand[334] and did provide professional training for British workers as mentioned before. Moreover, critical essays and articles published by prominent émigrés such as Vincent Korda or László Moholy-Nagy offered vital impulses for theoretical and practical discourses on the development of cinema – long before film studies was established as an academic discipline.[335] Regardless of such contributions of German-speaking filmmakers, the position of émigrés in the British film industry was hotly debated in the trade press throughout the 1930s. Whilst the end of the 1930s was dominated by critical voices, the first half of the 1930s, as this chapter has outlined, was largely more optimistic. Inspired by the rise in production and the great optimism in the wake of the quota legislation, the *Picturegoer Weekly* enthusiastically exclaimed 'Let Them All Come!' in November 1931 thereby taking an opposite position to Grierson a few years later. Featuring images of Renate Müller, Brigitte Helm and the American-born but German-trained Betty Amann, it argued that the increasing internationalisation of British studios would evidently lead to better standards and critical acclaim: 'Britain may soon be creating its own Garbos and Dietrichs – the rapidly growing foreign colony at Elstree will help tremendously in making British pictures world famous.'[336] Still about a year before the mass-immigration of German-speaking film personnel in 1933 and several years before the film crisis of 1936/37, a *Film Weekly* journalist equally appreciated the arrival of foreign experts:

> We should welcome American and Continental directors as long as they justify themselves by helping to make better and more widely acceptable British pictures. Men like Alexander Korda, Paul Stein, Mervyn LeRoy, and Rowland V. Lee should not be regarded with jealousy and suspicion simply because they do not happen to be British-born. Their skill and experience are their passports.[337]

Notes

1 See Julian Petley, 'Film Policy in the Third Reich', in *The German Cinema Book*, edited by Tim Bergfelder, Erica Carter and Deniz Göktürk (London: BFI, 2002), pp. 173–81 (p. 173).

2 The complex term 'anti-Semitism' will be used to refer to all forms of an

unusual hostility directed at Jews – whether it affected the political, economic or civic rights of Jews. For the problems and complexities involved in defining 'anti-Semitism' see Gavin I. Langmuir, *Toward a Definition of Antisemitism*, 2nd edn (Berkeley, Los Angeles and London: California University Press, 1996).

3 See Horak, 'German Exile Cinema, 1933–1950', p. 376.

4 See Siegfried Kracauer, *From Caligari to Hitler: A Psychological History of the German Film* (Princeton, NJ: Princeton University Press, 1947).

5 Cited in Petley, p. 178.

6 See Petley, pp. 178–9 and Hake, pp. 77–85.

7 See Joseph Goebbels, 'Rede vor den Filmschaffenden am 28 February 1942 in Berlin', cited in Gerd Albrecht, *Nationalsozialistische Filmpolitik* (Stuttgart: Enke, 1969), p. 500.

8 See Jan-Christopher Horak, 'German Exile Cinema, 1933–1950', *Film History*, 8.4 (1996), 373–89.

9 On the aryanization of Jewish film companies, see Jan-Christopher Horak, *Fluchtpunkt Hollywood: Eine Dokumentation zur Filmemigration nach 1933*, 2nd edn (Münster: MAkS, 1986), p. 8; Christoph Fuchs, 'In Labyrinth der Allianzen: Die Metamorphose des Fimenblabels "Cine-Allianz"', in *Aliierte für den Film: Arnold Pressburger, Gregor Rabinowitsch und die Cine-Allianz*, edited by Jan Distelmeyer (Munich: text+kritik, 2004), pp. 34–45 (pp. 37–40); and Martin Loiperdinger, 'State Legislation, Censorship and Funding', in *The German Cinema Book*, edited by Tim Bergfelder, Erica Carter and Deniz Göktürk (London: BFI, 2002), pp. 148–57 (pp. 151–2).

10 See Susan Tegel, 'The Politics of Censorship: Britain's "Jew Suss" (1934) in London, New York and Vienna', *Historical Journal of Film, Radio and Television*, 15.2 (June 1995), 219–45.

11 See *Neuigkeits-Welt-Blatt*, 23 October 1934. Cited in Tegel, p. 232.

12 Friedrich Porges, 'Film-Österreich in London', *Mein Film*, September 1935, p. 8. Translated by Ronald Walker.

13 *Cinématographie Française*, 22 July 1933. Cited in Phillips, pp. 51–2.

14 Horak, 'German Exile Cinema, 1933–1950', p. 377.

15 See Strickhausen, p. 251.

16 See Charmian Brinson, 'A Woman's Place . . .?: German-Speaking Women in Exile in Britain, 1933–1945', *German Life and Letters*, 51.2 (April 1998), 204–24 (p. 205).

17 See, London, *Whitehall and the Jews*.

18 Ibid., p. 13.

19 See J. M. Richie, 'German Refugees from Nazism', in *Germans in Britain Since 1500*, edited by Panikos Panayi (London and Rio Grande, OH: The Hambledon Press, 1996), p. 147–70 (p. 147).

20 Ibid., p. 148.

21 See ibid, p. 147.

22 'Contribution which His Majesty's Government in the United Kingdom is able to make to the Problem of Emigration from Germany and Austria', 11

July 1938, 'Intergovernmental Committee, Evian – July 1938, Technical Sub-Committee, CIE/CT/15', NA FO 919/9.

23 See Strickhausen, p. 253.

24 On emigration from the Third Reich to Britain see Gerhard Hirschfeld, 'Great Britain and the Emigration from Nazi Germany: A Historical Overview', in *Theatre and Film in Exile: German Artists in Britain, 1933–1945*, edited by Günter Berghaus (London and New York: Berg, 1989), pp. 1–14. Louise London has replaced previous figures for refugees admitted to Britain between 1933 and 1939 by an estimated number of 90,000. See London, *Whitehall and the Jews*, pp. 11–12.

25 See Higson, '"A Film League of Nations"', pp. 75–7.

26 See Gough-Yates, 'The European Film Maker in Exile in Britain 1933–1945', p. 218.

27 See Horak, 'German Exile Cinema, 1933–1950', p. 377.

28 See letters by the Home Office dated 29 September 1938 and 18 January 1939, NA HO 405/26547 236966.

29 Passport of Rudolph Kacser (aka Rudolf Katscher, later known as Cartier), NA HO 405/26875.

30 See Horak, 'German Exile Cinema, 1933–1950', p. 383.

31 See Doris Angst-Nowik, Jane Sloan and Cornelius Schnauber, *One-Way Ticket to Hollywood: Film Artists of Austrian and German Origin in Los Angeles* (Emigration 1884–1945) (Los Angeles: USC, [n.d.]).

32 Bergfelder, 'The Production Designer and the *Gesamtkunstwerk*', p. 22.

33 See ibid., p. 22.

34 See Jörg Schöning, 'All Hands Abroad: Kleines Lexikon deutschsprachiger Filmschaffender in Großbritannien 1925–1945', in *London Calling: Deutsche im britischen Film der dreißiger Jahre*, edited by Jörg Schöning (Munich: text+kritik, 1993), pp. 99–150 (p. 105).

35 See Bergfelder, 'The Production Designer and the *Gesamtkunstwerk*', p. 21.

36 Lo Hardy later committed suicide. Among her lodgers were the editor Stefan Lorant, the actresses Lilli Palmer and Irene Prador, the director Curtis Bernhardt, and script-writer Heinz Harald.

37 Marcus initially lived at 9 Queens Gate Terrace, London SW7 before he moved to Paddington. In January 1937 he first moved to 22 Lancaster Gate Terrace and in November 1937 to 43 Norfolk Square.

38 See Steffen Pross, *"In London treffen wir uns wieder": Vier Spaziergänge durch ein vergessenes Kapitel deutscher Kulturgeschichte* (Berlin: Eichborn, 2000), p. 91–4.

39 Cited in Phillips, p. 151.

40 Kevin Gough-Yates, 'Jews and Exiles in British Cinema', *Leo Baek Institute Yearbook*, 37 (1992), 517–41 (p. 520).

41 See ibid., pp. 533–4.

42 Police Report from 27 May 1938 on Paul Czinner (and Elisabeth Bergner), p. 10. NA HO 405/7511.

43 Ibid., p. 10.

44 Police Report from 1 January 1947, p. 3. NA HO 405/26875.
45 Police Report from 16 December 1938, p. 2. NA HO 405/2074 236967. See also the report on Walter Goehr from 6 June 1939, NA HO 405/5863 236966.
46 Metropolitan Police report on Lajos Biró from 16 December 1938, NA HO 405/2074 236967, p. 4.
47 See the file on Conrad Veidt, NA HO 382/8 236966.
48 See letter by G. L. Schwarz from 19 July 1940 and letter by Bartlett & Gluckstein, Solicitors, to the Aliens Department from 24 July 1940, NA HO 405/26875.
49 See letter from Alexander Korda to Geoffrey Lloyd from 9 June 1938, NA HO 405/2074 236967.
50 Letter from O. Locker-Lampson to S. D. R. Pimlott, Home Office, from 30 December 1938, NA HO 382/8 236966.
51 Letter from 26 January 1939, NA HO 382/8 236966.
52 Paul Marcus, *Pem's Personal Bulletins*, 7 September 1953; 21 April 1972. Cited in Gough-Yates, 'Jews and Exiles', p. 535.
53 See Brigitte Mayr, 'Carl Mayer: Years of Exile in London', in *Destination London*, pp. 195–203 (p. 201).
54 See Street, 'British Film and the National Interest, 1927–39', p. 30.
55 See Denis Gifford, *The British Film Catalogue*, 2 vols, 3rd edn (London and Chicago: Fitzroy Dearborn, 2001), I: *Fiction Film, 1895–1994*.
56 Horak, "German Exile Cinema, 1933–1950", p. 379.
57 On Lotte Reiniger's films see her *Sight and Sound* article 'Scissors Make Films' in which she explains her technique and delineates her career path. Lotte Reiniger, 'Scissors Make Films', *Sight and Sound*, 5.17 (Spring 1936), pp. 13–15.
58 'Notes of the Quarter', *Sight and Sound*, 4.15 (Autumn 1935), pp. 105–06 (p. 105).
59 '"The Robber Symphony": Film Fantasy to Music', *The Times*, 17 April 1936, film review, p. 10.
60 'Notes of the Quarter', p. 105.
61 René Dufuor (= Richard Dyck), '"Little Friend" – Studio Caumartin', *Pariser Tageblatt*, 8 February 1935, film review, p. 4. Translated by Ronald Walker.
62 Emile Grant (= Erich Kaiser), 'Kortner als Abdul Hamid: Erfolgreiche Pariser Premiere von „Abdul The Damned" im Marignan', *Pariser Tageblatt*, 30 August 1935, film review, p. 4.
63 See, for example, a manifesto by Maholy-Nagy published in *Sight and Sound*: László Maholy-Nagy, 'An Open Letter to the Film Industry and to All Who Are Interested in the Evolution of the Good Film', *Sight and Sound*, 3.10 (Summer 1934), pp. 56–7.
64 See Ryall, p. 39.
65 Horak, 'German Exile Cinema, 1933–1950', p. 379.
66 Tim Bergfelder, 'Introduction: German-speaking Emigrés and British Cinema,

1925–50: Cultural Exchange, Exile and the Boundaries of National Cinema',
in *Destination London*, pp. 1–23 (p. 10).

67 See *Wolfgang Suschitzky: Photos*, edited by Michael Omasta, Brigitte Mayr
and Ursula Seeber (Vienna: Synema, 2006) and *Wolfgang Suschitzky: Films*,
edited by Michael Omasta, Brigitte Mayr and Ursula Seeber (Vienna: Synema,
2010).

68 See Low, *Filmmaking in 1930s Britain*, pp. 93–4.

69 In this way producers in Britain used the full span of possible remakes as out-
lined by Robert Eberwein, 'Remakes and Cultural Studies', in *Play It Again,
Sam: Retakes on Remakes*, edited by Andrew Horton and Stuart Y. McDougal
(Berkeley: California University Press, 1998), pp. 15–33 (pp. 28–31).

70 On Arnold Pressburger's and Gregor Rabinowitsch's central role in the pro-
duction of multi-language productions in Europe, see *Alliierte für den Film:
Arnold Pressburger, Gregor Rabinowitsch und die Cine-Allianz*, edited by Jan
Distelmeyer (Munich: text+kritik, 2004).

71 See 'Notes of the Quarter', p. 105.

72 See Garncarz, 'Die Bedrohte Internationalität des Films', pp. 135–6.

73 Gerd Gemünden, 'Allegories of Displacement: Conrad Veidt's British Films',
in *Destination London*, pp. 142–54; Michael Williams, 'Anton Walbrook:
The Continental Consort', in *Destination London*, pp. 155–71; and Barbara
Ziereis, 'From "Alien Person" to "Darling Lilli": Lilli Palmer's Roles in British
Cinema', in *Destination London*, pp. 172–80.

74 See Gough-Yates, 'Jews and Exiles', p. 535.

75 C. A. Lejeune, 'The Private Lives of London Films', *Nash's Magazine*,
September 1936, p. 82.

76 Gough-Yates, 'The European Filmmaker in Exile in Britain, 1933–1945', p. 134.

77 Monja Danischewsky, *White Russian, Red Face* (London: Gollancz, 1966), p.
108–09. Episode cited in Gough-Yates, 'The European Filmmaker in Exile in
Britain, 1933–1945', p. 134.

78 Cited in Bergfelder, 'The Production Designer and the *Gesamtkunstwerk*', p.
33.

79 See Kevin Macdonald, *Emeric Pressburger: The Life and Death of a Screenwriter*
(London and Boston: Faber and Faber, 1994), p. 149.

80 Cited in Marion Berghahn, *Continental Britons: German-Jewish Refugees from
Nazi Germany* (Oxford and New York: Berg, 1988), p. 105.

81 Frank Jennings, 'Miss Palmer Faces a Problem', *Film Weekly*, 18 December
1937, pp. 13 and 33.

82 Salka Viertel, *The Kindness of Strangers* (New York: Holt, Rinehart and
Winston, 1969), p. 202.

83 See Hanns Eisler, *Composing for the Films* (New York: Oxford UP, 1947);
Sabine M. Feisst, 'Arnold Schoenberg and the Cinematic Art', *The Musical
Quarterly*, 83.1 (1999), 93–114; K. J. Donnelly, '*I Know Where I'm Going!*
Hearing Germanic Music in the Scottish Isles', in *Destination London*, pp.
220–29; and Florian Scheding, '"An Animated Quest for Freedom": Mátyás
Seiber's Score for *The Magic Canvas*', in *Destination London*, pp. 230–42.

84 Gough-Yates, 'The European Film Maker in Exile in Britain 1933–1945', p. 429.
85 See Pam Cook, *I Know Where I'm Going*, BFI Film Classics 65 (London: BFI, 2002), p. 36.
86 Cook, p. 36.
87 *Film Weekly*, 3 May 1935. Cited in Gough-Yates, 'Berthold Viertel at Gaumont British', p. 210.
88 On the way German film practitioners saw themselves, see *Werkstatt Film: Selbstverständnis und Visionen von Filmleuten der zwanziger Jahre*, edited by Rolf Aurich and Wolfgang Jacobsen (Munich: text+kritik, 1998).
89 Karl Freund, 'Die Berufung des Kameramannes', *Filmtechnik – Filmkunst*, 2 (20 January 1926), reprinted in Aurich and Jacobsen, pp. 19–25 (pp. 23–4). Translated by Ronald Walker.
90 Paul Rotha, 'The Art-Director and the Film Script', *Close-up*, May 1930. Reprinted in Paul Rotha, *Rotha on the Film: A Selection of Writings about the Cinema* (London: Faber and Faber, 1958), pp. 44–9.
91 Cook, p. 21.
92 Karl Freund, 'Der Kameramann', *Filmtechnik – Filmkunst*, 8 (16 April 1927), reprinted in Aurich and Jacobsen, pp. 88–92 (p. 92).
93 Geoff Brown, *Michael Balcon: The Pursuit of British Cinema* (New York: The Museum of Modern Art, 1984), p. 20.
94 See Edward Carrick, *Art and Design in the British Film* (London: Dennis Dobson, 1948), p. 12.
95 See Bergfelder, 'The Production Designer and the *Gesamtkunstwerk*', p. 29; Cook, pp. 49–50; and Junge's storyboards held by the BFI – most of which show the position of the camera in relation to the sets.
96 Rotha, 'The Art-Director and the Film Script', p. 44.
97 See Laurie Ede, 'Capital and Creativity: Notes on the British Film Art Director of the 1940s', *Screen*, 45.4 (Winter 2004), pp. 367–74 (p. 368).
98 A. Vasselo, 'Recent Tendencies in the Cinema', *Design for Today* (May 1935), pp. 170–74. Edward Carrick Collection, Harry Ransom Humanities Research Center, University of Texas at Austin, Box 29. Cited in Sarah Street, 'Extending Frames and Exploring Spaces: Alfred junge, Set design and Genre in British Cinema', in *Destination London*, pp. 100–10 (p. 102).
99 Siegfried Kracauer, 'National Types as Hollywood Presents Them', *Public Opinion Quarterly*, 13.1 (Spring 1949), 53–72 (p. 59).
100 Balcon, p. 99.
101 Cited in Taylor, 'Introduction', p. 8. Hitchcock's *The Man Who Knew Too Much* (Alfred Hitchcock, 1934) serves as a good example of the extent to which British films were altered by censors, see Stephen C. Schafer, *British Popular Films 1929–1939: The Cinema of Reassurance* (London and New York: Routledge, 1997), pp. 232–3.
102 See Jeffrey Richards, 'British Film Censorship', *The British Cinema Book*, 2nd edn, edited by Robert Murphy (London: BFI, 2001), p. 156.
103 See Schafer, p. 228.

104 See Gough-Yates, 'Berthold Viertel at Gaumont British', p. 208.

105 Cited in Jeffrey Richards, 'The British Board of Film Censors and Content Control in the 1930s: foreign affairs', *Historical Journal of Film, Radio and Television*, 2.1 (1982), 39–48 (p. 42).

106 Cited in Jeffrey Richards, *The Age of the Dream Palace: Cinema and Society in Britain 1930–1939* (London: Routledge and Kegan Paul, 1984), pp. 124–5.

107 BBFC Scenarios, BFI Special Collections Unit 154 and 162, May and June 1933.

108 On Breslauer's film, see *Die Stadt ohne Juden*, edited by Guntram Geser and Armin Loacker, Edition Film und Text 3 (Vienna: Filmarchiv Austria, 2000).

109 See Charmian Brinson, 'Facing the Facts: Relations with the "Heimat"', in *Changing Countries: The Experience and Achievement of German-speaking Exiles from Hitler in Britain from 1933 to Today*, edited by Marian Malet and Anthony Grenville (London: Libris, 2002), pp. 184–216 (p. 209).

110 See Wolfgang Benz, *Geschichte des Dritten Reiches*. Bundeszentrale für politische Bildung 377 (Munich: C.H. Beck, 2000), p. 159.

111 See Richards, 'The British Board of Film Censors and Content Control in the 1930s: foreign affairs', p. 41.

112 Low, *Filmmaking in 1930s Britain*, p. 69.

113 See James C. Robertson, *The British Board of Film Censors: Film Censorship in Britain, 1896–1950* (London, Sydney and Dover, NH: Croom Helm, 1985), p. 96.

114 See Richards, 'British Film Censorship', p. 158.

115 On the complex issue of Anglo-German film relations see Jo Fox, '"A Thin Stream Issuing through Closed Locke Gates": German Cinema and the United Kingdom, 1933–45', in *Cinema and the Swastika: The International Expansion of Third Reich Cinema*, edited by Roel Vande Winkel and David Welch (Basingstoke and New York: Palgrave, 2007), pp. 289–305.

116 See *Film-Kurier* (note that the journal is not paginated), 'London verbietet Hetzfilm', 6 December 1933, 'Londoner Hetzfilmverbot aufgehoben', 16 December 1933, 'Der englische Zensor trägt die Verantwortung für die Freigabe eines Hetzfilms', 20 June 1939, and 'Senator Ney erklärt – 20 Hetzfilme Amerikas gegen Deutschland: Churchills Filmgeschenk an Roosevelt und Stalin', 4 August 1941.

117 *The Times*, for example, wrote: 'above all the varied and extremely sensitive acting of Miss Bergner makes Catherine a real and fascinating person'. 'Leicester Square Theatre: "Catherine the Great"', *The Times*, 7 February 1934, film review, p. 10.

118 See the press clippings of British newspapers of March 1934 in the BFI Library. *The Times* also reported the controversy over the release of the film in Germany. See '*Catherine the Great* in Berlin: Nazi Campaign against Non-Aryan Actors', 7 March 1934, p. 12; '*Catherine the Great*: Nazi Disturbances in Berlin', 9 March 1934, p. 14; '*Catherine the Great*: Film Suppressed by the Nazis – Producers' Protest', 10 March 1934, p. 12.

119 See Klaus Völker, "'Aufklärung ist wichtiger als Verurteilung"': Zu Fritz Kortners Film *Der Ruf*, *FilmExil*, 3 (November 1993), 5–12.

120 On German-speaking exile theatre see Alan Clarke, "'They Came to a Country"': German Theatre Practitioners in Exile in Great Britain, 1938–45', in *Theatre and Film in Exile: German Artists in Britain, 1933–1945*, edited by Günter Berghaus Oxford and New York: Berg, 1989), pp. 99–119; and N. A. Furness, 'The Dramatist as Exile: Ernst Toller and the English Theatre', in *Theatre and Film in Exile: German Artists in Britain, 1933–1945*, edited by Günter Berghaus Oxford and New York: Berg, 1989), pp. 121–34.

121 See Pross, pp. 109–14; and Agnes Bernelle, *Schönberg – West End: Das Theater meines Lebens* (Cologne: Bollmann, 1997).

122 See Pross, p. 111.

123 On refugee plays that were critical of National Socialism or anti-Semitism, see Hugh Rorrison, 'German Theatre and Cabaret in London, 1939–45', in *Theatre and Film in Exile: German Artists in Britain, 1933–1945*, edited by Günter Berghaus (Oxford, New York and Munich: Berg, 1989), pp. 47–77.

124 See Horak, 'German Exile Cinema, 1933–1950', p. 379; and Richards, *The Age of the Dream Palace*, especially p. 296.

125 The self-imposed censorship of British production companies as a result of economic concerns bears many striking parallels to Hollywood's cautious stance before the Second World War. See Kracauer, 'National Types', pp. 55–6.

126 See Asper, 'Film', p. 962.

127 See Richard Falcon, 'No Politics!: "German Affairs" im Spionage- und Kostümfilm', in *London Calling: Deutsche im britischen Film der dreißiger Jahre*, edited by Jörg Schöning (Munich: text+kritik, 1993), pp. 77–88.

128 Robertson, *The British Board of Film Censors*, p. 95.

129 See James Chapman, 'Action, Spectacle and the *Boy's Own* Tradition in British Cinema', in *The British Cinema Book*, edited by Robert Murphy, 2nd edn (London: BFI, 2003), pp. 217–25 (p. 222).

130 See James Chapman, 'Celluloid Shockers', in *The Unknown 1930s: An Alternative History of the British Cinema, 1929–1939*, edited by Jeffrey Richards (London and New York: I. B. Tauris, 2000), pp. 75–98 (p. 75).

131 Macdonald, p. 150.

132 See Chapman, 'Celluloid Shockers', pp. 85–6.

133 See Falcon, p. 80, and Dennis Gifford, 'Silent Spies', *Journal of the Society of Film and Television Arts*, 24 (Summer 1966), 6–10.

134 Chapman, 'Action, Spectacle and the *Boy's Own* Tradition in British Cinema', p. 222.

135 See Chapman, 'Celluloid Shockers', pp. 93–4.

136 *Kinematograph Weekly*, 11 May 1933, p. 47.

137 *Picturegoer*, 20 May 1933. Cited in Sue Harper, "'Thinking Forward and Up"': The British Films of Conrad Veidt', in *The Unknown 1930s: An Alternative History of the British Cinema, 1929–1939*, edited by Jeffrey Richards (London and New York: I. B. Tauris, 2000), pp. 120–37 (p. 126).

REFUGEES FROM THE THIRD REICH

138 See Falcon, p. 82. For an analysis of Veidt's British roles and performance see Harper. Although Harper claims that Veidt's file is no longer in existence it can be found at the National Archives, Kew, under HO 382/8 236966.

139 Reginald J Whitley, 'Reginald J Whitley Reviews the Latest Films: Love – For Women: Guns – For Men!: "Dark Journey" (London Pavillion, To-Morrow', *Daily Mirror*, 25 March 1937), film review, p. 20.

140 *Dark Journey*, Screenplay, S. 7687, BFI Library. Cited in Harper, p. 133.

141 On Hitchcock's strategy of casting German-speaking actors to hint at Germany as the nation behind sinister plots in Britain despite a rigid BBFC censorship see Robertson, *The British Board of Film Censors*, pp. 94–5.

142 See ibid., p. 95.

143 Ibid., p. 95.

144 See Falcon, p. 84.

145 On a detailed analysis of *The Spy in Black* see also Moor, *Powell & Pressburger*, pp. 27–43.

146 Translated by Ronald Walker.

147 See Macdonald, p. 148.

148 See Moor, *Powell & Pressburger*, p. 31.

149 Andrew Moor, 'No Place Like Home: Powell, Pressburger Utopia', in *The British Cinema Book*, edited by Robert Murphy, 2nd edn (London: BFI, 2003), pp. 109–13 (p. 111).

150 *Mass-Observation at the Movies*, edited by Jeffrey Richards and Dorothy Sheridan (London: Routledge and Kegan Paul, 1987), p. 121.

151 See Falcon, p. 84.

152 See ibid., p. 85.

153 Moor, *Powell & Pressburger*, p. 28.

154 See Horak, 'German Exile Cinema: 1933–1950', p. 381.

155 Ibid., p. 382.

156 See ibid., p. 381.

157 Ibid., p. 383.

158 See Richards, 'The British Board of Film Censors and Content Control in the 1930s: foreign affairs', p. 41.

159 On the production costs of *Jew Süss* see E. G. Cousins, 'On the British Sets: The Worst Woman in Twickenham?', p. 30.
      Picturegoer, 12 May 1934, p. 30; Michael Balcon's remarks are cited in Kevin Gough-Yates, 'The European Filmmaker in Exile in Britain, 1933–1945', p. 27.

160 See Richards, 'The British Board of Film Censors and Content Control in the 1930s: foreign affairs', p. 41.

161 See ibid., p. 41.

162 G. A. Atkinson, 'Courage of "Jew Süss"', *Era*, 10 October 1934 (unpaginated press clipping, BFI Library).

163 See Sedgwick, 'The Market for Feature Films in Britain in 1934', pp. 19 and 34.

164 See *Neuigkeits-Welt-Blatt*, 19 October 1934. Cited in Tegel, p. 232.

165 See Tegel, p. 234.

166 Richards, 'British Film Censorship', p. 158.

167 Atkinson.

168 'JEW SÜSS (1934)', *Monthly Film Bulletin*, 1.9 (October 1934), film review, p. 81.

169 C. A. Lejeune, '"Jew Süss": A Costly Experiment in Horror', *Observer*, 7 October 1934, film review (unpaginated press clipping, BFI Library).

170 See Tegel, p. 225.

171 Emile Grant (= Erich Kaiser), '„Jew Süss": Im „Elysée–Gaumont"', *Pariser Tageblatt*, 7 December 1934, film review, p. 4. Translated by Ronald Walker.

172 Tegel, p. 220.

173 See Goebbels on 27 June 1940, *Goebbels Tagebücher: Sämtliche Fragmente*, edited by Elke Fröhlich, 4 vols (Munich: Saur, 1987), IV: *1.1.1940–8.7.1941*, p. 221.

174 See Tegel, p. 239.

175 See Tegel, p. 240.

176 *Punch*, 17 October 1934. Cited in Tegel, p. 227.

177 See, for instance, 'ABDUL THE DANMED (1935)', *Monthly Film Bulletin*, 2.15 (March 1935), film review, p. 22 and 'Regal Cinema: "Abdul the Damned"', *The Times*, 2 March 1935, film review, p. 10.

178 See review of *Abdul the Damned* in *The Sunday Times*, 3 March 1935 (unpaginated press clipping, BFI Library).

179 Emile Grant (= Erich Kaiser), 'Kortner als Abdul Hamid', p. 4.

180 See Robertson, *The British Board of Film Censors*, pp. 96–7.

181 See ibid., p. 97.

182 Richards, 'The British Board of Film Censors and Content Control in the 1930s: foreign affairs', p. 39.

183 On Szöke Szakall time in London during the production of *The Lilac Domino*, see 'Londoner Gespräch mit Szöke Szakall, *Mein Film*', 11 December 1936, p. 8.

184 Scene 235a, additional scene, 28 January 1937. Cited in Kevin Gough-Yates 'The European Film Maker in Exile in Britain', p. 46.

185 *Kinematograph Weekly*, 12 March 1936, p. 39.

186 Richards, 'The British Board of Film Censors and Content Control in the 1930s: foreign affairs', p. 45.

187 Cited in Phillips, p. 52.

188 See Rudolf Bernauer's Application for a Certificate of Naturalization, NA HO 405/2616 236967.

189 Metropolitan Police Special Branch report from 20 July 1949, NA HO 405/12865.

190 Metropolitan Police Special Branch report from 1 January 1947, NA HO 405/26875.

191 Cited in Volker Kühn, 'Nachwort', in Friedrich Hollaender, *Menschliches Treibgut*, trans. by Stefan Weidle (Bonn: Weidle, 1995), p. 348.

192 See Horak, 'German Exile Cinema, 1933–1950', p. 389, footnote 21.

193 'The British Board of Film Censors and Content Control in the 1930s: foreign

affairs', Historical Journal of Film, Radio and Television, 2.1 (1982), 39–48 (p. 42).

194 See Naficy, pp. 4–5.
195 Deniz Göktürk, 'Transnational Connections – Introduction', in *The German Cinema Book*, edited by Tim Bergfelder, Erica Carter and Deniz Göktürk (London: BFI, 2002), pp. 213–16 (p. 215).
196 Gerd Gemünden, 'From "Mr. M" to "Mr. Murder": Peter Lorre and the Actor in Exile', in *Light Motives: German Popular Film in Perspective*, edited by Randall Halle and Margaret McCarthy (Detroit, MI: Wayne State UP, 2003), pp. 85–107 (p. 99).
197 See Walter Benjamin, *Charles Baudelaire: ein Lyriker im Zeitalter des Hochkapitalismus. 2 Fragmente*, edited by Rolf Tiedemann (Frankfurt/Main: Suhrkamp, 1969).
198 Siegfried Kracauer, *Offenbach and the Paris of His Time* (London: Constable, 1937). Cited in Phillips, p. 113.
199 Greg Walker, 'The Roots of Alexander Korda: myths of Identity and the International Film', *Patterns of Prejudice*, 37.1 (2003), 3–25.
200 On the importance of musical films in 1930s British cinema, many of which were set in continental Europe, see Stephen Guy, 'Calling All Stars: Musical Films in a Musical Decade', in *The Unknown 1930s: An Alternative History of the British Cinema, 1929–1939* (London and New York: I. B. Tauris, 2000), pp. 99–118.
201 See Christian Cargnelli, '"Be Kvite Kniet, Everybody, *Please!*" Paul L. Stein and British Cinema', in *Destination London*, pp. 123–41.
202 'Regal Cinema: "Heart's Desire"', *The Times*, 22 October 1935, film review, p. 14.
203 On the collaboration between Stein and Tauber see Cargnelli, 'Wien Bilder', pp. 105–20.
204 Cited in Berghahn, *Continental Britons*, p. 105.
205 See Paul Marcus, *Pem's Privat-Berichte*, 17 November 1937, p. 65.
206 Viertel, *The Kindness of Strangers*, p. 202.
207 On Walbrook's attempts to learn English, see Wilson Kent, *The Millgate*, October 1938, p. 74. Cited in Gough-Yates, 'The British Feature Film as a European Concern' p. 153.
208 See 'Mr Anton Walbrook: Prince Albert of "Sixty Glorious Years"', *The Times*, 10 August 1967, Obituary, p. 8.
209 Tom Dysart, 'Anton Walbrook', *Film Weekly*, 26 December 1937, p. 21.
210 See unspecified BFI press cuttings on Anton Walbrook from 24 October and 24 November 1938. Cited in Moor, 'Dangerous Limelight', p. 87.
211 'Mr Anton Walbrook: Prince Albert of "Sixty Glorious Years"', p. 8.
212 'Oesterreich im Film', *Die Zeitung*, 8 January 1943, p. 7. Translated by Ronald Walker.
213 Christopher Isherwood, *Prater Violet* (New York: Random House, 1945; reprinted Minneapolis, MN: University of Minnesota Press, 2001), p. 96.
214 Isherwood, p. 47.

215 See Alfred Kerr to Rudolf Kommer, 21 July 1934. Alfred Kerr Archiv, Akademie der Künste Berlin.

216 See Deborah Vietor-Engländer, 'Alfred Kerr's Unknown Film Scripts Written in Exile: The Famous Critic and His Change of Genre', in *Ästhetiken des Exils*, edited by Helga Schreckenberger (= Amsterdamer Beiträge zur neueren Germanistik, 54 (2003)), pp. 123–39.

217 See Vietor-Engländer, p. 129.

218 See Alfred Kerr, *Eine Insel heißt Korsika* (Berlin: S. Fischer, 1933). The film manuscript is held by the Alfred Kerr Archive, Akademie der Künste Berlin.

219 Manuscript in the Akademie der Künste, Berlin. Translated by Ronald Walker.

220 Letter from Ivor Montagu to S. Chandos Balcon, 5 April 1935. Cited in Gough-Yates, 'Berthold Viertel at Gaumont-British', pp. 201–17 (p. 209). On the full scale of Viertel's problems at Gaumont-British see pp. 209–10.

221 Kerr to Berthold Viertel, 30 July 1935, Deutsches Literaturarchiv Marbach, 69.2512/2. Translated by Ronald Walker.

222 See Paul Marcus, *Pem's Privat-Berichte*, 17 August 1938, p. 48.

223 Dysart, p. 21.

224 Leonard Wallace, 'Meet Anton Walbrook', *Film Weekly*, 7 August 1937, p. 14.

225 The same applies to Wilcox's other 'Victoria' film *Sixty Glorious Years*. See Moor, 'Dangerous Limelight', p. 87.

226 See Moor, 'Dangerous Limelight', p. 87.

227 'A Film of Queen Victoria', *The Times*, 27 March 1937, p. 10.

228 Street, *British National Cinema*, p. 41.

229 Horak, 'German Exile Cinema, 1933–1950', p. 383.

230 See Reginald J. Whitley, 'Reginald J. Whitley Reviews the Latest Films: "Pagliacci" (Carlton Theatre)', *Daily Mirror*, 19 March 1937, film review, p. 28.

231 See Low, *Filmmaking in 1930s Britain*, p. 203.

232 See Horak, 'German Exile Cinema, 1933–1950', p. 383.

233 On Brecht's problems during the making of *Pagliacci*, see Wolfgang Gersch, *Film bei Brecht* (Munich: Hanser, 1975), p. 184.

234 See Martin Esslin, 'Some Recollections on Brecht and Acting', *Theatre Three*, 2 (1987), 9–20.

235 See Horak, 'German Exile Cinema, 1933–1950', p. 383.

236 Richard Dyer, *Stars* (London: BFI, 1979), pp. 142–9.

237 On reviews praising Cornad Veidt's performance see, for instance, *The Sunday Times*, 20 October 1935 and *Observer*, 20 April 1935 (unpaginated press clippings, BFI Library).

238 'The Passing of the Third Floor Back (British Made)', *Variety*, September 1935, film review (unpaginated press clipping, BFI Library).

239 Gemünden, 'From "Mr. M" to "Mr. Murder"', p. 99.

240 See Low, *Filmmaking in 1930s Britain*, pp. 176–7.

241 Gough-Yates, 'The British Feature Film as a European Concern', p. 158.

242 See ibid.

243 See *Film Weekly*, 27 June 1936. Cited in *London Calling*, p. 164.
244 See Gough-Yates, 'Jews and Exiles', pp. 517–43.
245 See London, *Whitehall and the Jews*.
246 See Norman Bentwich, *The Refugees from Germany, April 1933 to December 1935, etc.* (London: Allen & Unwin, 1936).
247 On a concise overview of books published on the issue see Sean Kelly, 'Review: Louise London, *Whitehall and the Jews, 1933–1948: British Immigration Policy, Jewish Refugees and the Holocaust*. Cambridge: Cambridge University Press, 2001', in *Reviews in History* (2001), http://www.history.ac.uk/reviews/paper/kellySean.html [accessed 25 December 2006].
248 See Bill Rubinstein, *The Myth of Rescue* (London and New York: Routledge, 1997).
249 See Martin Gilbert, *Auschwitz and the Allies* (London: Michael Joseph, 1981); David Cesarani, *Britain and the Holocaust* (London: Holocaust Educational Trust, 1998), ibid., *Justice Delayed* (London: Heinemann, 1992); and London, *Whitehall and the Jews*.
250 See Tony Kushner, 'The British and the Shoah', *Patterns of Prejudice*, 23.3 (Autumn 1989), 3–16; ibid., 'The Impact of the Holocaust on British Society and Culture', *Contemporary Record*, 5.1 (Autumn 1991), 349–75; and ibid., *The Persistence of Prejudice: Antisemitism in British Society During the Second World War* (Manchester and New York: Manchester University Press, 1989).
251 Marion Berghahn, *German-Jewish Refugees in England* (London: Macmillan, 1984), p. 103.
252 Marion Berghahn, 'German Jews in England', in *Exile in Great Britain: Refugees from Hitler's Germany*, edited by Gerhard Hirschfeld (Leamington Spa: Berg, 1984), pp. 285–306 (p. 294).
253 Carl Zuckmayer, *A Part of Myself*, translated by Richard and Clara Winston (*Als wär's ein Stück von mir*, Frankfurt/Main: Fischer, 1966; London: Secker & Warburg, 1970), p. 89. Cited in Gough-Yates, 'Jews and Exiles', p. 532.
254 Form A, Application for a Certificate of Naturalization, H.M. Stationary Office, p. 4. See, for instance, the application of Rudolf Bernauer on 22 January 1947, NA HO 405/2616 236967.
255 Letter from E Bloomfeld to the Home Office on 5 September 1938, NA HO 382/8 236966.
256 Ibid.
257 *The Fascist*, November 1932. See Gough-Yates, 'The British Feature Film as a European Concern', pp. 135–66 (pp. 150–1).
258 Paul Marcus, *Pem's Privat-Berichte*, 13 April 1938, p. 12.
259 Colin Holmes, *Anti-semitism in British Society, 1876–1939* (London: Edward Arnold, 1979), pp. 214–19. Cited in Gough-Yates, 'The European Film Maker in Exile in Britain, 1933–1945', p. 33.
260 Dolly Haas, 'Interview. Dolly Haas im Gespräch mit Gero Gandert', in *Exil: Sechs Schauspieler aus Deutschland: Mit Beiträgen von Gero Gandert, Karsten Witte und Angelika Kaps*, edited by Helga Balach and others, 6 vols (Berlin:

Stiftung deutsche Kinemathek, 1983), II: *Dolly Haas*, edited by Helga Balach, pp. 16–17.

261 See Gough-Yates, 'The British Feature Film as a European Concern', p. 151.
262 Collier, pp. 22–3.
263 See Bergfelder, 'The Production Designer and the *Gesamtkunstwerk*', p. 31.
264 Richard Shackelton, 'Trade Unions and the Slump', in *Trade Unions in British Politics: The First 250 Years*, edited by Ben Pimlott and Chris Cook, 2nd edn (London and New York: Longman, 1991), pp. 109–36 (p. 128).
265 *Report of the Proceedings at the 65th Annual Trades Union Congress,* Brighton, 4–8 September 1933, edited by Walter M. Citrine (London: Printing Society, 1933), p. 425.
266 See ibid., p. 446.
267 See ibid., p. 183.
268 See London, *Whitehall and the Jews*, pp. 2–3.
269 The unions represented at the conference were the National Association of Theatrical Employees (NATE), the Electrical Trades Union (ETU), the Musicians' Union (MU) and the Film Artistes' Association (FAA).
270 *Kinematograph Weekly*, 11 May 1933, p. 60.
271 *Cine-Technician*, May 1936, p. 23.
272 Nationalistic tendencies within British socialism can be spotted in the titles of influential socialist writings such as Henry Mayers Hyndman, *England for All: A Textbook of Democracy* (London: E.W. Allen, 1881), Robert Blatchford, *Merrie England* (London: Clarion Office, 1895) and ibid., *Britain for the British* (London: Clarion Press, 1902). Also see Stefan Berger, 'British and German Socialists Between Class and National Solidarity', in *Nationalism, Labour and Ethnicity, 1870–1939*, edited by Stefan Berger and Angel Smith (Manchester and New York: Manchester University Press, 1999), pp. 31–63.
273 Ralph Bond, 'The British Film Industry Between Life and Death', *Left Review*, March 1938. Cited in Jones, p. 77.
274 See Robert Benewick, *The Fascist Movement in Britain* (London: Allan Lane, 1972), p. 156; and Gough-Yates, 'The European Film Maker in Exile in Britain 1933–1945', p. 199.
275 See Tim Bergfelder, 'The Production Designer and the *Gesamtkunstwerk*', p. 33.
276 See Gough-Yates, 'The European Film Maker in Exile in Britain 1933–1945', p. 199.
277 ACT deputation from 13 July 1937, NA LAB 8/75 9820.
278 See ibid.
279 *Kinematograph Weekly*, 25 March 1937, cited in Gough-Yates, 'The European Film Maker in Exile in Britain 1933–1945', p. 180.
280 *Cine-Technician*, May 1936, p. 23.
281 *Kinematograph Weekly*, 3 September 1936, p. 5. Cited in Gough-Yates, 'The British Feature Film as a European Concern', p. 150.
282 NA LAB 8/75 136289. Cited in Gough-Yates, 'The British Feature Film as a European Concern', p. 141.

283 Horak, 'German Exile Cinema, 1933–1950', p. 377.

284 Police report on Paul Czinner from 27 May 1938, NA HO 405/7511, p. 10.

285 See the Ministry of Labour report for the year 1937, cited in *Cine-Technician*, July/August, 1938, p. 65.

286 According to the ACT, some film technicians had to work an average of around 100 hours per week, without overtime pay. See *Minutes of Evidence Taken Before the Committee on Holidays with Pay*, 1937/1938, London, HMSO, pp. 111, 115 and Jones, p. 62.

287 See the debates on 21 December 1932, 8 February 1934, 9 April 1935, 30 November 1933, 18 March 1937 and 21 July 1938.

288 The Minister of Labour, Alfred Brown, gave the number of 24 foreign film technicians that worked in Britain in mid-1938. See The House of Commons, 21 July 1938.

289 See Jones, p. 101.

290 On the files of Goldsmith and Pressburger (ACT Application for Membership No. 6090 and 3593) see Gough-Yates, 'The European Film Maker in Exile in Britain, 1933–1945', p. 232.

291 See *Cine-Technician*, May 1935, pp. 5–6; *Cine-Technician*, December 1936/ January 1937, 106–07; and *Cine-Technician*, January/February 1939, pp. 147–50.

292 See Street, 'British Film and the National Interest, 1927–39', p. 30. On the film crisis see also ibid., 'Alexander Korda, Prudential Assurance and British Film Finance in the 1930s', *Historical Journal of Film, Radio and Television*, 6.2 (1986), 161–79.

293 See Gifford, *The British Film Catalogue*, pp. 433–52 and 487–96.

294 On the cases of Alexander Korda and Max Schach see Bergfelder, 'The Production Designer and the *Gesamtkunstwerk*', pp. 31–2; Gough-Yates, 'The European Film Maker in Exile in Britain, 1933–1945', pp. 160–67; Street, 'Alexander Korda, Prudential Assurance and British Film Finance in the 1930s', 161–79; Low, *Filmmaking in 1930s Britain*, pp. 198–208 and pp. 218–29; and Naomi Collinson, 'The Legacy of Max Schach', *Film History*, 15.3 (2003), 376–89. On general information about the 1936/37 film crisis see Street, *British National Cinema*, pp. 9–10.

295 See Low, *Filmmaking in 1930s Britain*, p. 208.

296 Karol Kulik, *Alexander Korda: The Man Who Could Work Miracles* (London: W.H. Allan, 1975) p. 173.

297 See Helbig, *Geschichte*, p. 70.

298 See the contract between Alexander Korda on behalf of London Film Productions Ltd. and Marlene Dietrich dated Los Angeles, September 1935 (BFI London Film Productions Special Collection).

299 See Low, *Filmmaking in 1930s Britain*, p. 219.

300 The rushes appear in the 1965 BBC documentary *The Epic That Never Was* narrated by Dirk Bogarde, which is available at the National Film and Television (NFT) archives.

301 See Low, *Filmmaking in 1930s Britain*, p. 234.

302 See Jones, p. 15.
303 Bruce Hamilton Robert Lockhart, *The Diaries of Sir Robert Bruce Lockhart, 1887–1970*, edited by Kenneth Young, 2 vols (London: Macmillan, 1973–1980), I: *1915–1938* (1973), p. 392.
304 See *Kinematograph Weekly*, 13 January 1938, p. 139.
305 See Street, *British National Cinema*, p. 10; and Jones, pp. 14–15.
306 See Jones, p. 77.
307 *Daily Herald*, 4 November 1937. NA LAB 8/75 9820, note of a deputation from the ACT and British Association of Film Directors, 2 November 1937. Cited in Jones, p. 77.
308 Bergfelder, 'The Production Designer and the *Gesamtkunstwerk*', p. 33.
309 See ibid., p. 33.
310 Only after the war did he produce and/or direct numerous short music and documentary films.
311 For the case of Rudolph Cartier see Gough-Yates, 'The European Film Maker in Exile in Britain, 1933–1945', pp. 230–7.
312 Cited in Jones, p. 77.
313 See Bergfelder, 'The Production Designer and the *Gesamtkunstwerk*', p. 31.
314 'The Director', *Film Weekly*, 20 February 1932, p. 1.
315 For examples of pejorative depictions of Jewish filmmakers in Nazi publications see 'Der Mann mit der Zigarre', pictures of Jewish film personnel in the Nazi propaganda publication *Film-„Kunst", Film-Kohn, Film-Korruption: Ein Streifzug durch vier Film-Jahrzehnte*, edited by Carl Neumann, Curt Belling, Hans-Walther Betz (Berlin: Scherping, 1937). Reprinted in Helmut G. Asper, *Filmexil in Hollywood: „Etwas besseres als den Tod . . ." – Portraits, Filme, Dokumente* (Marburg: Schüren, 2002), p. 14.
316 Richard Griffiths, *The Fellow Travellers of the Right* (Oxford: Oxford University Press, 1983), p. 83.
317 Graham Greene, 'The Marriage of Corbal', *The Spectator*, 5 June 1936. Reprinted in: *The Pleasure Dome: Graham Greene – The Collected Film Criticism 1935–40*, edited by John Russell Taylor (London: Secker & Warburg, 1972), p. 80.
318 See, for example, London, *Whitehall and the Jews*, p. 6. On the anti-Semitism of Mosley's British Union of Fascists (BUF) see John Stevenson and Chris Cook, *The Slump: Society and Politics during the Depression* (London: Jonathan Cape, 1977), pp. 195–217.
319 See *Mornings in the Dark: A Graham Greene Film Reader*, edited by David Parkinson (Manchester: Carcanet, 1993). The issue is discussed by Bergfelder, 'The Production Designer and the *Gesamtkunstwerk*', p. 32.
320 Greene, p. 78.
321 Ibid., pp. 78–9.
322 Ibid. pp. 79–80.
323 Moor, *Powell & Pressburger*, p. 8.
324 *Kinematograph Weekly*, 3 January 1929. Cited in Gough-Yates, 'The European Film Maker in Exile in Britain 1933–1945', p. 168.

325 *Kinematograph Weekly*, 20 August 1936, p. 39.
326 *Kinematograph Weekly*, 26 November 1936, p. 37.
327 E. G. Cousins, 'On the British Sets: A Four-Foot-Two Hero', *Picturegoer Weekly*, 28 July 1934, pp. 26 and 28 (p. 26).
328 See E. G. Cousins, 'The Year on the British Sets', *Picturegoer Xmas Annual*, December 1934, pp. 15–17.
329 E. G. Cousins, 'On the British Sets: The Worst Woman in Twickenham?', *Picturegoer Weekly*, 12 May 1934, pp. 30 and 32 (p. 30).
330 Michael Balcon to Hermann Fellner on 24 June 1932 (BFI Michal Balcon Special Collection).
331 John Grierson, 'Aliens Stifle British Talent', *World Film News*, 3 September 1936, pp. 20–1. The author has been identified by Kevin Gough-Yates in an interview with the editor of *World Film News*, Hans Feld, on 12 July 1986. See Gough-Yates, 'The British Feature Film as a European Concern', p. 163, endnote 59.
332 Gough-Yates, 'The British Feature Film as a European Concern', p. 150.
333 Grierson, pp. 20–1. The article was reprinted in *Cine-Technician* as 'British Talent Stifled?, *Cine-Technician*, Oct/Nov, 1937, pp. 132–33.
334 See Gough-Yates' investigation of the 'Technical Section' of *Spotlight* for winter 1935, which shows that all major production companies in Britain employed at least one European cine-photographer. Gough-Yates, 'The British Feature Film as a European Concern', p. 143.
335 See Vincent Korda, 'The Artist and the Film', *Sight and Sound*, 3.9 (Spring 1934), pp. 13–16; and Maholy-Nagy, pp. 56–7.
336 Newnham, p.7.
337 *Film Weekly*, 20 February 1932, p.1. Cited in Kulik, p. 70.

3 *Dreaming Lips*, 1937. Courtesy of Deutsche Kinemathek, Berlin

4

'What a difference a war makes': German-speaking as 'emeny aliens' and valuable allies, 1939–1945

One of the main arguments against the naturalisation of foreign workers in the entertainment industry, as outlined in the previous chapter, was the high unemployment in Britain at the end of the 1930s. The beginning of war then aggravated an already difficult situation. Aside from the unions, individual letters to the Home Office illustrate a heightened anxiety towards foreigners that stemmed from the precarious situation on the labour market in some professions. In a letter of 7 October 1939 the London musician George Whitaker wrote to the Home Office that he 'and most of [his] musical colleagues at the Symphony Orchestras, and the West-End Theatre Orchestras, [who] are completely unemployed as the result of the War, . . . do not think it is in the National Interest that the enemy aliens [Walter Goehr, Ludwig Brav and Hans Mayer] should be either granted British nationality or allowed to work in times like the present'.[1] A day earlier the Musical Conductors' Association, possibly informed by Whitaker, wrote to the Home Office in respect of the same émigrés that it 'viewed with increasing alarm the influx of such aliens . . . and wishes to protest most strongly against the continuance of a competition by enemy aliens through naturalisation in time of war'. With regard to the case of the German conductor and composer Walter Goehr, the letter added that although he was a member of the Association, his election 'went through on what now appears to be an erroneous statement, namely that he was already a naturalised British subject. Non-British subjects are automatically debarred from membership.'[2] Needless to say the allegation of a false statement put forward in the letter, which was kept by the Home Office in Goehr's naturalisation file, might well have harmed his chances of obtaining British nationality.

Offering figures for the entire scope of the immigration, the Home Secretary himself acknowledged in the House of Commons on 21 November 1939 that the immigration of 11,000 German refugees had directly created jobs for 15,000 British workers.[3] Under the conditions of war the journal of the ACT – which had been critical of the employment of foreign film personnel throughout the 1930s – published an article which flagged up the valuable contributions of Germans and Austrians to the well-being of the British economy. The article, from spring 1941, suggests that the facts about friendly aliens, for example that 12 émigrés alone employed 1,200 people on the Team Valley Estate on Tyneside, should be of interest to ACT members in view of the recurrent controversy about foreign film technicians.[4]

Even if the hostility towards foreign film workers increased with the mass-purge of refugees from the Third Reich and the film crisis at the end of the 1930s, the striving after national unity in times of war eventually ended the lengthy controversy within the ACT over foreign film workers. While its trade journal *Cine-Technician* repeatedly featured articles about the union's campaign against the employment of émigrés in the 1930s,[5] it sympathises with 'friendly aliens' under the conditions of war. Underlining that much has changed since the time of the xenophobic rhetoric in some articles prior to the war, the journal now emphasised its solidarity with friendly foreigners. Otto Kanturek's obituary serves as a case in point: it recalls an instance when the native German cinematographer, in an altruistic act of comradeship and devotion to his unemployed British colleagues, deliberately left the country so that a British colleague in need 'was duly appointed to take his place'.[6] Moreover, the journal also published a report about aliens in Britain underlining their valuable contributions to the British economy and their courage as they, '[e]ven under the often depressing conditions of internment and compulsory idleness . . . continued to do what they could to prove their worth'.[7]

However, it seems myopic to believe that the latent, yet deep-rooted anti-alienism and anti-Semitism disappeared over night. Indeed, despite all official efforts to promote the image of a unified society, resentment against foreigners and Jews persisted during the war.[8] Although such antipathy was not generally shared within the film industry, this does not imply that British cinema was free from such notions. While the ACT clearly changed its policy towards émigré film personnel by more or less unconditionally acknowledging their contributions and valuable expertise, the newly appointed director of the Ministry of Information (MoI) Films Division, Kenneth Clark caused controversy with an interview in *Kinematograph Weekly*: 'We have got to win this war. The film will help to do it. It is perhaps the most important instrument of propaganda. If we lose the War – IF – let the essential non-British and Jewish element in the Industry realise what would happen to them under Totalitarian control.'[9]

The remark prompted indignation across the British cinema industry. Union representatives and producers alike called for an apology.[10] The European director of the distributor United Artists, George Archibald, for instance, attacked Clark's remarks in an open letter:

You argue that the Film Industry must help to win the war because Totalitarianism would be so unpleasant for what you oddly describe as the 'essential non-British and Jewish element in the Industry'. May I as a Scotsman assure you that I should find it no easier to accommodate myself to Totalitarianism than would my Jewish colleagues. I would add that in the Film Industry we do not think of a man as 'non-British' because he is Jewish.[11]

Using a similar sharp rhetoric, the Secretary of ACT, George Elvin, opposed Clark's comment in the same issue of *Kinematograph Weekly* claiming that his debut as head of the MoI Films Division is now overshadowed by remarks 'similar to those which fall so glibly from the mouths of the leaders of the forces against whom the war is being waged'. And he made clear that the ACT 'would never support an allegation that those [foreigners] who do work here and have adopted British nationality are less good citizens. . . . Similar allegations concerning the many Jews in the industry is [sic] an insult.'[12] Despite the strong condemnation of Clark's remarks, Elvin's phrasing, as Kevin Gough-Yates points out, is 'cautious and leaves open the possibility that foreigners who were not naturalized by 1940, i.e. the majority of refugees, may be less than "good citizens" and suggests that the ACT was not hostile to internment'.[13] All in all, however, the debate sparked by Clark's remarks illustrates a very marked turnaround in the ACT position. While the union's stance towards foreign and Jewish film professionals in Britain had been at best ambivalent during the 1930s, the war against Nazi Germany has turned aliens into allies. Yet besides the position of the union, the controversy surrounding Clark's remarks again raised general issues about the émigrés' position. In particular were they able to maintain their status within the industry even though the war turned many of them into 'enemy aliens'?

However, as tensions eased between the ACT and some émigrés, anti-Semitism and racism surged under the conditions of war. Writing to his wife Salka in California, the Jewish Viennese author, theatre and film director Berthold Viertel states that '[h]ere in England, papers are openly anti-Semitic'.[14] Viertel was not alone in his accusation of the press, which not only repeatedly propagated anti-Semitic ideas but also a deep suspicion towards everything foreign. François Lafitte, who was the first to write a book on the controversial internment of so-called 'enemy aliens', also uttered his concern that in 1940 'some newspapers systematically fostered anti-foreign feeling by inflammatory articles and misleading news items'.[15] Anti-alien and anti-Semitic comments not only stemmed from fascists or Nazi supporters but were part of 'daily discourse, literature and the press' during the inter-war years and well into the 1940s, as Tony Kushner has put it.[16] Not least because of the press coverage and the military success of the Wehrmacht on the continent, Mass Observation – which began to document public opinion and morale in 1937 – noted that already existing resentments towards foreigners and Jews increased during the late spring and early summer of 1940:

> The always latent antagonism to the alien and foreigner began to flare up. Nearly everyone, as previous research has shown, is latently somewhat antisemitic and somewhat anti-alien. But ordinarily it is not the done thing to express such sentiments publicly. The news from Holland made it the done thing all of a sudden . . . new restrictions on aliens corresponded with this feeling and were therefore widely welcomed.[17]

In order to examine the individual cases of refugees from Germany and Austria, tribunals were set up in 1939, which classified refugees in groups according to different criteria. Of altogether 73,000 individuals, approximately 1 per cent were classified as dangerous (class A) and immediately interned. There were 64,244 persons thought loyal (class C) and were at first exempt of all restrictions. Those who were neither thought dangerous nor loyal without doubt were placed into a special group (class B) with several restrictions such as a prohibition from travelling more than five miles outside the London area.[18] In a climate of xenophobia and fear of espionage and sabotage after the French, Dutch and Belgian war efforts failed in May 1940, Westminster resolved to intern thousands of German and Austrian exiles. Although the authorities sought to detain enemy aliens only, many of the internees were Jews or anti-Nazi activists who had fled Germany to escape persecution.[19] Among intellectuals and artists there were also a notable number of film personnel. Besides the actresses Annemarie Haase, Margarete Hruby or Gerard Heinz (Gerhard Hinze), the case of set designer Hein Heckroth exemplifies the tragedy of many interned émigrés and the drastic actions by the British authorities. Although Heckroth, who later was to create the stylised sets of *The Red Shoes* (Michael Powell and Emeric Pressburger, 1948), had no sympathies with fascism – his paintings were removed by the Nazis from galleries – he was arrested and shipped overseas on 10 July 1940 to be interned in Australia without any warning to his wife, child or employer.[20] Other interned film practitioners include author and director Rudolph Cartier, cinematographer Carl Kayser, actor and director Erich Freund, scriptwriters Emeric Pressburger and Heinrich Fraenkel, and set designer Alfred Junge.[21] In addition to the physical distress caused by internment, the psychological strains were severe. As Alan Clarke notes, in particular those who were subject to the atrocities in Nazi concentration camps feared similar ill-treatment now.[22]

Given that many interned Jews and anti-fascists had experienced the Nazi horrors, the practice of interning Nazi sympathisers and refugees at the same sites caused a lot of tension in internment camps in Britain and its dominions. In some cases staunch Nazi supporters maltreated and intimidated the other internees as they were housed together. In some instances, the authorities granted special rights (such as the freedom of assembly) to Nazis and not to anti-fascist internees.[23] Shipped overseas to a camp in Canada, the communist Wilhelm Koenen and the actor Gerard Heinz protested against the aggressive and threatening behaviour of Nazi internees only to be transferred to a detention centre originally reserved for Italian fascists. They were eventually released from detention after protests in Britain and a hunger strike by the remaining interned refugees of their Canadian camp.[24]

As the war progressed, many internees were gathered into camps to be deported to the dominions like the actor Heinz. This governmental plan, however, was gradually relaxed after a German submarine in July 1940 torpedoed the cruise liner *Arandora Star*. Requisitioned for war duties, the vessel left Liverpool on 1 July 1940 to take some 1,200 German, Austrian and Italian internees abroad.[25] The loss of 700 lives as a result of the attack caused public concern and fuelled criticism of British internment policy. No less a person than John Maynard Keynes, who tried to help several interned fellow economists, claimed he had 'not met a single soul, inside or outside government departments, who is not furious at what is going on'.[26] Winston Churchill's support for the policy of mass internment of enemy alien refugees notwithstanding, the growing concerns and increasing criticism led to the release of most internees towards the end of 1942. Interestingly, most refugees understood the measures of the British government to intern émigrés – even if they criticised the conditions in the camps. Writing for the American-based refugee newspaper *Aufbau* in January 1940, the exiled journalist and film and theatre critic Paul Marcus reports about the tribunals in Britain:

> In the meantime, the tribunals throughout the country have done their work and released the vast majority of the emigrants from those restrictions that it was necessary to impose upon them initially. Anyone designated a 'friendly alien' by those tribunals will now find it easier to get a work permit; he can sign on at the official employment exchange and will then have almost equal rights with his British counterparts.[27]

This view, however, is rather optimistic. While Marcus entirely omits what happened to those who were not declared 'friendly aliens', many of those émigrés who were eventually released from internment remained under surveillance[28] and found it difficult to gain work permits as cinema was seen as a vital and sensitive medium in the fight against Nazi Germany. Regarding Rudolph Cartier's naturalisation and authorisation to work in the film industry, one Whitehall official explicitly stated on 28 July 1944:

'We ought look very carefully at the establishment of aliens as directors of film companies.'[29]

With the intention of ensuring political and social stability, the Home Office was concerned with the political affiliations and personal financial status of individual émigrés. National Socialist affiliations were deemed as unfavourable as ties to communist or socialist circles and organisations. The political assessment criteria of the Home Office particularly hampered the prospects of naturalisation for political refugees. In their decisions Home Office officials relied on special reports on individual émigrés that were compiled by the police once a foreign national applied for naturalisation.

Heinrich Fraenkel's report, written after the war, mentions that he 'admitted having been a very ardent "fellow traveller" with the German communist party' only to stress that he had never been a party member and that 'he now [in 1949] realised that he had been very naive'.[30] Nine years earlier, in 1940, when the war turned progressively against Britain, the Home Office was not prepared to take any risks and had asked MI5 to observe the political activities of Fraenkel. After some initial problems (which involved some confusion about his identity as there seemed to have been another man with the same name and the temporary unavailability of an informer) they confirmed that Fraenkel was a communist sympathiser and, with more than a hint of a red scare, connected him with the filmmaker Ivor Montagu, a friend of Eisenstein and associate producer of Hitchcock's films:

> [Fraenkel] probably holds fairly advanced Left Wing views as he is a friend of long standing of Ivor Montagu, the prominent British Communist. Fraenkel's film work brought him into touch with the Soviet Film Industry in which he co-operated with Montagu. Fraenkel has also been connected with "Inside Nazi Germany" to which he had contributed articles under a nom de plume. We have no knowledge of his pro-Allied sympathies, and in view of his friendship with Montagu there might be some doubt about the latter.[31]

Since Montagu was a well-known and outspoken anti-fascist it seems incomprehensible why the association of Fraenkel with the communist filmmaker was seen as evidence of his lack of sympathy for the Allied cause in 1940. The above judgement is significant furthermore because it applies to a number of German-speaking émigrés who worked for Gaumont-British at one time or another such as Alfred Junge, Mutz Greenbaum, Joe Strassner, Berthold Viertel and many others. Under the aegis of Michael Balcon, who offered employment to many displaced personnel in the 1930s, Montagu served as an important link between British and foreign staff at Gaumont British because he spoke Russian and German fluently.[32]

Moreover, the police report fails to mention that Fraenkel left no doubt about his anti-Nazi orientation by publishing the book *The German People versus Hitler* (London: Allen & Unwin, 1940). in the very year of the report.

Despite economic difficulties, cases of xenophobia and thorough official surveillance as to émigrés' political beliefs, three developments proved to be beneficial for émigré film professionals. First, the BBC significantly expanded its staff from 4,900 at the beginning of war to 11,500 in 1945. Among them a significant number of refugees who worked as translators, conductors, composers and authors and also as speakers and actors for its German-language propaganda programmes.[33] Among other film personnel the actresses Lucie Mannheim, Sybilla Binder, Annemarie Haase and Hanne Norbert were contracted regularly.[34] Second, the relaxation of censorship prompted the production of anti-Nazi films such as the formerly rejected *Pastor Hall* (Roy Boulting, 1940), and thus offered much needed opportunities. Third, the MoI imperative to maintain a private 'flourishing British Film Industry, busy for the most part in producing, not propaganda films, but the normal entertainment film, produced, distributed, and exhibited through the ordinary commercial channels of the Industry'[35] helped German-speaking filmmakers to retain their position within British studios. Otto Kanturek, for instance, was working as chief lighting cameraman at Elstree before his tragic plane crash while filming *A Yank in the RAF* (Henry King, USA 1941). Other examples include the cameramen Erwin Hillier (Verity Films), Wolf Suschitzky (Paul Rotha Productions), Mutz Greenbaum (Ealing and Denham Studios – among others for RKO Radio British Productions, British National and Herbert Wilcox Productions) and Günther Krampf (Associated British and Ealing Studios), the scriptwriters Carl Mayer (Paul Rotha Productions), Wolfgang Wilhelm (Denham Studios – among others for Two Cities Films and RKO Radio British Productions), and the writer and producer Anatole de Grunwald (among others for Two Cities Films).

The war had a deep impact, moreover, on the émigrés' sense of belonging. Daniel Snowman, for instance, records that Emeric Pressburger, perhaps for the first time in years, felt that he was no longer a foreigner.[36] Despite the fact that he was initially interned as an enemy alien, he later recalled: 'Suddenly I had something in common with everyone I met.'[37] This new sense of community, which was shared by many German-speaking film personnel, had a deep impact on how they perceived their own displaced situation and how they participated in the fight against an enemy which had now also become the enemy of their country of domicile. Working for various production companies in Britain, many émigrés became actively involved in British propaganda in order to prove their allegiance to the

British war effort – a decisive criterion in the re-evaluation of their alien status and work permit claims.

British anti-Nazi films and German-speaking personnel

The Second World War not only had a seismic effect on the lives of émigrés but also fundamentally changed the modes of film production. Among other measures and developments, the BBFC eased some of its more stringent regulations and the newly established Films Division of the wartime MoI began to play a key role in the production of films. The combination of entertainment and political content, furthermore, led to an astounding boom in British cinema – both in terms of creativity and popularity.[38] This success has tended to be celebrated as a genuine national achievement. Charles Barr, among others, argued that by the end of the Second World War 'a positive reading of "mainstream" British cinema for the first time became convincingly available, both in Britain and abroad. It was a cinema unproblematically British in personnel (after a decade of foreign infiltration that was resented by many).'[39]

Notwithstanding all restrictions and the eventual internment of émigrés after 1939, the war also offered new opportunities. Actors with Germanic accents – a major disadvantage in previous years – were much sought after to appear in war films. The trajectory of actor Gerhard Hinze (Gerard Heinz) seems to illustrate well how wartime roles alleviated the situation of individual émigrés. Born in Hamburg in 1904, he began his career in the theatre in the northern German city where he also became a member of the German Communist Party. Interned by the Nazis in a concentration camp, he fled to Prague in 1935 and went to the Soviet Union until 1937. In 1938/39 he left Russia again via Prague for England where he sought work as an actor. After having been interned in Canada under atrocious circumstances he worked for the cabaret and theatre in wartime England. From 1942 he was repeatedly cast in films (*Thunder Rock*, Roy Boulting, 1943; *Went the Day Well*, Alberto Cavalcanti, 1942 and numerous postwar productions).

This section challenges the marginalisation of émigrés in previous critical accounts of British wartime cinema.[40] Rather than stressing the 'national' aspect of such films, the ensuing analysis draws special attention to the various contributions by German-speaking émigrés to British propaganda films or films with an implicit political connotation.[41] Having been able to fill important posts within the British film industry during the 1930s, German-speaking émigrés continued to play a key role in the making of wartime propaganda as can be inferred from the casts and credits of films such as *49th Parallel* (Michael Powell and Emeric Pressburger, 1941). In so doing, they shaped views on whom Britain was fighting and why. Many of the political statements by émigrés went beyond simplistic presentations of allies and enemies. Thus they contributed to the fact that by and large British Second World War propaganda, as Robert Murphy points out, shied away from the 'xenophobic chauvinism'[42] which had characterised the partisan media of the First World War. Many films even seem to differentiate between Nazis and 'good' foreigners or Germans by way of performances of émigré actors and actresses. By providing a *niche* for German-speaking actors, who of all film exiles experienced arguably the greatest loss of status, political films were important as they repeatedly featured émigrés as leads or in important supporting roles. Seen together with émigrés working in the film industry in other capacities, the contributions of actors show that film exile during the war cannot be described solely in terms of trauma, estrangement and paranoia but also as a creative encounter with another culture.[43]

The beginning of war marks a caesura not only in British and European film history but also in the lives of émigré film personnel. Whilst the war, in many respects, meant restrictions and hardships it also prompted a boom period of British cinema[44]. With new job prospects and less hostility from the cinema unions, many émigrés either maintained their positions within studios or eventually gained a foothold in the industry for the first time[45]. In view of such developments, the marginalisation of émigrés in previous critical accounts of wartime films – particularly those with a political message – must be challenged.[46]

Rather than stressing the 'national' aspect of such films, the ensuing analysis draws special attention to the various contributions by German-speaking émigrés to British wartime propaganda films or films with an implicit political connotation. Having been able to fill important posts within the British film industry during the 1930s, German-speaking émigrés continued to play a key role in the making of wartime propaganda as can be inferred from the casts and credits of films such as *49th Parallel*. The wartime films, too, demonstrate the way in which German-speaking émigrés were or were not able to wield influence over films by addressing political issues such as anti-Semitism, the holocaust and the nature of Nazism.[47]

Once the war with Nazi Germany broke out, many German-speaking exiles became actively involved in the British war effort. Some émigrés were recruited by Allied intelligence agencies because of their special language skills. The script writer and author Rudolf Bernauer, among others, was engaged in secret European operations for the US Army Office of Strategic Services (OSS).[48] Otto Kanturek, furthermore, became involved in the development of new weapons[49] and the Viennese author John Hans Kahan and Carl Lamac, who had already been a front-line cameraman for the axis-powers in the Second World War, took part in making promotional films for the army and the RAF.[50] Michael Powell recalled in retrospect that Anton Walbrook, for example, was one of the first stars to agree to appear in his *49th Parallel* (1941) because he was considered to be an enemy alien and wanted to show which side he was on.[51] Besides individual activities as military film professionals or secret agents, however, émigrés were excluded from joining the armed forces with only a few exceptions. Although Berlin-born Ken Adam was clearly just such an exception as a pilot for the RAF, many émigré artists were vital to British propaganda and to attempts to end American isolationist policies. Whilst cartoonists and caricaturists such as Joseph Otto Flatter published works that ridiculed Hitler and his policies in British newspapers,[52] German-speaking personnel participated in the majority of important wartime feature films with an anti-Nazi message. As their contributions to the 'war of information' against Nazi Germany were not without risks and sacrifices this certainly helped to prove their allegiance to Britain and the British.

The willingness of refugees to participate in the war of Britain did not remain unnoticed at Whitehall. In fact, their commitment in the war against Nazi Germany certainly helped individual German-speaking film personnel to ease some of the restrictions posed upon them at the beginning of war and eventually to take British nationality. In some cases, the MoI itself deemed the contributions of émigré film experts so important that it tried to support German-speaking film personnel in passport, residency and related matters. In a letter of 17 February 1941 an MoI official appealed directly to the Home Office, asking that the renowned cinematographer Otto Kanturek could immediately return to Britain from America:

> I am to state that Twentieth Century Productions are at present engaged on two films "Spitfire" and "William Pitt the Younger" which are regarded by this Ministry as being of definite propaganda importance. The shortage of skilled technical staffs [sic] is serious, and Mr. Kanturek is urgently wanted for work on both films. It is understood from M.I.5 that there is nothing against his return on security grounds.
>
> The Ministry of Information considers that the return of Mr. Kanturek is in the national interest, and that the work on which he will be engaged is of national importance. I am accordingly to request that you would be good enough to consider the Granting of re-entry permit to Mr. Kanturek.[53]

In order to strengthen the overall argument, the MoI also enclosed a letter from Kanturek's employer, Twentieth Century Productions Ltd., in which the company states that he is 'a definite asset to the film industry' and that his devoted allegiance to Britain and the war effort can clearly be seen in his past work. Tragically, the endeavour of the MoI came too late for Kanturek who died in a plane crash while filming *A Yank in the RAF* (Henry King, USA 1941).

Despite such individual tragedies the involvement of German-speaking émigrés in British films was an incisive one. They often offered different views on the events of war, the nature of the enemy and the allies' anti-Nazi coalition. With the outbreak of war, the film business initially suffered a severe drop in production output from 103 films in 1939 to about 60 to 70 films in the war years. The decline was the direct result of the conscription of about two-thirds of all employees in the industry, the requisition of half the studio space for war-related storage purposes and tax hikes.[54] Unlike the Third Reich, where cinema was seen as an integral part of propaganda throughout the 12-year Nazi rule, cinemas were initially closed in Britain once the war broke out. This drastic measure was deemed necessary by British authorities on grounds of unpreparedness. Although planning for war propaganda had begun as early as 1935, the close ties between censors and Westminster's appeasement policy as well as inter-departmental rivalry and personal animosities hindered these plans from being further developed. As a consequence, 'the role which the most significant mass media, radio and film, would play in wartime was still, astonishingly, undecided' by September 1939, as historian Philip M. Taylor points out.[55] Set up to inform the public during the war, the MoI appeared badly organised, even chaotic. Many of its Films Division staff, moreover, were not *au fait* with modes of film production.

The cinema's prospective value for propaganda purposes, however, led to the full reopening of film theatres in November 1939. The change of attitude can clearly be seen in the discussions and articles in trade papers and film journals of the time. In spring 1939 the London-based magazine *Sight and Sound* published a major article in which the president of a group of film trade journals, Martin Quigley, stated his views that film propaganda is out of place in any form. Once the war broke out, another article in the same journal called for cinematographic help for British interests under the heading 'Let the Screen Help!'.[56] In addition to numerous publications, many governmental organisations and official agencies also stressed the importance of motion pictures to the war effort. Much had changed since the First World War when decision-makers in the military and Whitehall had shared a profound distaste for the cinema, which they considered a low-brow, working class form of entertainment and which was seen as incapable of contributing to winning the war.[57] The Select Committee on National Expenditure, for instance, stated in a 1940 report: 'The wide distribution secured by commercial feature films gives excellent opportunities for disseminating, if not direct propaganda, an impression of the British attitude both to the issues of war and to war-time conditions.'[58] Looking for qualified personnel for its own propaganda productions, the MoI itself contracted a large number of German-speaking staff who, as foreigners, were not drafted, including Otto Kanturek, Anton Walbrook, Heinrich Fraenkel, Robert Neumann and Arthur Koestler to produce films such as *Lift Your Head Comrade* (1942), *These Are the Men* (1943) and *Information Please!* (1944).

In addition to its own engagement, however, the MoI sought to maintain a private film industry throughout the war in particular for the production of costly feature films. Or, as the MoI put it themselves, it is essential to maintain a private 'flourishing British Film Industry, busy for the most part in producing, not propaganda films, but the normal entertainment film, produced, distributed, and exhibited through the ordinary commercial channels of the Industry'.[59] For this purpose, it proposed to end the closure of motion picture theatres under the condition that effective measures of control were in place. The reopening of cinemas thus went hand in hand with increased governmental surveillance of the film industry as the outbreak of war profoundly changed censorship in Britain. Although the BBFC remained in service, its authority was restricted to moral matters as many responsibilities regarding censorship were transferred to the armed forces and the MoI.[60]

These changes had a deep impact on the production of films that were critical of Nazi ideology. Once cinematic appeasement had become obsolete, the pre-war ban on criticism of Germany and Japan was lifted. And, as one of the censors said in October 1939, 'during wartime our rule against the representation of living persons does not extend to enemy aliens'.[61] As a consequence many formerly rejected films such as *Pastor Hall*, the Soviet *Professor Mamlock* or the American anti-Nazi films *Confessions of a Nazi Spy*, *I Was a Captive of Nazi Germany* and *The Great Dictator* were released or rushed into production. This relaxation of previously stringent regulations was noted by refugees and the general public with content.[62] 'What a difference a war makes', commented the *Sunday Pictorial*.[63]

As the example of Otto Kanturek has shown, with the beginning of war the MoI also became actively involved in the release of interned German-speaking filmmakers and in their struggles with the Home Office and other authorities. The foreign experts were needed to meet the aims of the ministry as outlined by the first wartime Minister of Information, Lord Macmillan, in 1940. He issued a memorandum in which he explicitly put forward ideas for themes of feature propaganda films. Such films should revolve around plots that elucidate the purpose of war, the way Britain was fighting and the need for sacrifice for the war effort.[64] Even before this memorandum had been issued, émigré Alexander Korda was the first to make use of the changed political climate as he produced the earliest wartime propaganda feature *The Lion Has Wings* (Adrian Brunel, Brian Desmond Hurst, Michael Powell and Alexander Korda, 1939) which was shown in cinemas as early as November 1939. The MoI was certainly grateful for Korda's private initiative, particularly given the severe criticism MoI-produced films had to face during the first six months of war. If shown at cinemas at all, they 'ran the gauntlet of pungent and increasingly hostile criticism in the press, and produced constant complaints in and out of Parliament', as Francis Thorpe and Nicholas Pronay claim.[65]

Whereas emigrants in Hollywood were, according to Horak, not able to propagate ideas of a diverse, anti-fascist Germany,[66] the celebrity status of émigré stars in conjunction with the importance of German-speaking producers and scriptwriters in Britain facilitated such an influence. The films written by exile Emeric Pressburger are particularly significant here, dominated as they are by the 'masquerade of nationality . . . and the difficulties of being alien but not enemy, of being non-national' in the judgement of Antonia Lant.[67] Although still bound to portray a foreigner, Conrad Veidt in *Contraband* (Michael Powell and Emeric Pressburger, 1940) plays a sympathetic Dane who successfully tracks down German infiltrators in London during the war. The film highlights that the British were not alone in their fight by drawing upon the multi-national character of the anti-Hitler coalition. Furthermore, the film positions itself against Neville Chamberlain's appeasement policy. Thus the film was highly topical. Shortly before *Contraband* was released in the UK in mid-May, Chamberlain had resigned as Prime Minister after protests against his foreign policy caused by the Wehrmacht's occupation of neutral Denmark on 9 April 1940. In a symbolic scene, the film's Danish protagonists Captain Andersen and Mrs Sorenson (Valerie Hobson) manage to escape German spies and briefly hide in a storehouse full of residual busts of Chamberlain. Significantly, the hero prevails in the ensuing gunfight while the busts are destroyed – leaving the broken pieces to symbolise the failure of Britain's appeasement policy. *Contraband* is not the only British film, however, to sympathise with the continental-European victims of Nazi oppression. Two other 1940 émigré films also centre on foreigners who oppose Nazism: *Night Train to Munich (*Carol Reed, 1940) and *Dangerous Moonlight* (Brian Desmond Hurst, 1941*)*.

Otto Kanturek's cinematography created a threatening and dark atmosphere for Carol Reed's *Night Train to Munich* (1940), which is reminiscent of Hitchcock's British thrillers. The film tells the story of the Czech armour-plating inventor Dr Bomasch who tries to flee Prague when the Germans march into the city. On the way to Britain he and his daughter are caught by the Gestapo and brought to Berlin. With the help of an undercover

British agent, father and daughter manage to escape to neutral Switzerland. Although German émigré actors only play the part of villains (Frederick Valk a German officer at Munich station, the Viennese actor Hans Wengraf a concentration camp physician and Paul Henreid the Gestapo officer Karl Marsen), the production is an early example of films that were sympathetic to central European characters who contributed to the Allied war effort. However, unlike émigré films such as the wartime productions by Powell and Pressburger, *Night Train to Munich* is very much in the tradition of Hollywood anti-Nazi films as the film features a variety of stereotypes and myths. In a black-and-white manner, an English gentleman spy outwits all Nazi villains. Emblematic symbols like the enemy's boots, heel clicking, monocles, martial uniforms, swastikas and pictures of Hitler form part of the mise-en-scène, and, thus, clearly differentiate between friend and foe.

Dangerous Moonlight (Brian Desmond Hurst, 1941) combines escapism with propaganda in a story that includes romance, action and music. The film was a perfect example of what the MoI thought to be good propaganda. Shortly after his assumption of office, the second director of the MoI Films Division Kenneth Clark, outlined principles for the production of wartime films in *Kinematograph Weekly* that are central for an understanding of wartime film production.

> What we are fighting for must be 'put over' on the world by indirect methods, of which the filmic form is one. We do not want 'blah' of jingoism, but a concrete form embodied in the feature film as well as the documentary. We can make interesting entertainment pictures of propaganda value on topics which are to-day part and parcel of the national effort – the Convoys, Contraband Control, . . . and other phases of modern warfare.
>
> . . . I would add two things, firstly, no film is good propaganda unless it is good entertainment. A bad film transfers boredom to the cause it advocates. Secondly, it must be realised that the essence of successful propaganda is that people should not be aware of it. If you make people 'think' propaganda, their resistance to it is increased. . . . The greatest of the anti-German agents is Donald Duck. The whole ethics of Disney's work is that, while being superb entertainment, he portrays the popular hatred of regimentation and dragooning.[68]

Arguably less on account of Clark's principles and more because of economic reasons, British producers increasingly sought to offer a *potpourri* of genres in order to address a broad female and male audience. Such hybrid films adhered to a change in cinemagoers' preferences as 'the public couldn't sit through the ordinary talkie-talkie-tea-table picture. [People] wanted action, movement, colour, music, comedy – some sort of proxy release from our pent-up emotions.'[69]

The 1943 film *They Met in the Dark*, which was directed by Carl Lamac, co-written by Anatole de Grunwald, shot by Otto Heller and produced by Marcel Hellman, exemplifies the hybridity of many wartime feature films by mixing elements of musical romance with those of a Hitchcock-like suspense thriller. While it deals with the contentious wartime topic of espionage in Britain it features many music performances and a romantic subplot so as to enhance its appeal to a mass-audience. Made after the alien scare at the beginning of war, the film, moreover, draws on common fears about Nazi infiltrators. Otto Heller's sinister cinematography depicts the anxiety and agony of the early war years while the music scenes offer a relief from the war by means of popular escapist entertainment. What is interesting about *They Met in the Dark*, however, is the fact that the Nazi spy ring mainly comprises native British citizens. The film thus proposes that the war is not against a foreign nation but against a totalitarian ideology – a recurring theme of many émigré films. Together with Cavalcanti's well-known *Went the Day Well* (1942) in which even an oarsman of Cambridge's Jesus boat turns out to be a Nazi officer, it also draws on common beliefs that parts of the upper classes were Nazi-sympathisers.[70]

While *They Met in the Dark* challenges common fears of a foreign fifth column, other émigré films instead stress the valuable contributions of foreigners to the war effort. In *Dangerous Moonlight* émigré Anton Walbrook plays the Polish star pianist Stefan Radetzky who escapes from Warsaw when the Nazis attack Poland and in exile falls in love with an American heiress. The film clearly sets out to convince an American audience to join in the war against the Third Reich. In one scene, Radetzky's manager Mike leaves America to fight for the British. When he is questioned as to why he as an Irishman wants to do so after all the English have done to his ancestors, his answer 'that doesn't count when somebody else butts in' is a statement which implies that one has to leave old animosities aside when fighting an idea as evil as Nazism.

Moreover, Stefan Radetzky also wants to fight actively in the battle of Britain against the Nazis in a Polish division of the RAF despite his happy marriage and great success as concert pianist in America. At first, though, his wife Carol can convince him that he is an artist not a fighter and that he can do more by raising money by giving concerts. Yet after having performed the lushly sentimental *Warsaw Concerto*, Radetzky makes up his mind to fight actively in the Battle of Britain in a Polish division of the RAF. Composed especially for the film by Richard Addinsell and the uncredited Mischa Spoliansky, the emotional music makes him remember the plight of his people and the desire to return to his home country. In one of Walbrook's moving show-piece performances he explains to his wife (and all cinemagoers) why he has to fight:

Stefan: I'm joining our Air Force in England.

. . .

Carol: I don't know what's wrong with you tonight!
Stefan: I've tried, Carol, believe me, I've tried. Every time I'm telling myself
what a marvellous job I'm doing here in America. And every time I believe
it less. That's why I'm going. I have to. Something I can't explain, something I just can't help. But I know once I've done it, I'll feel alright inside.
Carol: I think it wrong. It's just a stupid waste.
Stefan: Life would be too easy if everybody said that. There would be no art,
no music left that would be worth fighting for.

His sensitive, yet passionate acting style and sometimes fragile screen
persona add an interesting nuance to the perception of foreigners in
British films. From his performances as the sympathetic Prince Albert
in Herbert Wilcox's *Victoria the Great* (1936) to the celebrated musician
in *Dangerous Moonlight*, Walbrook repeatedly played the roles of charm-
ingly melancholic outsiders. Rather than indulging in swift action he is
depicted as a taciturn if not introverted character who is repeatedly framed
by close-ups of his facial expressions. He is introduced by a superimposition of images that depict him staring into the camera in combination
with pictures that show the tragic circumstances under which he has met
his American wife amidst the rubble of Warsaw. While he silently mourns
over his comrades who were killed in action he almost motionlessly plays
the piano with a cigarette hanging carelessly from the corner of his mouth.
Whenever he speaks he does so very slowly giving emphasis and depth to
every single word. Andrew Moor pointedly describes his voice as 'subtly
modulated and rythmed tenor, tightening in moments of urgency into a
guttural, strangulated rasp.'[71] In contrast to stereotypes of the uncouth
'strange other' speaking loudly with a thick accent, he appears fragile,
receptive, cultured, eloquent and elegant. At variance with other German
or Austrian male stars in the late 1930s and early 1940s such as the salt-
of-the-earth Richard Tauber or the sinister Conrad Veidt, Walbrook is
deeply emotional and even cries at the end of the film when he finds a
letter of his wife in the belongings of his best friend who was killed in
action.

Being a refugee from the Third Reich is often attached to an obligation
to warn the British public against the perils of fascism. Given their experiences with National Socialism, refugees often add verisimilitude to the
argument when they challenge policies of appeasement or isolationism.
When Walbrook as Radetzky in *Dangerous Moonlight* is accused by his
American wife Carol of throwing his talent and life away by joining the
RAF, he replies:

Stefan: Now, you must begin to forget who I am – an exile, a man without a country of his own.

Carol: How can you say a thing like that after how you have been treated here.

Stefan: But that's why. Carol, can't you see? I am happy here, everybody's kind. It's so easy to forget all about my country and my people.

While this dialogue is contemporaneous with British efforts to end American isolationism, the events of war support Stefan's position that challenges the idea that going to fight is but 'some patriotic notion'. In the context of wartime cinema, *Dangerous Moonlight* is an example of the MoI's increasing support for the incorporation of 'friendly foreigners' into feature film projects. In its endeavour to propagate the conflict with Nazi Germany as 'The People's War' in which all strands of British society are united in the fight against the common enemy,[72] foreigners became valuable allies.

In addition to the 'good foreigner', British films also featured roles for 'good Germans'. In so doing, they offered a nuanced picture that significantly differed from British and American mainstream anti-Nazi films that commonly featured a variety of stereotypes in a black-and-white manner. As the following examples illustrate, British émigré films such as *Pastor Hall* (Roy Boulting, 1940) *49th Parallel* (Michael Powell, 1941) and *The Life and Death of Colonel Blimp* (Michael Powell, 1943) all have a German protagonist and clearly distinguish between Germans and Nazis. In fact, they often underline Nazi cruelties by explicitly showing how the Nazis deal with 'good Germans'. In this way, German-speaking émigrés together with British colleagues helped to prevent MoI plans of an 'anger campaign' against Germans from being put into practice using feature films. Being part of a general Home Morale Campaign of 1940, the MoI's General Production Division planned a campaign 'designed to increase the anger felt by the British people towards the Germans and Germany with the purpose of ensuring maximum determination to see this war through to victory'.[73] The implementation of the plan would also have further exacerbated the situation of German-speaking émigrés in Britain. The strategy for the campaign 'Anger in Action' reads as follows:

The Germans are by race and nature a nation of bullies. They are and have always been the gangsters of Europe. Always they have been the same, treacherous swaggering race – overbearing in triumph, whining when defeated. . . . The only way to deal with a bully is to face up to him and fight him. This German bully who much prefers beating-up helpless little nations now has to tackle us. But we have smashed him before by standing up to him and we will smash him again in the same way. Nothing else is possible. This treacherous cowardly bully will not leave one single generation to live in peace. Our lives, our children's lives will not be worth living whilst Nazi Germany stands.

British men and women . . . together we shall hit this Nazi beast so hard that it will never rise again.[74]

While the MoI campaign was pretty much in the vein of the chauvinistic hate propaganda of the First World War, the British media was somehow reluctant to follow its suggestions. In an article on the situation of emigrants in Britain for the exile newspaper *Aufbau,* German émigré Paul Marcus, for instance, reported that English newspapers called for a clear distinction between German refugees and Nazis.[75] The cinema industry with its numerous German-speaking employers and employees did not follow the suggestions of the proposed MoI hate campaign either.

Positioning themselves against racist hatred in any form, many émigré feature films of the era accentuate the fact that a significant number of Germans were themselves victims of Nazism. The drama *Pastor Hall* (1940) is a case in point. Based upon a play by Ernst Toller, a well-known playwright in Germany who had been expatriated by the Nazis for his pacifist ideas and affiliations with communist circles, the film tells the story of the persecution and martyrdom of the German pastor Martin Niemöller, who was sent to Dachau concentration camp.[76] Although Niemöller had fought for Germany as a U-boat captain in the First World War, he was eventually interned after his religious beliefs had led him to preach regularly against Hitler and the Nazi movement. Having been banned before the war by the BBFC on the grounds that the film's 'exhibition at the present time would be inexpedient',[77] the film adaptation was rushed into production shortly after the beginning of war. It drastically depicts how German fascists deal with dissident voices within the Third Reich. The violence of the concentration camp scenes showing the whipping of Pastor Hall, and the penning of inmates like animals into small and damp cells, anticipate the Allied postwar footage of the Nazi death mills. Still unfamiliar with such drastic images, a *Daily Mirror* critic notes that *Pastor Hall* is a 'very good and well-acted picture, but the accentuation of the prison camp horrors makes me very doubtful of its entertainment appeal'.[78]

Not least because of its actuality and the 'artistic validity of Ernst Toller's play on which the screen-script is based, . . . *Pastor Hall*', in the judgement of exile Klaus Mann, 'surpasses the American output in intellectual seriousness and moral authority'.[79] Likewise, historian Nicholas John Cull regards the film as the 'most eloquently anti-Nazi film' of the war.[80] The audience's response certainly backs such judgements that the film was well received. Minister of Information Duff Cooper, for instance, wrote to the film's distributors: 'I believe that *Pastor Hall* is a great film showing the nature of our present struggle. I hope it will be widely seen.'[81]

The opening scenes of *Pastor Hall* depict an idyllic rural community in

Southern Germany; the imagery resembles that of many popular British pre-war musical comedies (e.g. *Heart's Desire*, 1935) which also presented a nostalgic and serene view of Alpine life. However, the Nazis soon destroy the harmonious atmosphere. The film conveys this visually, through military uniforms that do not fit the peaceful village life, and through sound, as the cheerful melody that accompanied the beginning of the film gives way to the military tunes of storm-troopers marching through the streets. The gloomy cinematography by Mutz Greenbaum identifies the National Socialists as unemotional and blunt characters while Pastor Hall, played by Wilfrid Lawson, appears as a caring father figure. The intimacy created in several scenes with Hall is pointedly contrasted by the cold and claustrophobic atmosphere generated by the Nazi intruders.

Greenbaum, a prominent lighting expert, particularly relied on the creation of chiaroscuro effects through tones of black and white as a means of infusing settings with a specific mood. This becomes particularly evident in his striking juxtaposition of scenes that depict Pastor Hall amongst his family and friends, using flat lighting to create a homely feeling through an even distribution of light and shade, with sequences featuring Nazi characters that employ low-key lighting to evoke a menacing ambience. The cinematography thus underlines the threat emanating from the storm-troopers who are, among other things, responsible for the suicide of a village girl who is pregnant by a young Nazi who has no intention of marrying her, and also for the death of a village boy as the result of an internal Nazi power struggle.

Apart from the high contrast that characterises sequences like the conversation of Hall with the storm-trooper leader in the pastor's study prior to his internment, Greenbaum also employs other forms of symbolism as a means of visual characterisation. His film shots contain Nazi insignia throughout the film and he, very strikingly, applies back lighting to place objects such as the barbed wire or the prison bars of the concentration camp in silhouette. When Pastor Hall is trying to calm the pregnant girl, he is shot in close-up, holding her head gently against his shoulder and shielding her with his hand, while the back lighting through the lattice windows of her room throws a cage-like shadow on the wall, illustrating her hopeless situation. The projection, furthermore, literally foreshadows Pastor Hall's own situation later in the film by resembling the bars of his concentration camp cell, which is filmed in a similar way.

Throughout the film the victimisation of 'good Germans' invites a non-German audience to sympathise and even identify with the oppressed community, above all with Pastor Hall who seeks to comfort the villagers. This active identification of British cinema-goers with Hall is furthermore encouraged when he preaches against Nazi ideology for the last time in the final scene of the film, and the camera position changes from that of the congregation below to a straight-on angle: Hall speaks directly to the cinema audience rather than to the fictional characters. The intended identification with the oppressed villagers is also achieved by means of commonalities that establish links between the German village and the British audience. The mise-en-scène of the picturesque rural locale, for instance, shares many characteristics with the English pastoral tradition – a tradition that was central to wartime representations of Britain.[82] The fact that the protagonist, despite the traditionally Catholic denomination of Southern Germany, is a protestant priest, also eases the process of persuading an English audience to identify with the religious village community and its pastor.

By engaging the audience's empathy for the German victims of Nazism, *Pastor Hall* adheres to a general pattern of émigré propaganda films: that the fight against Nazism is not a fight against a people, but rather a fight against an ideology. Consequently, a new Germany after the war is deemed possible – a belief further emphasised by the title sequence which explicitly dedicates the film 'to the day when it may be shown in Germany'. Through the character of Heinrich Degan played by Bernard Miles, the film suggests that some Germans were seduced into National Socialism rather than being staunch supporters of Hitler's ideology and could thus be re-educated. Degan, who joins the SS because he has been unemployed for a long time, gets shot while he helps Pastor Hall to escape from the concentration camp.

A survey carried out by Mass-Observation among 31 MoI officials documents how successful *Pastor Hall* actually was in getting its message across. Among a general approval for the film's drastic depictions of acts of violence committed by Stormtroopers as this may increase the determination to fight Nazism, the report found that an 'overwhelming number' of the audience claimed that the film made them detest the Nazi apparatus and not the German people as such.[83] This was a significant achievement in that public opinion generally turned against Germans. Whilst in 1939 only 6 per cent of the people questioned in a survey by the British Institute of Public Opinion had the opinion that the war was being fought against the German people rather than their leaders, this number had risen to 50 per cent by the end of 1940, roughly at the time of *Pastor Hall*'s general release.[84]

The reception of the propaganda film in the all-important US market was equally successful despite some initial pessimism. The *Documentary Newsletter* had claimed that

the film has been admired for certain intrinsic production qualities, but it is observed that concentration camps and other European cruelties create only a sense of distance in the native mind and a feeling of 'Thank God we emigrated from Europe to a decent country'. . . . Jewish maltreatment, concentration camps, sadistic lashings are, one is afraid, old stuff, alien, slightly discredited and do not command people's deepest attention.[85]

However, reports from New York City paint a different picture. When *Pastor Hall* premiered in 1940 to critical acclaim in the American metropolis, the screening incited spontaneous anti-Nazi riots in Times Square.[86] Moreover, American journalists at a press preview are said to have 'gasped at some of the incidents depicted here, shuddered during the concentration camp sequences, told each other afterward that this picture has more impact and shock than any treatment of the subject to date'.[87] Thus, an American audience, in particular in a multi-cultural environment with a high proportion of Jewish residents, was not nearly as indifferent to the plight of central European critics of National Socialism as the *Documentary Newsletter* article fears. Indeed, the success of British propaganda pictures such as *Pastor Hall* and *49th Parallel*, which were intended for the US market as part of the general British campaign against American neutrality, certainly influenced American views on a war they knew principally, as Nicholas John Cull points out, through British eyes.[88]

Two German-speaking film émigrés engaged in the production of *Pastor Hall* appear in the film's credits under an alias: Using the surname Reiner, Anna Gmeyner co-wrote the script, and the composer Hans May is billed as 'Mac Adams'. It remains difficult to reconstruct their contributions in detail, owing to the paucity of primary sources regarding the production process. What can be ascertained from contemporary newspaper reviews, however, is that Gmeyner added 'little bits'[89] to Toller's original play, accentuating the brutalisation of concentration camp detainees.[90] While it is difficult to reconstruct the exact contributions of all émigrés involved – with the exception of Gmeyner's script – the presence of émigré filmmakers, nonetheless, permeates the film through resonances of their own social experience as victims of Nazi oppression and refugees. Besides its strong anti-Nazi message, *Pastor Hall* actually discusses exile as a way of evading Nazi persecution – an unorthodoxy at the beginning of war when the topic of refugees was still seen as very problematic.

In order to change public opinion in the US and end its isolationist policy, the MoI directly supported another émigré anti-Nazi film: *49th Parallel*. Written by Emeric Pressburger, it tells the story of a stranded Nazi U-boat crew trying to make their way to the US via Canada after their submarine has sunk. A key sequence illustrates the difference between Germans and Nazis. After the peaceful and hospitable Hutterite community has offered the Nazi crew at large food and accommodation

– being neither aware of their identity nor their intentions – the Nazi leader tries to convince the settlement of the Third Reich's cause. In his speech, which not coincidentally resembles the way Hitler addressed the public, he praises 'the greatest idea in history, the supremacy of a Nordic race' and asserts a shared German culture by calling the Hutterites 'brothers'. The Hutterites, however, refrain from joining the submarine crew in paying tribute to the Führer by shouting 'Heil Hitler!'. In an emotional speech written specifically for him by Pressburger, Walbrook, who plays the Hutterites' leader, stresses the difference between celebrating German cultural heritage and being a Nazi – representing not only the fictional Hutterite settlement in Canada, but also the whole German-speaking émigré community:

> You call us 'Germans', you call us 'brothers'. Yes, most of us are Germans, our names are German, our tongue is German, our old handwritten books are in German script, but we are not your brothers. Our Germany is dead. However hard this may be for some of us older people, it's a blessing for our children. Our children grow up against new backgrounds, new horizons, and they are free. . . . No, we are not your brothers.

In addition to *49th Parallel* other films also drew upon the transnational character of the anti-Hitler coalition as the MoI increasing supported the idea of including 'good foreigners' in feature film projects. Whilst foreigners were seen as valuable allies, in many British wartime films émigrés take the place of admonitory voices warning Britons and Americans of the perils of fascism. A good example of this is *The Gentle Sex* (Leslie Howard, 1943) starring the German actress Lilli Palmer as the refugee Erna Debruski. In the film that draws upon the valuable contributions of women to the British war effort, she is part of a group of women who join the Auxiliary Territorial Service (ATS). Returning from an important mission, Erna passionately explains why the war must be won by all means: 'I know what freedom is because my people have lost it. . . . You still don't understand what this war really means, . . . in spite of all the bombs and air raids. They are nothing. . . . My country is gone . . ., my father was shot for fun . . ., my younger brother was handsome – I never forget his face when they were done with him.' Whilst the film was primarily intended to enhance the status of women in uniform,[91] it also underlines the pivotal role taken by foreigners in the fight against Nazism.

Arguably the most important film in terms of representation of foreigners and Germans is *The Life and Death of Colonel Blimp*. The film again owes much to the émigré filmmakers involved – above all Pressburger who was introduced to Powell by Korda himself before the war sharing as they did not only a devotion to art cinema but also to the traditions of continental cinema and culture'. Talking about his collaboration with the émigré Pressburger in an interview with Ian Christie, Michael Powell clearly admits that it was his production partner who was responsible for a lot of the generosity shown to the Germans.[92]

Under the umbrella of the Rank Organisation, their independent production outfit The Archers, which they established in 1943 after their success with *49th Parallel*, was allowed a greater degree of artistic licence than most mainstream wartime companies, giving the film émigrés involved the opportunity to exert an influence on their films. The unprecedented resources of J. Arthur Rank, whose rise from a Yorkshire miller to film mogul is one of the most extraordinary success stories of British cinema history, not only included financial contributions but also access to studios (Denham and Pinewood), distributors (General Film Distributors) and cinema circuits (Gaumont and Odeon), all of which were controlled by Rank.[93] In the film magnate's endeavour to gain national and international recognition and critical acclaim, the Archers became one of the cornerstones of Independent Producers, an élite school for visionary filmmakers set up by Rank during the war.

The leading role of Theo Kretschmar-Schuldorff was, as Powell recalls in his memoirs, especially written for Walbrook,[94] whilst Alfred Junge was responsible for the lavish sets. In particular his accurate designs representing the German capital, including Prussian military uniforms and the clothes of conservative-nationalistic student fraternities shown in a Berlin café and duel in the opening scenes, became a hallmark of *The Life and Death of Colonel Blimp*.[95] Other German-speaking personnel involved in the production include costume designer Joseph Bato and actors Carl Jaffé, Albert Lieven and Ferdy Mayne.

Some of the dialogue is in German without any translation or subtitles, giving the picture a sense of authenticity. By telling the story of a cross-national friendship between a British (Clive Candy, the Colonel Blimp of the title) and a Prussian officer (Theo Kretschmar-Schuldorff) from around 1900 to the Second World War, the film deals with the problem of how a civilised European country could unconditionally follow Hitler's inhumane ideology. The view expressed by Clive Candy's wife while she and her husband are visiting Theo in a First World War POW camp in Britain can be seen as a *leitmotif* of the film and one of the main questions German-speaking émigrés asked themselves:

> I was thinking how odd they [the Germans] are, queer, for years and years they are writing and dreaming beautiful music and poetry – all of a sudden they start a war. They sink undefended ships, shoot innocent hostages and bomb and destroy whole streets in London, killing little children. And then

they sit down in the same butcher's uniform and listen to Mendelssohn and Schubert.

In many respects Pressburger, who wrote an original script early in 1942,[96] had his own life and career in mind when he invented this story about a man who comes to Britain as a refugee from Nazi Germany after having lost his family. But *The Life and Death of Colonel Blimp* was also a very personal film for the other émigrés involved as discourses on exile, displacement, foreignness and otherness can be found throughout. Set designer Alfred Junge was interned as an 'enemy alien' at the beginning of the war and had just been released from a camp in Huyton near Liverpool when filming started.[97] The odd mix of claustrophobia and lively cultural activity that marks the POW camp in *Blimp* thus, one might argue, would not coincidentally resemble the experiences of many German-speaking émigrés who were classified as 'enemy aliens' and set up theatre groups and organised concerts and lectures in internment camps.[98] Given all the émigré-related issues dealt with in the film (border-crossings, immigration tribunals, internment, cross-cultural friendships, diasporic life), Paul Marcus rhetorically asked whether it was a coincidence that his old Berlin acquaintances Pressburger and the composer Allan Gray were involved in the production.[99]

The Life and Death of Colonel Blimp, by and large, avoids one-dimensional characterisations of Germans. Notwithstanding the unwelcoming interrogation by the immigration officer and his own previous internment, Kretschmar-Schuldorff leaves no doubt about his allegiance to Britain; he even wants to enlist in the armed forces. However, unlike Radetzky in *Dangerous Moonlight* he is refused on account of his alien status. Meant to epitomise the determination and beliefs of German-speaking refugees in the immediate aftermath of xenophobic hysteria and internment, the more balanced view of émigrés in *Blimp* owes much to Pressburger's dramatis personae. Having modelled many sequences in the film on his own experiences, he commented in 1970:

> I who lived for quite a while in Germany and had German friends, I wanted to express this feeling of mine that though my mother had died in a concentration camp and I was preconditioned about the whole thing, I always believed . . . that there were good Germans . . . who didn't have to go away from Germany but chose to go away.[100]

Being in many respects, as Pressburger's biographer Kevin Macdonald argues, Emeric's 'screen alter ego',[101] Kretschmar-Schuldorff is exactly this kind of a good German who chooses to leave Germany behind. Walbrook's own émigré status once again contributes to the authenticity of his performance. Among other scenes this is particularly evident when he is interrogated at the immigration tribunal. The film sympathises with the refugee rather than with Her Majesty's officer – this is achieved through the interaction of Pressburger's script, Junge's set design, Bato's make-up and Walbrook's acting style, which emphasised the increasing fragility of the once energetic and proud Kretschmar-Schuldorff. While he is standing in front of the immigration officer who sits behind an elevated desk barely looking at him, grey-haired Theo appears bowed and fragile. In a similar way to his performance in *Dangerous Moonlight*, Walbrook brings forward his case very slowly and wearily as he explains in detail how the Nazis have ruined his life and family.

The Life and Death of Colonel Blimp, however, became notorious not so much for its description of Germans and émigrés as for the unsuccessful attempt to ban the film by Winston Churchill.[102] Here, the role of Kretschmar-Schuldorff as a 'good German' was only one aspect of the Prime Minister's disapproval. He primarily disliked the depiction of the British forces as the film criticises the mindset of old-school officers who would rather lose a war than give up the ideals of sportsmanship and gentlemanly conduct. Further criticism appeared in journals and newspapers of the time. A reviewer in *Tribune*, for example, rejected the character of Kretschmar-Schuldorff as a 'refugee intellectual [who] cluttered up the place with long meanderings'.[103] Further criticism came from members of the far political right, namely the sociological critics E. W. and M. M. Robson. In a pamphlet titled *The Shame and Disgrace of Colonel Blimp* they condemn the film as 'the most disgraceful production that has ever emanated from a British studio'.[104] Moreover, in another publication on cinema they make the case that all films by Powell and Pressburger demonstrate 'a rabid anti-Britishism which was almost pathological in its intensity'.[105] Although little seems to be known about the Robsons and their Sidneyan Society it appears too simplistic to dismiss them as 'a minor curiosity of Powell-Pressburger scholarship' as proposed by Ian Christie.[106] Rather than marginalising the Robsons' hysterical condemnation, which might seem as paranoid and irrational hatred today, their interpretation of Powell's and Pressburger's work, as Chapman argues, was at the time 'simply the most extreme of several similar readings'.[107] While it remains difficult to give details about the possible circulation of the Robsons' publications it can be inferred from reactions to their pamphlet on *The Life and Death of Colonel Blimp* in the trade journal published by the ACT that it was at any rate well known in film and cinema circles where it caused some controversy. Yet although *The Shame and Disgrace of Colonel Blimp*, which sold for two shillings and six pence, received a more or less unfavourable review in *Cine-Technician*, the main point of criticism is not the Robsons' one dimensional Germanophobic reading of Powell's and Pressburger's film but rather their line of argument and style of presentation:

> Here [in *The Shame and Disgrace of Colonel Blimp* the Robsons'] argument is developed in an attack on poor *Colonel* Blimp, which the authors see as a cunning and subversive attempt to laud everything German and pour sour scorn on everything English. . . .
>
> Now I don't think anyone would particularly want to defend Emeric Pressburger as a script writer. There is certainly something fishy about his Squadron Leader X or U-Boat Captains striding unscathed through the stupid democracies, and I suppose there can be few people who know as little as he does about the real life of this country. . . . Meanwhile, I'm afraid all this extravagance, over-simplification, muddled thought and attempt to see the English as a "race" has ruined what might have been a good pamphlet. For I think they've got a good case here, at bottom, and their writing is always lively.[108]

Again, through its trade journal, the ACT can be accused of xenophobic resentment as this review uses the opportunity to mention Pressburger's status as an immigrant as a negative. Following a response by the Robsons in the next issue of *Cine Technician*, in which they point out that the review made a number of unjust allegations by putting 'up a number of Aunt Sallies of his own imaginative creation and shying at them with a terrific amount of misspent gusto', the reviewer once again expresses his basic agreement with their ideas as he writes 'I hope readers of the *Journal* will also read the *Blimp* pamphlet (it's well worth it)' in order to make up their own mind.[109]

Despite a number of vocally negative views, however, the majority of film critics were in favour of *Blimp*. Viewers, as Maroula Joannou records, even seem to have embraced Kretschmar-Schuldorff's character as they saw 'his impassioned appeal to English justice [as] the apotheosis of the film'.[110] Not least because of the film's box office success in Britain, where it was one of the top box office films of 1943 alongside the American exile film *Casablanca*, it had an influence on the perception of German victims of Nazism.

While many wartime films dealt with Nazi atrocities and the need to stand together in the 'Battle of Britain', the persecution of Jews was generally not referred to as a cause of war. In fact, most films avoid the issue by either making Christians the victims of Nazi oppression (as in *Pastor Hall* or *49th Parallel*) or by not giving any reasons for the persecution at all: although one can guess why Erna Debruski's family in *The Gentle Sex* was harassed by the Nazis, the film actually omits whether they were actually Jews. As Garth S. Jowett and Victoria O'Donnell note, it remains one of the most controversial problems for any account on information policy during the Second World War to explain why the issue of German concentration camp victims in general and that of Jews in particular received very little or no public recognition until the end of the war. Neither wartime feature films, documentaries nor newsreels explicitly dealt with the issues and so it was not until the liberation of concentration camps and the subsequent showing of atrocious black-and-white newsreel footage that most Anglo-American audiences were confronted with what happened.

The neglect of Jewish protagonists was, with few exceptions, politically motivated.[111] While anti-Semitic feelings flared up regularly and Britain was generally seen as a country of refuge for continental Jews for a limited period of time only where refugees were expected to move on to the US or South America,[112] British officials and the film industry were generally anxious to stress that Britain was fighting for herself and democracy rather than for Jews who were commonly considered to be 'aliens *whether or not they were citizens*'.[113] While anti-Semitic rhetoric was notable throughout the 1930s and the beginning of war, it increased significantly from late 1942 to the end of war, as Sonya Rose has shown.[114] It seems that the commercial film industry and its sponsors (namely the MoI) were anxious about generating a flood of anti-Semitic commentary and public refusal in the event that they made films with Jewish protagonists.

Against the trend of neglecting the plight of European Jewry in commercial feature films, Sidney Gilliat's *The Rake's Progress* (1945) not only explicitly mentions the precarious situation of Jews on the continent but also draws attention to Britain and the British who choose to turn a blind eye to their dilemma. Lilli Palmer plays the part of a young Jewish Austrian woman, Rikki Krausner, who desperately tries to flee Vienna after the *Anschluss* in what is perhaps the only British film that explicitly refers to the dramatic life-threatening situation of Jews in countries under Nazi control, their desperate attempts to seek refuge in other countries, and the reluctance of British authorities to offer any help by easing immigration restrictions. In order to leave Nazi controlled Austria, Krausner tries to convince the British playboy Vivian Kenway (played by Palmer's husband Rex Harrison) to marry her so she will be given a British passport. Her dramatic condition is made obvious by the visualisation of the threat in a scene that shows her talking to Kenway about the marriage arrangements (i.e. his financial reward for marrying her) and then zooms out through the window towards a daunting Nazi rally in the streets outside their hotel. In her desperation, she successfully proposes to pay all debts for the penniless cosmopolitan roué if he marries her so she can leave the country for Britain.

Not only does *The Rake's Progress* offer a remarkably direct account of the plight of European Jews and their forced emigration, it also records the indifference of some Britons towards the pogroms in Germany and Austria.

In the role of the good-for-nothing idler, Rex Harrison convincingly plays an Oxford drop out who becomes a grand prix driver in order to finance his exorbitant lifestyle. His race entry in Vienna, however, is cancelled because of the Hitler-Mussolini pact and the annexation of Austria by the Third Reich. Able neither to pay for his excessive hotel bill with the expected prize money nor to extricate himself from the precarious situation, he agrees to marrying the Jewish girl primarily (if not solely) because she offers to straighten out his debts. Once the just-married couple get to Britain, however, the newly arrived foreign girl has problems being accepted. Deeply suspicious of his son's motives, Kenway's father asks: 'Foreign I gather . . .?'. After the reply that she was indeed Austrian, he comments disapprovingly: 'I took it for granted that you marry a British girl somehow.' Rikki Krausner's otherness is thereby two-fold according to common attitudes in Britain at the time: she is Austrian and Jewish. The film thus depicts the negative sentiments against Jews of foreign descent, which ran deep in wartime Britain. Speaking also for many other readers, as the editor pointed out, a letter by a North-West London woman printed by the *New Statesmen and the Nation*, for instance, complained about the 'ill-mannered and unsocial behaviour of a percentage of foreign Jews'.[115] In a similar way, the writer Naomi Mitchison expressed her view in 1943 that she had 'a certain suspicion of Jews, and when one reads of what is happening [to them on the continent] one has a tendency to think it serves them right before one can catch oneself up'.[116]

Even if Rikki Krausner in *The Rake's Progress* is eventually given a British passport because of her marriage to Vivian Kenway, the ending of the film does not offer reconciliation for the Jewish protagonist. Whereas the Jewish woman tries her best and even feels great affection for her husband, he falls in love with his father's British secretary upon which Rikki Krausner eventually commits suicide. Following this tragic development, the frame narrative of *The Rake's Progress*, in which Vivian Kenway is a soldier in the Second World War, offers a further interesting aspect. While he seeks to redeem himself by his self-sacrificing fight against the Germans, the film suggests that Britain (or at least a certain caste of upper-class gentlemen for which Kenway stands) is paying the price for its appeasement policy and indifference towards the plight of the European Jewry which had guided their policies and actions in the years before the war.

Representation of émigrés after the declaration of war

Among all films made by German-speaking émigrés in Britain, the films of Michael Powell and Emeric Pressburger especially featured many roles of outsiders. Indeed, the films of *auteurs* such as Powell and Pressburger added depth and ambiguity to social and cultural concepts such as national identity and nationhood. While the two filmmakers, according to Gough-Yates, worked together on most production processes the 'concentration on relationships, the dispiriting desolation that the central characters often feel [and which was often the result of their displacement and alienation] are entirely Pressburger's'.[117] As Maroula Joannou, moreover, writes in her analysis of Englishness in the work of Powell and Pressburger, it was in particular the latter who was responsible for the positive and patriotic representation of the English character which 'draws attention to the multiple, hybrid, and diverse identities that have always existed side by side with the dominant ideas of Englishness, the latter functioning to reproduce the marginal status and suspicion of the immigrant and the asylum seeker'.[118] By transcending existing genre conventions the creative duo of Powell and Pressburger once again underline that their oeuvre must be placed at the centre of an assessment of exilic and diasporic filmmaking in Britain. Transnationality, boundaries, clash of cultures, ethnicity, exile and diaspora are recurring motifs in a large part of their work including *The Spy in Black*, *Contraband*, *49th Parallel* (1941), *The Life and Death of Colonel Blimp* (1943), *A Canterbury Tale* (1944), *I Know Where I'm Going* (1945), and *Black Narcissus* (1947).

The lives of both Powell and Pressburger were characterised by international itineraries infusing the fictional plots with actual momentum. While the former lived some time on the European continent and had already made a film set on a remote Scottish Island, *The Edge of the World*, in 1937, Pressburger had left his native Hungary for Berlin via Stuttgart and Prague. Having started his script-writing career in the Weimar Republic during the 1920s one of his early published stories was evocatively called 'Travelling' and he gained his first screen credit for Robert Siodmak's film *Abschied* (*Farewell*, Germany 1930). The persistent theme of border-crossings is not restricted to territorial or physical journeys in their films. By scrutinising concepts of identity and redrawing national and cultural boundaries the journeys also acquire metaphorical meanings, as they become philosophical and psychological ones.[119]

I Know Where I'm Going, for instance, is a filmic *tour de force* about a modern Mancunian woman who travels to a small Scottish island to meet the rich industrialist she sets out to marry. What seems to be a simple story is in fact a multi-layered narrative, which deals with wider issues by comparing and contrasting love with materialism, modernity and tradition and urban life with the countryside. The film also deals with distant spaces and imagined homelands – both literally and metaphorically. The protagonist Joan, a modern, young and aspiring woman leaves her familiar environment, the urban metropolis. While she masters hectic city life very well, the unfamiliar Highland milieu poses some problems. What was initially planned as a brief trip becomes an odyssey when the journey is repeatedly interrupted by forces of nature. Compelled to stay some time in a seaside village, she appears as a stranger. In stark contrast to the city where she is a mobile woman who moves in the same pace and style as her surroundings she neither understands Gaelic nor the unfamiliar customs of the close-knit village community. In addition, the forced nature of her stay before she reaches the final destination can, once again, be interpreted as a representation of the itinerary of émigré film-makers. Thus, many refugees shared Joan's fate when she sits on her suitcase waiting for a chance to continue her journey. When the storm also blows the journey out of her hands, leaving her in the unknown territory with nothing but her few belongings, she finally decides to take shelter. What begins as a stopover soon turns into a lengthy stay. The uncontrollable forces of nature in the film resemble the unruly political situation German-speaking refugees confronted on their flight from the Third Reich.

Apart from Emeric Pressburger, who was co-author, co-producer, and co-director of the film, other émigrés also participated in the making of *I Know Where I'm Going*: Erwin Hillier was responsible for the imaginative cinematography, the musical score was written by Allan Gray and was conducted by Walter Goehr. Moreover, the long-time set designer of Powell and Pressburger's production company The Archers, Alfred Junge, built the meticulously crafted sets at the Denham studios. Both the German-speaking expatriates' own experience with displacement as a state of mind and their understanding of cinematic expressionism as a means of projecting internal conflicts externally, arguably enabled them to add a psychological momentum to the film. Indeed, Weimar cinema's legacy of foregrounding elements of mise-en-scène and camera angles with the aim of making visible mental states and intense emotions is noticeable here. The combination of Junge's set design and – above all – Erwin Hillier's camera and unusual lighting techniques plays a crucial role in the interpretation of the film. Territorial and metaphorical journeys are particularly evident in Hillier's penchant for doorways and windows that visualise the characters' passage as central motif of *I Know Where I'm Going*. What is more, many scenes were filmed against the light so that characters are depicted as silhouettes against the rough nature of the Scottish seascape, where the film's outdoor scenes were shot so as to exemplify the elemental struggles of its narrative. Erwin Hillier, who had worked with Fritz Lang in Germany, also used deep-focus photography and low-key lighting to create atmospheres as semantic markers. Hereby the film gains a sophistication and ambiguity that is far more than 'unworthy romantic nonsense about an ancestral curse' in the wording of one critic.[120] The camera and lighting techniques, as Pam Cook argues, were applied to create uncertainty within a mysterious, Gothic atmosphere and to picture the border crossing theme between 'one world and another, between exterior (light, knowledge, reason, objectivity) and interior (darkness, demons, irrationality, subjectivity)'.[121] In a key scene at the end of the film, when the male lead Torquil MacNeil enters a ruined castle, he is filmed at a straight-on angle in an expressionist style. The only light comes from behind while the camera is positioned in the dark, where the protagonist confronts a spell that was cast on his family carved into a stone. Here, the threshold of the 'forbidden' castle represents his internal struggle to overcome his family trauma. When his love for Joan appears to have overcome the spell, the surrounding nature appears accordingly welcoming.

For Joan their love also changes things for the better. By placing her at the centre of the story as a figure of identification, *I Know Where I'm Going* reverses the German refugee émigré tale by putting an English subject into the position of a stranger with all the struggles involved. Yet, while many films emphasise the problems of being away from home, *I Know Where I'm Going* also draws upon positive effects of the diaspora. In fact, the unfamiliar Scottish environment has a cathartic effect on Joan. Instead of following her initially materialistic motives that have led to her decision to marry a rich industrialist, she decides in favour of love and sets aside her longing for financial wealth. Thus Powell and Pressburger's film suggests that despite all oppositions such as England/Scotland and cities/countryside there are some universal values shared by all. Innate moral values and emotions such as honesty, trust, moderation, love, and friendship, can, according to the narrative, transcend national, territorial and cultural boundaries. Thus, they enable foreigners and outsiders to interact with the people in their new environment.

Pam Cook goes one step further as she interprets the recurring use of trick photography and rear projections as filmic representations of memory processes. According to her convincing analysis, the cinematic technique of superimposition that creates multi-layered images on the silver screen is similar to the way our human mind recalls the past.[122] Seeing composite images as a metaphor for memory, Cook claims that *I Know Where I'm Going* deals with displaced identities

> through an exploitation of memory which acknowledges that place or 'home' are inevitably coloured by distance and the passage of time, and can never fully be recovered. 'Scotland' literally becomes a screen against which is played out the loss of homeland, and the re-collection of images of home that characterises the diasporic experience.[123]

Whereas some émigré films provide dystopian accounts of foreign lives in Britain, *I Know Where I'm Going* offers a rather positive outlook which becomes manifest in its happy ending. By drawing upon his and his fellow exiles' experiences, scriptwriter Emeric Pressburger thus infuses the film with an autobiographical psychological momentum whilst dealing with themes of dislocation, alienation, trauma and themes of assimilation. Unlike many other émigré films that were made before the war including *Victoria the Great* and *Heart's Desire*, however, Pressburger, under the impression of war with Nazi Germany, offers an optimistic outlook of the émigré psyche by proposing the possibility of successful assimilation to new surroundings. As the film gains a quasi-therapeutic function of allowing émigrés both on and off the screen to revisit their own situation, it achieves a complexity that challenges all genre conventions. It is in fact the 'exile tale' that is to a great extent responsible for the film's appeal that combines an original cinematography and rich production values fused with psychological processes and states of mind.

Arguably, however, the positive outcome of the marriage of an English woman and a Scottish man in *I Know Where I'm Going* was only made possible because they are in the end both British. Filmic representations of continental Europeans suggest that here the differences were not so easily overcome. As a result mixed marriages and relationships between émigrés and British citizens were generally ruled out in filmic plots. Owing to xenophobic resentment and racial demarcations only same-sex friendships such as that of the best friends in *The Life and Death of Colonel Blimp*, Theo Kretschmar-Schuldorff and Clive Candy occasionally form part of narratives.

The 1943 feature film *The Demi-Paradise* (Anthony Asquith), which was produced and written by the Russian-born German-speaking émigré Anatole de Grunwald, revolves around a Russian engineer who comes to Britain where he works on a valuable icebreaking ship propeller. Similarly to other foreign characters coming to Britain (such as Albert in *Victoria the Great*) he first finds England to be an inhospitable country. So his first impressions are dominated by the unpleasant weather and the unfriendliness of the native population. However, while the foreign expert encounters various – often mythical – strands of English culture and society, he not only revaluates many common prejudices about England but also, like Albert in *Victoria the Great*, falls in love with a young British girl. The romance ends, though, when he returns home without her. Like many narratives of the 1930s and 1940s with foreign protagonists, *The Demi-Paradise* presupposes that foreigners stay in Britain for a limited period of time only and ultimately intend to go back to their native country.

The émigrés' relationship with their former *Heimat* is part of numerous films. *Pastor Hall*, for instance, illustrates the problems refugees faced in exile. In one of the daunting concentration camp scenes – shot by Mutz Greenbaum using, on the one hand, low-key lighting to increase the claustrophobic atmosphere and, on the other, close-ups to give inmates a face and personality – a Jew tells the others why he is in the camp although he had already been safely in exile in France:

> Every morning in Paris I went for a walk. . . . One morning in April I saw birds on the branches of a tree, everything smelled of spring and everybody was laughing and happy for their reason. And I, I don't know why, suddenly I felt homesick. I couldn't bear the thought of everybody speaking in a foreign language.

By locating the exile of victims of Nazism in France and the USA the story of German refugees becomes palatable in a British film at the commencement of war. In the context of an alien scare in Britain that led to the mass-imprisonment of foreign nationals at the beginning of war, moreover, a contemporary audience may also have interpreted the plight of the prisoners in *Pastor Hall* as a criticism of Westminster's current policy of internment. In this regard it is important to note that the film personalises the plight of refugees and illustrates the reasons for their dire situation. This was particularly important as exiles were treated as an anonymous group by parts of the British right-wing press, which often did not differentiate between Nazi sympathisers and Nazi opponents. Yet, notwithstanding the dire conditions of internment and all the hardships of life in the British diaspora, the plight of internees in the concentration camp depicted in *Pastor Hall* make the difficult situations of exiles seem all the better.

Another film made by the Boulting brothers, *Thunder Rock*, deals with exile from a rather different angle. Released at the end of 1942, the complex film echoes the political situation in both the Pacific and the European arena of war. Its protagonist David Charleston is a disillusioned journalist who retreated from his profession and active involvement in politics when his editors and the British public showed a considerable lack of interest in his early warnings against the perils of Fascism in Italy, Germany and Spain. In his endeavour to withdraw himself from the world, he finds refuge on Thunder Rock, a remote lighthouse in the middle of Lake Michigan. Without books, films, newspapers and radio he imagines the captain and passengers of a ship which sank near Thunder Rock in 1849 as the characters for a new book. While Charleston hopes that his novel about the tragic shipwreck would not involve any politics, the conversations with his dramatis personae (who all appear as real persons in the film) eventually all end up dealing with socio-political affairs. Being all immigrants, the passengers left Europe to find a better life in America but drowned when their ship went down. Through a series of flashback sequences the film depicts the events that caused them to leave the 'Old World'. While the British characters emigrated for reasons of poverty and injustice, the Austrian family of Dr. Kurtz left because their lives were under serious threat. The use of new and pioneering methods of anaesthetics had caused upheaval in his hometown. Threatened by an intimidating mob Dr. Stefan Kurtz (Frederick Valk), his wife Anne Marie (Sybilla Binder) and daughter Melanie (Lilli Palmer) are forced to leave the country. As in *Broken Blossoms* before the war, the violent crowd not coincidentally resembles the images of anti-Semitic Nazi rallies in Germany and Austria. The stormy and rainy passage of the immigrants' ship, furthermore, looks like the ship passages in other émigré films such as *Victoria the Great,* highlighting the strains of transnational journeys. The sunken immigrant vessel in the film also evokes an interesting parallel to the *Arandora Star* incident, which caused the death of hundreds of émigrés.[124]

Intertwining the complex narrative with discourses of emigration and displacement, *Thunder Rock* sides with the foreigners (as did the previous Boulting brothers' film *Pastor Hall*). In one of the showcase speeches given by émigré actors in films dealing with émigré themes, Dr. Kurtz, played by Frederick Valk with a stern facial expression, defends his reluctant decision to leave his home country. Inasmuch as his case may describe the reasons behind American immigration during the nineteenth century, his words, questioning any theodicy, acquire a contemporaneous meaning in the wake of mass emigration of artists and scientists from Germany and its occupied territories:

> [The] world grows dark and men and justice shrink like little rivers when there is no rain. God looks down, but he's no longer the God of mercy. He sees us now fleeing across oceans and continents, deserting our fatherlands and all our deepest dreams. The triumph of science, the progress of education, equality of men and women, these are the banners we leave on the field. He sees us now, groping about in an alien land, for all the second prizes: wealth, security, peace of mind.

In a similar way to other wartime films made by or with émigrés, the Austrian family members serve as admonitory voices urging Charleston to go back to England and fight for his country. Whereas the captain, the Kurtz family and the other immigrants cannot return home or fight for their beliefs simply because they died 90 years ago, Charleston, under the conditions of total war, has an obligation to help fight Nazism. Convinced by the fictional immigrants created in his own mind, the film eventually ends with Charleston giving up his self-enforced isolation by leaving Thunder Rock. Just before his departure, the ship passengers leave his mind. Melanie Kurtz, played by the émigré star Lilli Palmer, reminds him about the joy of being alive despite living through troubled times because the living have the opportunity to work and to fight for their beliefs. While this closing statement in the film is meant as an encouragement to all audiences, it offers an alternative reading. Delivered by Palmer's gentle and emotional voice, which displays a slight foreign accent, the message can well be read as a statement of support for refugees.

Together with only a few other cinematic examples, the self-enforced isolationism of Charleston in *Thunder Rock* stands out as an interesting variation of the common exile theme in that the alienated character is English rather than foreign. In the majority of films, though, foreigners play the part of the lone, isolated and unattached individual. *The Red Shoes* (Powell and Pressburger, 1948) vividly captures this mood and state of affairs through the figure of the Russian ballet master Boris Lermontov, who was modelled after the expressionist impresario-autocrat Sergei Diaghilev, who became a prominent exile after the Russian revolution. Indeed, the story about the 'incompatibility of "life" and "art"' (Andrew Moor)[125] is the point of departure for an examination of the émigré artist's story. Although made after the war, the script was initially written by Pressburger for Korda in 1937 and captures the international make-up of the British culture industry of the 1930s. Among other things, Pressburger's original script incorporated ideas of the contemporary ballet master and prominent German émigré Kurt Jooss.[126] Although the 'realistic' aesthetic was replaced by a more fantasy-like mise-en-scène in the film, it nevertheless places an émigré artist at the centre of the narrative: the exotic and somewhat alien character of Lermontov played by Anton Walbrook. Whilst this complex film allows for metaphorical readings, Lermontov's ballet company can be read as an example of other creative activities and cultural spheres under the leverage of foreigners. Hence Andrew Moor argues that the 'Ballet Lermontov is held up as a mirror for The Archers' own company, and the film suggests communalities between ballet and cinema as art forms'.[127] Indeed, reading the world of ballet in *The Red Shoes* as an allegory for the film business seems compelling in view of the scenes of grand premieres, stars, elegant dinner parties and gossip. Thus the diegetic Lermontov ballet, which is depicted as having both drawn upon, and enriched the world of British dance, shares many parallels with British cinema. The pompousness of the soiree at the beginning of the film when Boris Lermontov meets the young dancer Vicky for the first time not coincidentally evokes a film business party that brings together upper-class society, businessmen and wilful artists. In a reflection of Alexander Korda's international aspirations, the Lermontov Ballet Company tries to reach an international audience by performing in London, Paris and Monte Carlo. In his autobiography Michael Powell acknowledges the intentional parallels between Korda and Lermontov that illustrate the close correlation between the international acclaimed ballet producer and émigré film mogul suggested by the film.[128] The frequent change of settings furthermore bears striking similarities to the cosmopolitan nature of the film business with its many freelance film professionals. Indeed the performing arts theme itself alludes to the constant nomadic existence of touring professionals. As a recurring subject matter in numerous émigré films (see *Pagliacci*, *Heart's Desire*, *The Robber Symphony*, *First a Girl*), it is itself part of the topos of exilic and diasporic cinema.

While the Boris Lermontov of the film is at the top of his profession, which allows him an exquisite lifestyle and his lavish Monte Carlo Villa, he is nevertheless a loner. His own solitude forms a stark contrast to the theatre performances of his critically acclaimed work. Singled out by his enigmatic aura and yearning for total control, he incorporates many characteristics commonly attributed to German-speaking film person-nel. It is in particular Alfred Junge's work ethos which resembles that of Lermontov as it is characterised by a similar admiration for artistic and organisational excellence coupled with a slight contempt for impatience. In Powell's recollection, at least Junge is described as follows: 'Alfred was a Prussian, a great disciplinarian as well as a great organiser. He hadn't a second to waste.'[129] Keeping in mind that Pressburger was eagerly learn-ing English when he wrote the original film script for Alexander Korda in 1937, the solitude and taciturnity of Lermontov, moreover, mirrored his own situation as it did with Walbrook who personified the Russian ballet impresario.[130] Rather than a dystopian exploration of displacement and the diaspora, however, the fact that Lermontov is solitary but not lonely and taciturn but not inarticulate suggests that his situation is tempera-mental and not enforced upon him.

One of the many scenes that support a reading of *The Red Shoes* as a self-reflexive film about filmmaking as well as about the diaspora is the cocktail party where Lermontov first meets Vicky. Appearing aloof and reluctant to join in the conversations, he takes a seat to observe the guests. The unorthodox camera position, which frames him from behind following his look at the social gathering, mimics the position of a theatre or cinema audience. The observing gaze of the camera here is once again that of the émigré *flâneur*: separated from the others, it stresses Lermontov's status as outsider as he sits alone on a sofa, unattached to society. Echoing a duality of responses to German-speaking artists in Britain during the 1930s and 1940s that ranged from admiration to fierce opposition, Anton Walbrook's performance as Boris Lermontov is that of an enigmatic, sometimes despotic, foreign genius. Scenes in which he enters the stage from behind a curtain (during a performance), steps out of the darkness (during an orchestra audition) or sits in a dim and silent room further support his solitude that stems from his artistic obsession in combination with his nomadic, unattached lifestyle. His transnationalism, which resembles his off-screen alter ego Diaghilev, is furthermore stressed by his nonchalant performances on an international stage in which he fluently speaks Russian, English and French.

Although originally written in the 1930s, Powell's and Pressburger's ballet classic galvanised the euphoric mood and optimism in the aftermath of the war. By combining a fantasy narrative, lavish costumes, artistic dance performances with what the original trailer labelled the 'glamour of the South of France in exquisite Technicolor',[131] *The Red Shoes* encapsulates the longing of a postwar audience for escapist entertainment. As Michael Powell observes in his memoirs: 'I think that the real reason why *The Red Shoes* was such a success, was that we had all been told for ten years to go out and die for freedom and democracy . . . and now the war was over, *The Red Shoes* told us to go and die for art.'[132] While the film portrays foreignness as an eternal character trait through the figure of Lermontov, his solitude and alienation is the result of his own decision to live for his ideal of *l'art pour l'art* rather than any external political repercussion. Although the foreigners in *The Life and Death of Colonel Blimp* or *The Gentle Sex* were forced into exile by totalitarianism or the events of war, Lermontov has chosen his life as expatriate artist. Even if this multi-layered film corresponds to the general theme of displacement that had featured many of Powell's and Pressburger's earlier films, the end of war, so it seems, has fundamentally changed the conditions of the diaspora from a politically enforced situation to a deliberate life choice.

Rather than painting a dystopian picture of England as a country of loss, trauma, and displacement for foreigners, as films such as *Heart's Desire* or *Victoria the Great* suggest, some films also paint a positive picture. In fact, many films made with émigré participation cherish England as a country of freedom and security – often in stark contrast to romanticised images of the former *Heimat*. As foreigners, émigrés were able to compare their old habitat with their new British environment. Given their tragic encounter with National Socialism, they often drew upon fundamental values of Anglo-American culture such as freedom of speech, security, democracy and diversity – but above all as a refuge from persecution by the Nazis. Although foreign characters in émigré films repeatedly seem to be forlorn in unfamiliar environments, they often manage to assimilate in the end as they overcome their displacement and disorientation. In this

THE CONTINENTAL CONNECTION

process, these films echo the fact that many refugees or other immigrants from German-speaking countries settled in Britain and, after some initial problems, embraced English culture. A significant number found a new home and even sought to become British citizens. For some members of the émigré community, perhaps most notably Alexander Korda, this led to a strong feeling of identification with the English way of life, its mannerisms and eccentricities. In his witty account of continental Europeans and their fascination of Englishness, Ian Buruma, for instance, describes Korda admiringly as a 'Jewish showman with his Savile Row suits, his chauffeur-driven Rolls and his suites at the Dorchester Hotel. . . . [H]e saw the British Empire as an example of gentlemanly administration.'[133] Korda's admiration for England was also visible in his work as producer. Apart from the image of Big Ben and the famous words 'London Film Production presents . . .', at the beginning of his films, many narratives deal with Englishness, the British heritage and the Empire. This holds especially true for the genres of historical epics (in particular the many biopics) and Empire Films. His film *Sanders of the River*, for instance, is attributed to 'that handful of white men' whose dedication and commitment in their rule over the Empire 'is an unsung saga of courage and efficiency'.

As a typical upper-class comedy made during the war, *The Demi-Paradise* sketches a harmonious, reverential picture of Britain through the eyes of a Russian engineer as outlined before. Once he encounters various English characters, he fundamentally changes his negative preconceptions to the point that he associates Britain with democracy, community, unity, and plurality.[134] Though *The Demi-Paradise* does not deny frictions in British society – hence the film's title – the good qualities clearly outnumber the drawbacks. At the end, the once sceptical foreigner Ivan Kouznetsoff perceives the country and its people as warm and kindly with a love for sports and a sense of humour, liberty and fairness.[135] The foreigner's perspective is central to quite a few wartime narratives as a comparative approach reveals. In films such as *The Demi-Paradise*, *The Gentle Sex* or *The Life and Death of Colonel Blimp* the perspective of a foreigner adds verisimilitude to a celebration of Britain and her ideals without reverting to the jingoism that characterises more simplistic strands of wartime cinema. While foreigners in films gradually discover the merits of their new country of domicile and associate themselves with Britons, their roles continue to be marked by their otherness as they, more often than not, become allies but not true Britons.

The central position of foreigners, which in most cases had the approval of the MoI, simultaneously influenced the way some related issues such as immigration, internment and xenophobia were treated in films. While the refugee theme, as shown earlier, was a contentious issue during the first months of war, the circumstances fundamentally changed as of mid-1940. The *Arandora Star* incident in July 1940 marks a turning point of government policy and public opinion regarding refugees from Nazi Germany. Following the tragic event, internees who were deemed less dangerous were gradually released and Whitehall sought to stress that friendly aliens were part of the anti-Hitler coalition.[136] For this purpose, the MoI specially produced the documentary *Lift Your Head Comrade* (1942) for the home and American markets. Written by the Hungarian German-speaking refugee Arthur Koestler, the film seeks to publicise the fact that some formerly classified 'enemy aliens' enrolled in a special military unit and so became part of the British armed forces.[137]

The new conditions could also be felt in the private feature film industry. Whilst émigrés from the Third Reich had commonly played foreign spies and mysterious foreigners up to 1940, their otherness was now constantly toned down as they increasingly became part of the 'People's War'. While Germanic accents were still used to portray secret agents and saboteurs, the repertoire of foreign allies progressively served to emphasise similarities rather than differences. Filmmakers such as Powell, Pressburger and Leslie Howard repeatedly sought to point out that Britain and her Allies were fighting the Third Reich and Nazism but not Germans as such. As refugee filmmakers contributed to the battle for Britain, their foreignness disappears into the background in the endeavour to construct a general sense of communal unity. Or in other words, the notion of 'the people's War', which still exists in popular memory as a historical moment when everybody was united in the fight against Nazism, turned many filmic refugees into valuable allies.[138] Examples are Theodor Kretschmar-Schuldorff in *The Life and Death of Colonel Blimp* (Michael Powell, 1943), Stefan Radetzky in *Dangerous Moonlight* and Erna Müller in *The Gentle Sex* (Leslie Howard, 1943), played by Anton Walbrook and Lilli Palmer respectively.

Whereas Kretschmar-Schuldorff already had a good friend in Britain and was accustomed to the English way of life from the time when he was a POW in the First World War, Erna Müller had more problems integrating into British society. In an endeavour to underline the great contributions of women to the war effort and to fight existing chauvinism against female soldiers, *The Gentle Sex* tells the story of seven women, representing a cross-section of wartime Britain, who join the Auxiliary Territorial Service (ATS). While documentaries such as *Listen to Britain* (Humphrey Jennings and Stewart McAllister, 1942) made by the Crown Film Unit for the MoI depicted women in allegedly 'male' blue-collar jobs in factories, Whitehall was also keen to promote women in uniform as British men were drafted into the military. Owing to the shortage of 'manpower', émigré women were particularly targeted and positively encouraged to enter the labour market (if they had not already done so) and to join the auxiliary forces. In fact, as early as 1941 an official leaflet labelled 'Information relating to the General Welfare of Refugees from Nazi Oppression' stated that anti-fascist émigrés, besides entering nursing, agricultural or domestic work, could also enlist in the ATS and the Women's Auxiliary Air Force (WAAF).[139]

Although *The Gentle Sex* is, strictly speaking, not an émigré film because none of the off-screen personnel was a German-speaking immigrant, the casting of Lilli Palmer adds a refugee's perspective to the film. From the opening sequence at a train station that introduces the main protagonists, Erna Müller is set apart as apparently the outsider. In accordance with her foreign name, her worn clothes without jewellery, simple hairdo, and face without make-up, the voice-over narrator presents her as the 'foreign looking one – whose face is so lost, yet so angry'. The fact that *The Gentle Sex* begins at a train station and that the women meet in a compartment on their way to basic ATS training refers to a general phenomenon of films dealing with the diaspora and exile. The only places for refugees – be it in fiction or real life – to meet Britons are public places. With few exceptions, like that of Kretschmar-Schuldorff, they had no British friends on arrival. Locations where refugees and British people commonly meet in films thus include trains, shops, buses, sidewalks, parks, etc.

After having hardly spoken a word during the trip to their basic training camp, Erna Müller is the only one who praises the food served as 'absolutely delicious' while the others find it a bit like a simple school dinner. Moreover, when given her new uniform she is happy and moves as if she was wearing the latest *haute-couture* from Paris. In comparison to the other women, her behaviour and looks hint at what she must have been through as a refugee. At first, however, the others do not seem to understand her at all. She remains the foreign outsider. Her situation, the film suggests, is as much her own fault as that of the fellow female recruits. While her taciturn character does not help at all to make friends, the other women initially show little interest in her and her story. What is more, the different cultural background also hampers her integration. At a cheerful concert evening after basic training all the women sing popular British songs. Although Erna Müller wants to join in, she does not know the lyrics of the songs she probably hears for the first time.

Yet, despite all problems assimilating, Erna Müller does not encounter any form of refusal – notwithstanding her continental background. Rather than one-sidedly referring to the difficulties of many exiles, *The Gentle Sex* promotes the assimilative power of British society. At the same time as the other women in her division put aside existing class boundaries, Erna Müller finally overcomes her ethnic and cultural otherness and becomes a respected part of the group and a valuable member in the fight against Nazism. An important step towards integration is a scene in which she opens up and tells the others about her plight. She describes the cruelty of the Gestapo that has killed her family and the love of her life, Paul. For the other girls – and with them the cinema audience – who have not yet learned about the atrocious capabilities of Nazism other than the bombings of British cities, Erna Müller's graphic accounts help them to understand her deep sadness. The anonymous plight of German Jews and other continental refugees, which for many Britons was no more than a recurring theme in the papers, finally gets a face. Through empathy, the other women are able to bond with the foreigner regardless of all differences. The human tragedy and the common fight against the Third Reich prove powerful enough to tear down all boundaries.

Rather than endorsing the idea of communalities between Britain and her allies, numerous other accounts of the time were investigating the exceptionality of England and the English. Anthologies of poetry such as Collie Knox's *For Ever England* which includes works by many authors ranging from Kipling, Shakespeare, Wordsworth, etc. were meant to underline British cultural achievements.[140] In order to show people why it is worth fighting for England and English culture, many publications and articles were drawing upon stereotypical and idealised descriptions of what many saw as the essence of Englishness: the Church of England, public schools, Oxbridge and the quintessentially English game of cricket. Many of the images of rural England are represented by a set of universal tropes that evoke an idealised place of wholesomeness and comfort. Following the same pastoral tradition as *The Demi-Paradise*, Powell and Pressburger's *A Canterbury Tale* (1944) revives images of an idyllic rural England coupled with the affirmative depiction of traditions and pre-war values.[141] In a similar way to other films by Powell and Pressburger, the film praises the beauty of the countryside and positions itself against the mass media, consumerism, and city life. Unlike earlier fictional works that use the contrast of actual events and idealised descriptions for the purpose of emphasising the horrific realities of war, *A Canterbury Tale* is 'an exploration of the spiritual values for which England stands, testimony to the belief that the roots of the nation lie in the pastoral and to the idea of England as synonymous with freedom.'[142] Or, as presented in the press book, the film is 'a new story about Britain, her unchanging beauty and traditions. . . . Those who see it and are British will [think]: "These things I have just seen and heard are all my parents taught me. That is Britain, that is me."'[143] Besides being a pastiche of pastoral novels and paintings, the film also deals with issues of displacement through the character of American GI Bob Johnson, who is a stranger in Britain.[144]

The journey of the American protagonist through Kent acquires a psychological momentum as he seeks to understand England. In the scenes in which he is depicted in common settings of exile cinema – such as train stations, trains, and hotels – the film visualises his displacement. Besides his status as traveller, his otherness is constantly underlined by his pronunciation, his uniform (the chevrons on his arm point in the opposite direction from sergeant's stripes in the British Army), and a characteristic American corn-cob pipe. As an outsider, Bob Johnson, like the town girl in *I Know Where I'm Going*, observes the peculiarities of the British countryside – many of them equally unfamiliar to the film's intended urban audience. Notwithstanding his alienation he is fond of Britain and tries to understand the people and culture of his new environment. As a native speaker of English, however, he has a not insignificant advantage over émigrés from Germany or Austria such as Josef Steidler in *Heart's Desire*. Indeed, unlike dystopian accounts of exilic and diasporic lives, *A Canterbury Tale*, as the plot advances, increasingly develops into a story of successful assimilation.

Although the strangers in the film, GI Johnson and perhaps even more his American friend Mickey, are somewhat parodic figures in their naive views of England and their tourist-like behaviour, they retain a positive persona throughout the film. In line with official MoI policies, *A Canterbury Tale* stresses the common ground between Britain and her allies. Made with a British and an American audience in mind Powell and Pressburger seek to strengthen the cross-Atlantic alliance by exemplifying the close ties between the two English-speaking nations. Rather than abstract values and morals like a belief in the liberal freedoms of democracy a common ground comes to life through the character of Bob Johnson, who more and more becomes part of the close-knit village community in the English hinterland – which the film portrays as the backbone of England and the model of a harmonious society. Here, the film follows a fad of the time in using a conventionalised set of tropes depicting rural England as an unspoiled pre-industrial idyll that provided a symbolic role model for the whole nation. During the war, such depictions increasingly acquired a political significance.[145] Compared with the pre-war years, a significant change took place. While many 1930s British pictures evoke beautiful images of southern German or Austrian rural landscapes, in wartime such images were restricted to Britain and its allies only (compare, for instance, the Canadian Hutterite farming community in *49th Parallel*). This had far-reaching consequences for German-speaking actors in Britain. While they frequently found employment in one of the many films set at nostalgic alpine villages like *Heart's Desire* or *Waltz Time* before the war, this opportunity ceased to exist with the disappearance of this genre. In some cases, the only remaining roles for accented actors were those of enemy soldiers in propaganda films.

As with exile cinema in general, travelling is a central motif of *A Canterbury Tale* that deals with a modern-day pilgrimage against the background of a society that is worth fighting for. While the threat of Nazi Germany is clearly visible in the rubble of destroyed houses in Canterbury, 'pilgrimage' is a metaphor for the common fight against the Third Reich. 'The People's War' thus defends rural England and all it stands for. As an important symbol, Canterbury cathedral combines these values as it 'borrows from a tradition of English pastoralism to find strength in the past through the invocation and reinforcement of a mythical old England', as Andrew Moor observes.[146] Yet, the cathedral and the pilgrimage theme can also be interpreted as the pursuit of what makes up the essence of England. Thus the quest of the film's hero Bob Johnson among other things represents and comments on the situation of foreigners in Britain and their attempts to become part of English society and culture.

As with most films made by Powell and Pressburger's production company The Archers, the casts and credits of *A Canterbury Tale* feature an astonishing number of German-speaking personnel. Although actors from Austria or Germany were not cast in leading roles – as in many of their other films – the cameraman (Erwin Hillier), the scriptwriter (Emeric Pressburger himself), the composer (Allan Gray, i.e. Josef Zmigrod), the conductor (Walter Goehr), and the art director (Alfred Junge) had all worked in Berlin. Many of them started their careers there and, as apprentices or students, worked with leading representatives of Weimar culture such as Fritz Lang, Reinhold Schünzel and Arnold Schönberg. The international collaboration in The Archers' team of production had a major impact on how issues of nationality and culture were treated. Above all the close collaboration between Powell and Pressburger extended to all production processes from the early planning stages to the actual shooting; a special position that is reflected by that unique credit 'written, produced, and directed by Michael Powell and Emeric Pressburger'. Under the umbrella of the Rank Organisation, which later also sponsored Marcel Hellmann of Excelsior Films, their independent film company The Archers had a greater artistic freedom than most mainstream wartime productions which allowed the other émigré film professionals involved to exert an influence on the film.[147]

Just as in other films made by Powell and Pressburger, a chief characteristic of *A Canterbury Tale* is the special emphasis that is laid on the hybrid nature of culture and the inter-connectedness between cultures.

THE CONTINENTAL CONNECTION

Not everyone was partial to so much internationality and plurality – especially since the film is not hammering home a simple message. Although Ernest Betts in *The Sunday Express* praises in particular Erwin Hillier's cinematography as a 'miracle' and acknowledges the attractiveness of the film, its complex plot and dual focus are the source of some irritation: 'The faults of the picture are mystification and obscurity. Is this film about Anglo-American relations, is it a hymn to England, or what? I don't know.'[148]

In a manner reminiscent of many German-speaking film professionals who sought employment in Britain, Bob Johnson's language skills, curiosity, openness, and knowledge are the main preconditions for his integration. In a similar way to many technicians from Germany and Austria – who were among the most successful émigré groups in Britain – he first achieves recognition in the village community by way of his technical understanding: while the former were widely accepted for their knowledge of art history or optics, Bob Johnson is appreciated for his wood-cutting know-how. Talking to the local joiner, both men discover that regarding working with wood the same rules apply in England and Bob Johnson's part of America where his father is a cabinetmaker. Their interest in lumber and craftsmanship transcends national boundaries – as does the military vocabulary and the officer's code of honour in *The Life and Death of Colonel Blimp*. After their conversation, the American GI is asked over for dinner at the joiner's house; an invitation that clearly marks the acceptance of the foreign visitor. Likewise, German-speaking art directors and technicians gained recognition and the respect of their British colleagues through their expertise. Both *A Canterbury Tale*'s art director and cinematographer, Alfred Junge and Erwin Hillier, for instance, had studied painting and learned their craft starting from the bottom in German studios before they helped to transform British modes of film production. Arguably the technical terminology (i.e. the rules of optics) that was universally acknowledged in world cinema eased the assimilation process. In this respect it can be explained why technicians and art directors had fewer problems integrating than film personnel who relied heavily on the English language and culture such as actors and script writers. Moreover, as the examples of Alexander Korda or Emeric Pressburger show, many of the most successful émigrés showed a great willingness to adapt to their new environment. While the former appeared more British than the British in his manners and exquisite suits, the latter's identification with England and its customs can, for instance, be deduced from his great interest in English football and staunch support for Arsenal FC. Evocatively the happy ending of *A Canterbury Tale* is followed by closing credits over underlying images of boys playing football. If one agrees with Hamid Naficy's thesis that exilic and diasporic films are inseparable from their creators, Pressburger's passion for English football and admiration for British culture are visible in this ending. The film here proposes a reconciled relationship between the foreigner and Britain.

Although the English countryside is by and large seen as a rural utopia, combining Pressburger's nostalgic memories of growing up on a farm in Hungary with a celebration of those elements which were perceived as typically English, *A Canterbury Tale* also parodies such a positive view. In so doing Powell's and Pressburger's film, the intertextual title of which alone suggests artificiality and constructedness by referring to Chaucer's collection of tales from the fourteenth century, differs significantly from uncritical pastoral depictions of rural England. Perhaps comparable with Stella Gibbons' comic novel *Cold Comfort Farm* (1932), *A Canterbury Tale* mocks the romanticised English country community that can be found in representations of the pastoral ideal. The local magistrate Colpeper, for instance, initially appears as a friendly and respectable member of the rural community but soon turns out to be 'the Glueman', a criminal who attacks young women by pouring glue into their hair. In addition, Powell and Pressburger's film also features a 'village idiot' as part of the country personae – another character who does not quite fit the topos of rural England as a contemporary Arcadia. In a similar way, the name of the rural village 'Chillingbourne' also contradicts the pleasant atmosphere created by the film while the title itself underlines the general artificiality and self-referentiality of the story. The England portrayed in *A Canterbury Tale* is constructed and may not be 'real'.

The production context of the film also counteracts the idyllic England created by the film at first glance. Pressburger himself was not allowed to leave London for on-location filming in Kent.[149] Against the background of the internment of so-called 'enemy aliens' and the strict territorial restrictions imposed upon émigrés, the film invites an ambivalent, critical reading. While the foreigner Bob Johnson discovers the positive aspects of his new temporary home, other aliens were, at least outside the cinemas, denied this experience. What can be seen here is that exile cinema self-consciously interrogates concepts such as Englishness and national identities rather than taking on unquestioned images of the new host country.[150] This at least partially explains the discontinuities and ruptures of an otherwise 'perfect' filmic England in *A Canterbury Tale*. Yet, within the ambivalent strands of exilic filmmaking, ruptures and ironic discontinuities, as the film also shows, do not contradict a general acceptance and appreciation of English ideas and values. This holds especially true for things which come closest to representing the alien's perception of Englishness.

While it is a common phenomenon of exile cinema to call into question concepts of nationhood and cultural identities rather than simplistically celebrating them, many émigré films feature critical voices directed against the adopted homeland and its policies. In addition to criticism that is inscribed metaphorically and subliminally, some filmic treatments also express rather apparent disapproval, in particular of Whitehall's restrictive immigration policies and hesitant pre-war actions to help European Jews. What at first seems a dilemma (criticising the country that offered refuge), is more exactly a demonstration of the pluralistic nature of the British film industry – an industry which was not even nationalised in times of war. From the position of go-betweens and outsiders, many émigrés in fact combined constructive criticism with pledges of allegiance to their new home. Indeed through their engagement in British films German-speaking émigrés illustrate Gerd Gemünden's and Anton Kaes' understanding of 'displacement and disorientation as (admittedly forced) opportunities for self-examination and social critique'.[151]

Again *The Life and Death of Colonel Blimp* as a key wartime émigré film serves as a good example. It differs from most mainstream films made during the Second World War. The film repeatedly frustrates generic conventions and challenges national clichés and expectations.[152] Like other film scripts written by Pressburger discourses on exile, foreignness and otherness can be found throughout the film. A scene of a stage version of Joyce's novel Ulysses, which alludes to Western culture's best-known émigré traveller Odysseus, is an obvious case in point.[153] Adding a level of critical reflexivity and abstraction, the stage in fact creates what may well be regarded as a *tableau vivant* of exile. The view expressed by the immigration officer in the film draws directly upon the many problems exiled filmmakers had to face: 'You may be an anti-Nazi, you may not – in times like these one enemy in our midst can do more harm than ten across the Channel.'

One year after having already played a German political refugee in the successful London theatre play *Watch on the Rhine*, Walbrook again slips into this role when he was cast in what was to remain the only explicit wartime filmic account of the immigration process. As Theo Kretschmar-Schuldorff, Walbrook is interrogated by a British tribunal in *The Life and Death of Colonel Blimp*. The scene embodies many of the anxieties of exiles and is central to any assessment of how films represented the situation of refugees. In the way that it echoes the experiences of British 'enemy aliens' who went through various monitoring sessions themselves, the tribunal in *The Life and Death of Colonel Blimp*, which decides whether or not the sympathetic Kretschmar-Schuldorff will be granted refuge in Britain, acquires actuality and authenticity. Referring to this scene in the film, Pressburger remarked in an interview:

I had the same kind of experience [in immigration control] obviously. England is a very, very difficult country for foreigners to come to. Of course, when I came my intention was to stay in England but you have to lie straight away . . . you're not only dying to stay in England, you can't go anywhere else. And . . . to the question, 'How long do you intend to stay here?' You mustn't say, 'I intend to stay forever' . . . so you answer, 'Six months', and then you extend the six months. . . . I believe that anyone that comes to the country under the same circumstances cannot love the Immigration Officers.[154]

Besides Powell and Pressburger a number of émigré films seem to confirm Naficy's argument that the representation of the diaspora and exile have a tendency to emphasise 'claustrophobia and temporality, and it is cathected to sides of confinement and control and to narratives of panic and pursuit. While the idyllic open structures of home emphasize continuity, these paranoid structures of exile underscore rupture.'[155] Yet, rather than essentialising accounts of exile and the diaspora as loss and trauma, other films have called for a more holistic representation of the émigré experience. Particularly those narratives which engage with transnational culture often proposed a more complex scenario. While the émigré experience undoubtedly caused numerous hardships it also enabled both German-speaking film professionals and their diegetic screen personae to engage with a new, sometimes fascinating culture.

Notes

1 Letter from George Whitaker to the Home Office on 7 October 1939, NA HO 405/15863 236966.
2 Letter from the Musical Conductors' Association to the Home Office on 6 October 1939, NA HO 405/15863 236966.
3 See Dorothy Frances Buxton, *The Economics of the Refugee Problem* (London: Focus, 1939), p. 7. Cited in Gough-Yates, 'The British Feature Film as a European Concern', p. 168.
4 See *Cine-Technician*, March/April 1941, p. 41.
5 See, among other articles and reports of the union's annual general meetings, 'Foreign Technicians: The Policy of the Association of Cine-Technicians', *Cine-Technician*, February 1936, p. 88, 'And Still They Come', *Cine-Technician*, August-October 1936, p. 39 and p. 41. See also the reply 'David B. Cunynghame, Production Manager, London Films, says "And Still We Need Them"', *Cine-Technician*, December 1936/January 1937, p. 108, and 'British Talent Stifled?', *Cine-Technician*, October/November 1937, pp. 132–3.
6 *Cine-Technician*, July/August 1941, p. 96.
7 *Cine-Technician*, March/April 1941, p. 41.
8 See Rose, *Which People's War*, pp. 92–106.

9 *Kinematograph Weekly*, 11 January 1940, p. C4.

10 Gough-Yates, 'Jews and Exiles', p. 532.

11 *Kinematograph Weekly*, 15 January 1940, p. 5.

12 Ibid., p. 5.

13 Gough-Yates, 'The European Film Maker in Exile in Britain, 1933–1945', p. 33, footnote 4.

14 Quoted in Viertel, pp. 224–5.

15 Lafitte, pp. 26–8.

16 Kushner, *The Persistence of Prejudice*, p. 11.

17 Cited in Bernard Wasserstein, *Britain and the Jews of Europe, 1939–1945*, 2nd edn (London and New York: Leicester UP, 1999), p. 81.

18 See François Lafitte, *The Internment of Aliens* (London: Penguin, 1940; reprinted London: Libris, 1988), p. 62.

19 On the internment of 'enemy aliens' see, for example, Peter Gillman and Leni Gillman, *'Collar the Lot!': How Britain Interned and Expelled its Wartime Refugees* (London: Quartlet Books, 1980); Ronald Stent, *A Bespattered Page: The Internment of 'His Majesty's Most Loyal Enemy Aliens'* (London: André Deutsch, 1980); *'Totally un-English?': Britain's Internment of 'Enemy Aliens' in Two World Wars*, edited by Richard Dove (= Yearbook of the Research Centre for German and Austrian Exile Studies, 7 (2005)).

20 See Lafitte, p. 79 and Gough-Yates, 'The European Film Maker in Exile in Britain 1933–1945', p. 420.

21 See Tim Bergfelder, 'The Production Designer and the *Gesamtkunstwerk*' p. 31; and Gough-Yates, 'The European Film Maker in Exile in Britain 1933–1945', p. 411 and p. 425. On Heinrich Fraenkel, see the file in the National Archives: NA HO 405/12865.

22 See Alan Clarke, "Theatre behind Barbed Wire: German Refugee Theatre in British Internment", in *Theatre and Film in Exile: German Artists in Britain, 1933–1945*, edited by Günter Berghaus (Oxford and New York: Berg, 1989), pp. 189–222 (p. 190).

23 See ibid., pp. 191–2.

24 See ibid., p. 193.

25 See Richard Dove, *Journey of No Return: Five German-speaking Literary Exiles in Britain, 1933–1945* (London: Libris, 2000), p. 182.

26 John Maynard Keynes to Francis C. Scott, 23 July 1940, *The Collected Writings of John Maynard Keynes*, edited by the Royal Economic Society, 30 vols (London: Macmillan, 1971–1989), XXII (1978): *Activities 1939–1945: Internal War Finance*, edited by Donald Moggridge, pp. 190–91. Cited in London, *Whitehall and the Jews*, p. 171.

27 Paul Marcus, 'Londoner Notizen', *Aufbau*, 5 January 1940, p. 3. Translated by Ronald Walker.

28 See, for instance, the National Archive files on Katscher/Cartier (HO 405/26875), Rudolf Bernauer (HO 405/2616), Lajos Biro (HO 405/2074) and Paul Czinner (HO 405/7511). All files were opened by the Home Office at the author's request.

29 Handwritten note from 28 July 1944. NA HO 405/26875.

30 Police Report from 20 July 1949 on Heinrich Fraenkel, p. 7. NA HO 405/12865.

31 Letter from 31 December 1940, NA HO 405/12865.

32 See Kevin Gough-Yates, 'Berthold Viertel at Gaumont-British', in *The Unknown 1930s: An Alternative History of the British Cinema, 1929–1939*, edited by Jeffrey Richards (London and New York: I. B. Tauris, 2000), pp. 201–17 (p. 209).

33 See Stefan Howald, 'Life as an "Enemy Alien"', in *Changing Countries: The Experience and Achievement of German-speaking Exiles from Hitler in Britain from 1933 to Today*, edited by Marian Malet and Anthony Grenville (London: Libris, 2002), pp. 152–60 (p. 155); and Kevin Gough-Yates, 'The BBC as a Source of Employment for Film Workers and Composers during the War', in *Literatur und Kultur des Exils in Großbritannien*, edited by Siglinde Bolbecher and others, Zwischenwelt, 4 (Vienna: Verlag für Gesellschaftskritik, 1995), pp. 215–40.

34 See Brinson, 'A Woman's Place . . .?:', p. 217.

35 Note on MoI film policy, 3 October 1939, NA INF 1/194.

36 See Daniel Snowman, *The Hitler Emigres: The Cultural Impact on Britain of Refugees from Nazism*, 2nd edn (London: Pimlico, 2003), p. 155.

37 Cited in ibid., p. 155.

38 See Philip M. Taylor, 'Introduction', in *Britain and the Cinema in the Second World War*, edited by Philip M. Taylor (New York: St. Martin's Press, 1988), pp. 1–14 (p. 6).

39 Charles Barr, 'Introduction: Amnesia and Schizophrenia', in *All Our Yesterdays: 90 Years of British Cinema*, edited by Charles Barr (London: BFI, 1986), pp. 1–26 (pp. 10–11).

40 Besides Barr see *Britain and the Cinema in the Second World War*, edited by Philip M. Taylor (New York: St. Martin's Press, 1988) and Anthony Aldgate and Jeffrey Richards, *Best of British: Cinema and Society from 1930 to the Present* (London and New York: I. B. Tauris, 1999), pp. 57–93.

41 In accordance with established practice of scholars, the term 'propaganda' will be used throughout this article 'not in the popular pejorative sense, but as a specific term to describe the act of mass persuasion', Nicholas John Cull, *Selling War: The British Propaganda Campaign Against American 'Neutrality' in World War II* (New York and Oxford: Oxford University Press, 1995), p. xi.

42 Robert Murphy, *Realism and Tinsel*, p. 9.

43 See Gemünden and Kaes, p. 3.

44 See Taylor, 'Introduction', pp. 1–14 (p. 6).

45 A number of exiles, in fact, used the outbreak of war to stress their contempt of Nazism, offering their help to state institutions such as the newly established Ministry of Information (MoI). See, for instance, the case of Cartier whose solicitors contacted the Home Office, emphasizing, among other things, his willingness to become engaged in anti-Nazi propaganda. See Letter by Bartlett & Gluckstein, solicitors, to the Under-Secretary of State, 24 July 1940, NA HO 405/26875.

46 Besides Barr see *Britain and the Cinema in the Second World War*, edited by Philip M. Taylor (New York: St. Martin's Press, 1988) and Anthony Aldgate and Jeffrey Richards, *Best of British: Cinema and Society from 1930 to the Present* (London and New York: I. B. Tauris, 1999), pp. 57–93.

47 Given that wartime production was not so different from genre preferences of 1930s British cinema, émigrés not only appeared in the now thriving war or combat films but also continued to contribute, among others, to consume melodramas, spy thrillers and historical films.

48 See letter from 26 April 1945 about the termination of Bernauer's engagement for the OSS, NA HO 405/2616 236997.

49 According to a letter by Kanturek's solicitors he invented an anti-aircraft projectile, an infra-red beam apparatus and an anti-tank weapon which were all under consideration by the War Office or members of the armed forces. See letter from Griffinhoofe and Brewster, Solicitors, to the Home Office of 25 June 1940, p. 1. NA HO 405/26547 236966.

50 See Schöning, 'All Hands Abroad', pp. 119 and 122.

51 See Michael Powell in an interview with Kevin Gough-Yates on 22 September 1970. Gough-Yates, *Michael Powell in Collaboration with Emeric Pressburger*, unpaginated.

52 See Rosamunde Neugebauer, 'Anti-Nazi-Cartoons deutschsprachiger Emigranten in Großbritannien: Ein spezielles Kapitel Karikaturengeschichte', in *Ästhetiken des Exils*, edited by Helga Schreckenberger (Amsterdamer Beiträge zur neueren Germanistik, 54 (2003)), pp. 93–122.

53 NA HO 405/26547 236966.

54 See Jürgen Berger, 'Listen to Britain: Strukturen und Arbeitsweisen der Films Division des Ministry of Information 1939–45 – Ein Beitrag zur Administrations- und Produktionsgeschichte britischer Filmpropaganda' (unpublished doctoral thesis, University of Konstanz, Germany, 2001), p. 34; and Political & Economic Planning (PEP), 'The British Film Industry – A Report on its History and Present Organisation, With Special Reference to the Economic Problems of British Feature Film Production' (London: PEP, 1952).

55 Taylor, 'Introduction', p. 8.

56 Andrew Buchanan, 'Let the Screen Help!', *Sight and Sound* 8.31 (Autumn 1939), pp. 87–8.

57 On opposition to cinema in the First World War see Nicholas Reeves, 'Official British Film Propaganda', in *The First World War and Popular Cinema: 1914 to Present*, edited by Michael Paris (New Brunswick, NJ.: Rutgers University Press, 2000), pp. 27–50 (pp. 29–30).

58 Thirteenth Report from the Select Committee on National Expenditure (London: His Majesty's Stationery Office, 1940), p. 5. Cited in James Chapman, *The British at War: Cinema, State and Propaganda, 1939–1945* (London and New York: I. B. Tauris, 1998), p. 58.

59 Note on Policy of Ministry of Information with regard to films, 3 October 1939. NA INF 1/194.

60 See Richards, 'British Film Censorship', p. 158. See also ibid., 'Wartime Cinema Audiences and the Class System – The Case of *Ships With Wings* (1941)', *Historical Journal of Film, Radio and Television*, 7.2 (1987), 129–41, and James Robertson, 'British Film Censorship Goes to War', *Historical Journal of Film, Radio and Television*, 2.1 (1982), 49–64.

61 Cited in Taylor, 'Introduction', p. 9.

62 See Paul Marcus, *Pem's Privat-Berichte*, 9 August 1939, p. 54.

63 *Sunday Pictorial*, 1 June 1941, cited by Richards, 'British Film Censorship', p. 158.

64 The memorandum is reproduced in *Powell, Pressburger and Others*, edited by Ian Christie (London: BFI, 1978), pp. 121–24. See also *Best of British*, p. 57. On the MoI and home front morale see Ian McLaine, *Ministry of Morale – Home Front Morale and the Ministry of Information in World War II* (London, Boston, MA and Sydney: Allen & Unwin, 1979).

65 Francis Thorpe and Nicholas Pronay, *British Official Films in the Second World War* (Oxford: Oxford UP, 1980), p. 21. Cited in Taylor, 'Introduction', p. 10.

66 See Horak, 'Wunderliche Schicksalsfügung', p. 266.

67 Antonia Lant, *Blackout: Reinventing Women for Wartime British Audiences* (Princeton: Princeton UP, 1991), p. 197.

68 *Kinematograph Weekly*, 11 January 1940, p. C4.

69 C. A. Lejeune, 'A Filmgoers Diary', cited in *Red Roses Every Night*, edited by Guy Morgan (London: Quality Press, 1948), p. 69.

70 See Jeffrey Richards, 'National Identity in British Wartime Films', in *Britain and the Cinema in the Second World War*, edited by Philip M. Taylor (New York: St. Martin's Press, 1988), pp. 42–61 (p. 49).

71 Andrew Moor, 'Dangerous Limelight: Anton Walbrook and the Seduction of the English', in *British Stars and Stardom: From Alma Taylor to Sean Connery*, edited by Bruce Babington (Manchester and New York: Manchester University Press, 2001), pp. 80–93 (p. 83).

72 On the 'People's War' as a promoted wartime ethos see Rose, *Which People's War?*.

73 General Production Division, 'Anger' Campaign, 17 June 1940, NA INF 1/849, p. 2. Cited in Berger, p. 91.

74 Berger, p. 91, footnote 23.

75 See Paul Marcus, 'Die Situation der Emigranten in England', *Aufbau*, 1 November 1939, pp. 11–12 (p. 11).

76 A comprehensive summary of the plot can be found in James C. Robertson, *The Hidden Cinema: British Film Censorship in Action, 1913–1975* (London and New York: Routledge, 1993), pp. 74–8.

77 Cited in Richards, 'The British Board of Film Censors and Content Control in the 1930s: foreign affairs', p. 42.

78 '"Pastor Hall" (Carlton Theatre, W.)', *Daily Mirror*, 24 May 1940, p. 13.

79 Klaus Mann, 'What's Wrong With Anti-Nazi Films?', *Decision* (August 1941). Reprinted in *New German Critique*, 89 (Spring/Summer 2003), 173–82 (p. 177).

80 Cull, p. 49.

81 Robertson, *The Hidden Cinema*, p. 77.

82 See Richards, 'National Identity in British Wartime Films', pp. 45–6.

83 MO File Report 162: 'Pastor Hall', 2 June 1940, *The Tom Harisson Mass-Observation Archive* (London: Harvester Press, 1983), microfiche. Cited in James Chapman, 'Why we fight: *Pastor Hall* and *Thunder Rock*', in *The Family Way: The Boulting Brothers and British Film Culture*, edited by Alan Burton, Tim O'Sullivan and Paul Wells (Trowbridge: Flicks Books, 2000), pp. 81–96 (p. 86).

84 On wartime public opinion and the Germans see McLaine, pp. 137–70; and John Ramsden, *Don't Mention the War: The British and the Germans Since 1890* (London: Little, Brown, 2006).

85 'The Other Side of the Atlantic', *Documentary Newsletter*, September 1940, p. 4.

86 See Cull, p. 50.

87 Robertson, *The Hidden Cinema*, pp. 77–8.

88 See Cull, p. 201.

89 C. A. Lejeune, '"Pastor Hall": A British Picture', *Observer*, 21 January 1940. Cited in Chapman, 'Why we fight: *Pastor Hall* and *Thunder Rock*', p. 84.

90 See Chapman, 'Why we fight: *Pastor Hall* and *Thunder Rock*', p. 84.

91 On the role of women in wartime Britain see Sonya O. Rose, 'Sex, Citizenship, and the Nation in World War II Britain,' *American Historical Review*, 103.4 (October 1998), 1147–76.

92 See Ian Christie and R. Collins, 'Interview with Michael Powell: The Expense of Naturalism', *Monogram*, 3 (1972), pp. 32–8 (p. 33).

93 See James Chapman, '"The true business of the British movie"? *A Matter of Life and Death* and British Film Culture', *Screen*, 46.1 (2005), 33–49 (p.35).

94 See Powell, p. 406.

95 It is thus perhaps more than a footnote to film history that the ritualistic, dramatic build-up and the meticulously crafted sets made a long-lasting impression on the young Martin Scorsese, who modelled parts of his acclaimed *Raging Bull* (1980) after these scenes. See Martin Scorsese, 'Foreword', in *Arrows of Desire: The Films of Michael Powell and Emeric Pressburger*, edited by Ian Christie (London: Waterstone, 1985), pp. 10–13 (p. 12).

96 See Ian Christie, '*Blimp*, Churchill and the State', in *Powell, Pressburger and Others*, edited by Ian Christie (London: BFI, 1978), pp. 105–20 (p. 105).

97 See Michael Powell in an interview with Kevin Gough-Yates on 22 September 1970. Gough-Yates, *Michael Powell in Collaboration with Emeric Pressburger*, unpaginated.

98 See Clarke, 'Theatre behind the Wire', pp. 189–222 and Georg W. Brandt, 'Thespis Behind the Wire, or Entertainment in Internment: A Personal Recollection', in in *Theatre and Film in Exile: German Artists in Britain, 1933–1945*, edited by Günter Berghaus, (Oxford and New York: Berg, 1989), pp. 223–29.

99 Paul Marcus, 'Leben und Tod des Colonel Blimp', *Aufbau*, 16 July 1943, p. 12.

100 Pressburger, cited in Gough-Yates, 'The British Feature Film as a European Concern', p. 156.
101 Macdonald, p. 218.
102 For a critical survey of the history of the film see James Chapman, '*The Life and Death of Colonel Blimp* (1943) Reconsidered', *Historical Journal of Film, Radio and Television*, 15. 1 (March 1995), 19–54; and Anthony Aldgate and Jeffrey Richards, pp. 79–93.
103 Review in *Tribune*, 19 June 1943. Cited in *Powell and Pressburger: The Life and Death of Colonel Blimp*, edited by Ian Christie (London: Faber, 1994), p. 59.
104 E. W. Robson and M. M. Robson, *The Shame and Disgrace of Colonel Blimp: the True Story of the Film* (London: The Sidneyan Society, 1944), p. 3.
105 E. W. Robson and M. M. Robson, *The World is My Cinema* (London: Sidneyan Society, 1947), p. 65.
106 Ian Christie, *A Matter of Life and Death*, BFI Film Classics (London: BFI, 2000), p. 65.
107 Chapman, '"The True Business of a British Movie"?', p. 45.
108 Given that the review has not yet been considered by the existing literature, it seems necessary to cite the review at length. *Cine Technician*, September/October 1944, pp. 92–3.
109 Letter from the Robsons to the editor, *Cine Technician*, November/December 1944, p. 120.
110 Maroula Joannou, 'Powell, Pressburger, and Englishness', *European Journal of English Studies*, 8.2 (2004), 189–203 (p. 196).
111 On the representation on Jews in British cinema in the 1930s and during the war, see Gough-Yates, 'Jews and Exiles in British Cinema', pp. 517–41.
112 See Louise London, 'British Immigration Control Procedures and Jewish Refugees 1933–1939', in *Second Chance: Two Centuries of German-speaking Jews in the United Kingdom*, edited by Werner E. Mosse et al., (Schriftenreihe wissenschaftlicher Abhandlungen des Leo Baeck Instituts, 48) (Tübingen: Mohr, 1991), pp. 458–518.
113 See Rose, *Which People's War?*, p. 105.
114 See ibid., pp. 98–106.
115 Cited in 'A Miserable Position', *Jewish Chronicle*, 5 March 1943, p. 10. The *Jewish Chronicle* closely observed the growing anti-Semitism in Britain, see Wasserstein, p. 130.
116 Mass Observation Archive (MOA), DR M1534, March 1943. Quoted in Tony Kushner, 'Remembering to Forget: Racism and Anti-Racism in Postwar Britain', in *Modernity, Culture and the Jew*, edited by Bryan Cheyette and Laura Marcus (Cambridge: Polity Press, 1998), pp. 226–41 (p. 227).
117 Kevin Gough-Yates, 'Pressburger, England and Exile', *Sight and Sound*, 5.12 (1995), 30–55 (p. 34).
118 Joannou, pp. 189–203 (p. 191).
119 See Naficy, p. 6.
120 'Entertainments: "I Know Where I'm Going" – The Western Isles', *The Times*, 14 November 1945, film review, p. 6.

121 Cook, p. 44.
122 See ibid., pp. 48–9.
123 Ibid., pp. 48–9.
124 See Dove, *Journey of No Return*, p. 182.
125 Moor, *Powell & Pressburger*, p. 200.
126 See ibid., p. 201.
127 Ibid., p. 199.
128 See Powell, p. 614.
129 Ibid., p. 228.
130 Ibid., p. 611.
131 Ibid., p. 203.
132 Ibid., p. 653.
133 Ian Buruma, *Voltaire's Coconuts or Anglomania in Europe* (London: Weidenfeld & Nicolson, 2000), p. 245.
134 See David Lusted, '"Builders" and "The Demi-Paradise"', in *National Fictions*, edited by Geoff Hurd (London: BFI, 1984), pp. 27–30 (p. 28).
135 See Richards, 'National Identity in British Wartime Films', pp. 50–2.
136 See Dove, *Journey of No Return*, p. 182.
137 See Andreas Klugescheid, '"His Majesty's Most Loyal Enemy Aliens": Der Kampf deutsch-jüdischer Emigranten in den britischen Streitkräften, 1939–1945', in *Jüdische Emigration zwischen Assimilation und Verfolgung, Akkulturation und jüdischer Identität*, edited by Claus-Dieter Krohn (= *Exilforschung: Ein Internationales Jahrbuch*, 19 (2001)), pp. 106–27.
138 See Moor, 'Dangerous Limelight', p. 82.
139 On the role of German-speaking women in exile in Britain during the war, see Brinson, 'A Woman's Place . . .?', pp. 204–24.
140 See Aldgate and Richards, p. 60.
141 On Powell and Pressburger's work and the pastoral tradition, see Moor, *Powell & Pressburger*, pp. 85–102.
142 Anthony Aldgate and Jeffrey Richards, pp. 61–2.
143 *A Canterbury Tale* press book, BFI microfiche.
144 See Gough-Yates, 'Exiles and British Cinema', p. 174.
145 On the political implications of the division of city and countryside see Rose, *Which People's War?*, pp. 198–218; and John Taylor, *A Dream of England: Landscape, Photography and the Tourist's Imagination* (Manchester: Manchester University Press, 1994), pp. 198–211.
146 Moor, *Powell & Pressburger*, p. 95.
147 Pressburger was thus euphoric about the opportunity to work for Rank shortly after his release from internment. See Geoffrey Macnab, *J. Arthur Rank and the British Film Industry* (London and New York: Routledge, 1993), p. 91.
148 Ernest Betts, 'You'll like this U.S. sergeant in a truly British film: *A Canterbury Tale*', *Sunday Express*, 14 May 1944, film review, p. 6.
149 See Powell, p. 443.
150 See Moor, 'No Place Like Home', pp. 109–13.
151 Gemünden and Kaes, pp. 3–4.

152 See Street, *British National Cinema*, p. 52–5.
153 On theatre performance and the theme of exile in *The Life and Death of Colonel Blimp* see Moor, 'No Place Like Home', p. 112.
154 Cited in Gough-Yates, 'The British Feature Film as a European Concern', p. 156.
155 Naficy, p. 5.

4 *The Spy in Black*, 1939. Courtesy of Deutsche Kinemathek, Berlin

5

Conclusions: The legacy of German-speaking filmmakers in Britain

This study has demonstrated that the many German-speaking émigrés working in and around London played an important part in the development of British national cinema from the late 1920s to the end of the Second World War and beyond. It has outlined how Film Europe – with its numerous and multi-facetted pan-European joint ventures and co-operation treaties – helps to explain the various contacts and close relations between the British and continental film industries. In the wake of the UFA crisis and the positive economic situation in Britain as a result of the protectionist regulations introduced in 1927, many German-speaking film practitioners found employment for the major English production companies, which admired filmmakers such as Ewald André Dupont, Alfred Junge, Oscar Werndorff, Mutz Greenbaum and Werner Brandes for their technical and artistic expertise. Before the mass purge of film personnel as a result of state anti-Semitism in Nazi Germany the arrival of continental film workers from Germany and Austria increasingly changed the look of British films in terms of visual imagery, technical innovation and storylines. Among other things, they introduced apprenticeship schemes, streamlined production processes, raised technical standards (as can be seen in highly mobile cameras), put more importance on elements of mise-en-scène and infused films with exoticism and internationalism. In addition to the cosmopolitan feel of the films that were often set at transcultural locations and the junction points of Europe, a striking feature is open depiction of sexuality and nudity. The trajectories of individual film professionals during the cosmopolitan co-operation labelled 'Film Europe', which started as a movement to challenge Hollywood's market hegemony, thus undoubtedly paved the way for many of the mainly Jewish exiles after 1933.

With the increasing numbers of German-speaking émigré film personnel coming to Britain after 1933 and again in 1938, a growing number of voices uttered concerns that the foreign workers were employed to the detriment of British staff working for the film business. In addition to many restrictions imposed upon foreign nationals in the cinema industry and elsewhere,

Whitehall interned many German-speaking émigrés at the beginning of war. Yet despite all the hardships and an 'alien scare' after the first triumphs of the *Wehrmacht* on the continent, the position of the UK government and public opinion towards German-speaking refugees was altogether ambivalent. Whereas a high number of émigrés were interned under miserable conditions, Britain also saved many lives as it offered refuge to numerous people from Nazi-Germany. And although xenophobic tendencies and antipathy, in particular on the part of the trade unions, cast a shadow over the reception of refugees, the great number of non-governmental organisations along with significant private engagement offered support to many exiles and helped film professionals and artists to show the British public a picture of the other, democratic and liberal Germany in the tradition of the Weimar Republic.

The living conditions of individual refugees underscore the great diversity of film émigrés. While the unfamiliar environment and restrictions imposed upon immigrants by the authorities caused problems for all German-speaking film personnel in Britain, those exiles who more than others relied on the language (i.e. actors and script writers) suffered particularly severe loss of income, status and artistic expression. Yet it is myopic to limit accounts of the British diaspora to hardships. The various activities of émigrés – outside the cinema industry as well as in the numerous films in which they participated – give evidence of a rich and vivid émigré life in Britain. As the new country of domicile offered opportunities to many German-speaking film personnel, Britain in turn benefited much from the continental film workers and artists. As the casts and credits of the era illustrate, the majority of big-budget films were in fact produced by or with the participation of German-speaking émigrés.

The high figure of German-speaking émigrés who worked in the relatively small British film industry in Greater London from 1927–1949 casts serious doubt on the existence of a self-contained national film industry. In fact, the numerous contributions of foreign personnel to narratives, aesthetics, technical innovation, organisation of work and the introduction of training and apprenticeship schemes suggest that this period of filmmaking was – all restrictive measures aside – dominated by transnational cross-fertilization. This book, therefore, is part of a trend of film scholarship to question the notion of national cinema as a closed entity. It argues that the increasing international prominence of British films particularly in the course of the 1930s is inextricably linked to the assimilative power of English production companies on the one hand and the achievement of their German-speaking employees on the other. Despite all undeniable problems of migration, this study illustrates that the complex processes of cultural adaptation need to be described as enriching and dynamic.

The departure from Germany or Austria marks a decisive point in the lives of all émigré filmmakers who came to Britain involuntarily as refugees. This explains why most of their work showed a lifelong preoccupation with issues of displacement, national character and cultural affiliation. Prompted by the atrocities during the war, moreover, films made by and with émigré increasingly dealt with the question of how the people in their former homeland, some of them neighbours or friends, could have been responsible for the Holocaust. By dealing with a wide range of films made by or with German-speaking émigrés, it was argued in this book that films covering diasporic and exilic themes as well as politics to varying degrees were not the exception but rather the norm. Repeatedly the hybrid and diverse identities that are prominent in many of these films put marginalised groups such as foreigners, asylum seekers and immigrants at the centre of interest. Whether émigrés participated in the production of popular genre cinema or films that gradually transcended mainstream conventions (most notably in the stylised feature films of Powell and Pressburger which may be seen as an antithesis of the aesthetics of British realist filmmaking), it was they who often included notions of exile and the diaspora in films. So these German-speaking foreigners underline the fact that the filmic texts cannot be isolated from their creators. The subsequent approach of reading émigré films against their historical background and the trajectories of those responsible for their making, that was favoured here, places the author of a filmic text and the production context at the centre of attention. It must be stressed, however, that the complex studio production of the 1930s requires a multiple-author model in which individual contributions are not always clear-cut. This book nevertheless shows how experiences of mobility and life in the diaspora – whether voluntary or forced – influenced the aesthetics and narratives of the British cinema from the late 1920s to the early postwar period and beyond. Reading émigré films against the background of their own displaced living conditions has proven a useful method to make visible the accented style which, as Naficy argues, 'helps us to discover commonalities among exilic filmmakers that cut across gender, race, nationality and ethnicity . . ., genres and authorship'.[1]

As the films repeatedly echo the physical and psychological states of the film personnel involved in their making, they commonly engage with nostalgic recollections of the homeland (as in the many Austrian romantic comedies such as *Heart's Desire*) and criticism of the new country of residence or their own uprooted, dislocated identities (as in *Victoria the Great* or *Broken Blossoms*). As a major contribution of German-speaking film professionals to British cinema, such auto-biographical references to exile and diaspora generally support Hamid Naficy's judgment that representations of displaced lives often centre around social-psychological dilemmas associated with cultural displacement and loss. Through narratives that often engage with feelings of panic and pursuit the structures of exilic and diasporic films underscore rupture and uprooted living conditions.[2] Yet this rather negative verdict, which undoubtedly applies to many British films that draw a rather dystopian picture of life in the diaspora, is counteracted as well. Many films made by or with émigrés also celebrate (or at least acknowledge) the traditions and values of their new country of domicile. Besides commenting on Britain, many narratives moreover also deal with diasporic living conditions and the country émigrés had to leave behind. The rise of Nazism frustrates filmic accounts of the old home country Germany and Austria as an unspoilt idyll. As shown, many émigré films coalesce criticism against the Third Reich with an analogous emphasis on the merits of England as a country of refuge. By focussing on transnational existences, concepts of nationality, recollections of the *Heimat* and the new country of domicile, British émigré films represent the full scale of the complex psychological process of immigration and life in the diaspora with its lasting effects on the displaced psyche. The films, thereby, give insight into the minds of German-speaking émigrés that were subject to an assortment of contrasting and conflicting experiences of the old and the new, assimilation processes, loss, trauma, persecution, generous welcome gestures and the emergence of a hybrid identity.

Talking about favourable and unfavourable accounts of exile it must therefore be stressed that few films offer homogeneous representations. It speaks for the quality of many British films made with German-speaking émigrés that they very often refrain from black-and-white images in favour of more nuanced depictions. In collaboration with their British and international colleagues their films are, apart from a few exceptions which confirm the rule, the product of continuous negotiation and of the investigation of nationhood, cultural affinity and migration rather than commonplaces and simplistic statements. As outsiders their texts often took a different perspective – sometimes interrogating mainstream ideas on puristically defined national identity. Films such as *The Life and Death of Colonel Blimp* and *The Gentle Sex* indeed show that cherishing the values of one's new home country does not mean naive or uncritical patriotism.

Foreign actors playing foreign characters in films made by foreign personnel charged British films with a noticeable cosmopolitan feel. Underscoring a general tendency to avoid subtitles in 1930s and 1940s cinema, many émigré films comprise lengthy dialogues in German without any translation adding authenticity to the story of displacement and dislocation of refugees from the Third Reich. By infusing the British cinema with self-reflexive cosmopolitan and disorientating styles, foreign languages, travellers and cultural go-betweens, the films are ethnically coded. This means that in British films made by or with German-speaking personnel, like in other accented cinemas, 'more than not, the actor's ethnicity, the character's ethnicity, and the ethnicity of the star's persona coincide'.[3]

Besides accounts of displacement and the diaspora, another characteristic of British films made with German-speaking émigrés after 1933 were the numerous explicit or implicit political statements against totalitarianism in general and Nazism in particular. Once the war broke out, moreover, filmmakers from Germany and Austria were vital to the production of propaganda films. Indeed, particularly those production companies run by émigrés and which employed a great number of German-speaking film practitioners were at the forefront of making films with an anti-Nazi message. Korda's London Film Productions, Powell's and Pressburger's The Archers and Michael Balcon's Gaumont-British are exemplary. Sometimes, most of the senior staff involved in the production of a single British film consisted of German-speaking émigrés. Through their presence and expertise they not only contributed to the high production values of many British films of the era, they also influenced storylines of films and ways of representation. By way of the performances of exile actors such as Anton Walbrook émigrés moulded public images of good continentals who opposed Hitler and all he stood for. They thereby challenged nationalistic attitudes that tended to condemn Germans lock, stock and barrel. In fact, the contributions by German-speaking immigrants can thus partially explain the nuanced depictions of Germans and foreigners in British films despite a general tendency towards scapegoating the 'foreigner'. Repeatedly in British wartime films German and Austrian exiles underwent a significant transition from enemy alien to foreign ally. So it does not come as a surprise that it is a refugee who in *The Life and Death of Colonel Blimp* informs the British audience about the serious threat posed by Hitler: 'This is not a gentleman's war. This time you are fighting for your existence against the most devilish idea ever concocted by the human brain – Nazism! And if you lose there won't be a return match next year, perhaps not even for a hundred years!'

By differentiating between 'democratic' and 'totalitarian' Germans rather than demonising a whole people, German-speaking film practitioners in Britain furthermore helped to propagate the idea that a new peaceful Germany was possible once the war was over. The speeches Emeric Pressburger wrote for Anton Walbrook, for instance, serve as important statements as they are the voice of the 'other', democratic and humanistic Germany in the realm of cinema. As in Korda's *Rembrandt* (1936), the magus-like characters played by Conrad Veidt and Walbrook, which form an aspect of continuity in the otherwise diverse oeuvre of Powell and Pressburger,[4] can in fact well be seen as a positive counterpole to the exploitation of historical personalities in Third Reich cinema as historical and ideological predecessors of the *Führer* (as in *Bismarck*, 1940; *Robert Koch*, 1939; *Rembrandt*, 1942; *Andreas Schlüter*, 1942; *Der große König*, 1942 and *Diesel*, 1942).

Through fictional characters émigrés aided in warning against the Nazi threat and promoting ideas of democracy and freedom as fundamental British values. Whilst émigré film personnel partly assimilated into British culture, stressing communality rather than divergence, they ultimately remain outsiders aware of their foreign origins. Yet, as Andrew Moor observes in connection with Anton Walbrook, 'with Nazism reserved as the only significant "other" [they become] unthreateningly different.'[5] The film analyses of this study have demonstrated that British films made by émigrés interrogate nationhood and challenge puristically defined notions of national cinema. The narratives of British exile films, at variance with other British productions, combine otherness with Britishness and thereby depict a hybrid émigré identity in which different traditions and influences coalesce.

Postscript: Postwar émigré careers and the question of remigration

When the Second World War ended so did the exile of all German-speaking refugees. And although the unconditional capitulation of Nazi Germany meant that former refugees could theoretically return home, only a minority eventually returned to their former *Heimat*. The individual reasons for this were as manifold as the diverse experiences in exile. As such, the decision of whether to stay or to leave was based on how émigrés considered their current and future situation in Britain on the one hand and in their former home countries on the other.

Owing to the social, political and arguably even the economic situation in Britain from the mid-1940s to the 1950s, the prospects of leaving the country appealed to very few émigrés. Having largely lived in the country for more than a decade, they had often found a new home. Émigrés, indeed, made new friends, learned the language, got accustomed to the culture, and in many cases found steady work following years of initial hardship. The way in which many former refugees had gained a foothold in the British film and media industries, too, meant that they were by now highly regarded and often firmly established figures. This is not to say that émigrés working in the film business did not experience any problems. Some genres in which émigré film personnel particularly prospered since the early 1930s, most notably costume dramas and literary adaptations, declined as part of a wider postwar trend towards cinematic realism that culminated in Free Cinema movement in the mid-1950s, on the one hand, and cost-effective popular Ealing comedies on the other. Yet, there still were many opportunities in popular postwar genres such as war films and thrillers. The late 1940s and 1950s, too, offered new employment opportunities in the fledgling medium of television where technical experts and persons with overseas' contacts and language skills were much sought after as the successful television of Rudolph Cartier among others illustrates.[6] As West Germany, moreover, became an important export market for British films, a number of film companies on Wardour Street employed émigrés to communicate with German distributors and to prepare promotional material for the German market. The German-Jewish film critic Hans Wollenberg, once editor of the trade journal *Die Lichtbildbühne* in the Weimar Republic, was instrumental in organising Ealing's promotional campaign for the German release of its *Dead of Night* (Alberto Cavalcanti, Charles Crighton, Basil Dearden and Robert Hamer, 1945).[7] More generally, the contributions of émigrés to the war effort (not least through their visibility in wartime films) and the postwar revelation of Nazi atrocities against Jews and other minorities improved the standing of émigés in postwar Britain. Whitehall alleviated their position, too, by changing its immigration policies. Naturalisation was now in many cases offered to those who were previously denied British citizenship.[8] As a consequence, the overall situation was fundamentally better for émigrés than in the US, where many German-speaking artists such as Brecht, Eisler and director William Dieterle increasingly came under suspicion by the HUAC committee.

Whereas the overall circumstances were largely favourable to émigrés in Britain, the situation in the different occupation zones in Germany and Austria was less welcoming. The beginning of the Cold War, for instance, complicated matters and exacerbated the already difficult political and economic situation. Above and beyond the general uncertainties, the rebuilding of the German film industry was slow and far from being unproblematic. The end of war did not mark the beginning of a fundamentally new German cinema as postwar German film shared many of its characteristics and, perhaps most importantly, its personnel with Third Reich cinema.[9] This is especially true for the western occupational zones where those who had remained in the Third Reich generally dominated most postwar film productions. With Arthur Brauner only one formerly exiled Jewish producer returned offering employment opportunities specifically to fellow émigrés in 1950s West Germany.[10] This meant that retuning émigrés, more often than not, had to work closely with those who had to varying degrees co-operated with the former regime and who were disinclined to welcome retuning émigrés.

As the enmity towards the outspoken anti-fascist Marlene Dietrich after the war demonstrates, the German and Austrian public was equally hostile, chastising particularly those who have been helping the Allies. Whether because of shame and guilt or open racial antipathy, the postwar German and Austrian media often played their part in repressing the sensitive issue of exile. Hence many encounters between former refugees and those who had remained in the Third Reich are characterised by deep mistrust and awkwardness. In her autobiography, published not in Germany but in Switzerland in 1974, Lilli Palmer told the story of how she was greeted by leading representatives of the German film industry after the war, asking her innocuous questions about her latest film, her family or future plans rather than how she felt being back in Germany after all these years.[11] If returning British émigrés sought to be accepted in postwar Germany, as this and other examples show, they generally had to accept that politics and the Nazi past were to be avoided. Those who complied could be presented as internationally acclaimed German stars in return.[12] This, however, was the exception rather than the norm. Referring to the negative responses towards émigrés particularly in the western zones, Helmut G. Asper draws a very bleak picture: 'If by emigration one means that film émigrés were able to take up positions in film production commensurate with their pre-1933 position and importance after their return, then no remigration . . . of exiled directors and producers to West German film took place'.[13] Even if the situation was somewhat different in the Soviet zone with its newly-founded Deutsche Film AG (DEFA), jobs there were almost exclusively given to staunch Socialists such as Konrad Wolf who typically had been in exile in Moscow and not in London.

The reaction towards émigrés, which was at best indifferent, thus helps to explain why only two films by former refugees dealing with themes of displacement, German guilt, and the disillusionment of returning émigrés were produced in Germany in the immediate years after the war. These were *Der Ruf* (1949), written by Fritz Kortner and directed by Josef von Báky, and *Der Verlorene* (The Lost One, 1951), written and directed by Peter Lorre. In a similar way to Wolfgang Koeppen's novel *Das Treibhaus* (The Hothouse, 1953), in which a former émigré who fails to play an active role in the restructuring of a new Germany eventually commits suicide, both films tell the story of individuals who optimistically returned to Germany only to find that there was little hope for a new democratic country. Following the public rejection as a response to the sensitive plots and the involvement of former émigrés, both films ultimately proved to be economic failures.[14]

Although topics such as the Nazi-enforced migration of mainly Jewish artists, professionals and intellectuals were not strictly taboo, they were – in contrast to a number of films ranging from *Trümmerfilme* (rubble films) to the popular *Heimatfilm* that refer to German refugees expelled from the former east of the Third Reich by the Soviet Army – [15] often treated subtly and often in the form of obscure plots that foreground other conflicts.[16] In contrast to the situation in Britain, where a number of postwar films and television dramas thematised the problems of people displaced from continental Europe as a result of Nazi terror and the beginning of the Cold War such images were largely absent from German screens.[17] In the American, French and British zones and later the Federal Republic of Germany, this development was further aggravated by a penchant for escapist entertainment. Although the history of postwar West German cinema cannot be described adequately as coherent, linear and conformist, commercially successful films nevertheless tended to ignore explicit references to present German problems, thereby underlining a widespread filmic depoliticisation.[18]

The renunciatory reaction towards former refugees and their stories – particularly in the western zones and later in the Federal Republic – was not only restricted to homecoming exiles but also impacted those émigrés who participated in films that were shown in Germany. When regional and national newspapers, for example, covered the German release of *The Red Shoes*, the reviews in the press were varied. Several critics demonstrated their low esteem of British cinema and its émigrés. The *Berliner Zeitung*, for instance, called the film a laughable parody and ironically concluded, alluding to German-speaking émigrés, that British cinema still needed to import a few good directors. In a similar way, *Berliner Blatt/Die neue Zeitung* saw a 'horrible film' ('scheußlicher Film'), a parody even, which featured a performance by Walbrook which was hardly bearable a decade and a half ago ('was vor eineinhalb Jahrzehnten schwer erträglich war').[19] Others were full of praise for what they regarded as a superb artistic achievement.[20] Among them were a few reviews that even specially mention Walbrook's performance by comparing it to the acclaimed roles he had played before he left Germany in *Maskerade* or *Der Student von Prag*.[21] The *Neue Zeit* in Berlin also clearly identifies with Walbrook and Albert Bassermann by calling them 'one of our best'.[22] Such acknowledgments, however, did not mean that the reviews were characterised by a relaxed attitude towards émigrés. Their exile status and the reasons for their flight is evaded as it was in other reviews featuring émigrés. Whilst critics repeatedly acknowledge the participations of former German film stars, they generally fail to explain why they appear in such quantity in the cast and credits of British films. Unlike actors and acresses, whose cultural roots were specially foregrounded in promotional material, the originas of émigré technicians, designers, writers and producers were hardly mentioned in press releases and reviews and thus remained largely unknown in Germany.

The at best indifferent reaction to émigrés thus helps to explain why so few refugees were involved in the British re-education efforts, despite the fact that a number of émigrés had initially offered to play an active role in the restructuring of a new democratic and humanitarian Germany. Berthold Viertel, for instance, put together a concept of how émigrés could participate in the reorganisation of the German theatre and film culture as early as 1944 for the Council for a Democratic Germany.[23] Symptomatically for the experiences of other émigrés, however, his concept was never implemented. Unlike in the American and Soviet occupation zones, where émigrés played a more prominent role in the re-education programmes and media policy, Westminster and Whitehall were largely sceptical as to their usefulness. Not only was the majority of all Germans opposed to former exiles, but Westminster had also been bewildered by the heterogeneity of the German-speaking émigrés in London for some time.[24] As to the postwar British cultural policy for Germany, wartime strategy documents had already laid out that the aim to promote a positive 'British way of life' required émigrés to 'work as much as possible behind the scenes or under appropriate cover'.[25] The fact that they were neither peceived as English or British nourished official doubts as to their usefulness to project a positive image of the UK's values and culture. As people who were perceived as neither sufficiently British nor German or Austrian enough after having spent years abroad, émigrés were figuratively caught between two stools as Gabriele Clemens states.[26]

Even if a minority of émigrés eventually remigrated to Germany or Austria, this does not imply that their impact on early postwar life in the former Third Reich was insignificant. In contrast to official institutions and policies, private film enterprises viewed émigrés rather favourably as a means of product differentiation and marketing material. In fact, émigrés were consciously used as a sales argument for British distributors in Germany. As the promotional material held at the Frankfurt Film Museum archive suggests, some marketing campaigns for British films focussed on émigré stars. An important aspect of the promotion for the *The Queen of Spades* (Therold Dickinson, 1949) by its German distributor Omnium Film, for instance, featured posters and creative playcards as flyers that all promised a 'Reunion with Anton Walbrook (Adolf Wohlbrück)'. In the same vein, the promotional material that was released on the occasion of Kortner's return to Germany – after years of exile in Britain and Hollywood – emphasised that the film was a very personal project:

> The driving force in this film is Fritz Kortner. *Der Ruf* is a passionate testimony for the country of his mother tongue, for the country of his artistic roots, for the country of undestroyable ties – Germany! The homesickness of the university professor returning to Germany [played by Kortner in the film] was his homesickness, and the character's attempt to reconnect to the homeland was his own attempt.[27]

Arguably more than other distributors, Rank's Eagle-Lion-Film in British-occupied Hamburg tried to use the popularity it hoped émigrés still enjoyed in Germany and Austria. Walbrook's and Bassermann's past success before exile, as such, was used as a sales argument for *The Red Shoes*. Besides celebrity cutouts featuring large images of Walbrook and Bassermann (rather than the female lead Moira Shearer), a booklet was posted to cinemas introducing the émigré star: 'Who, at the time, did not sincerely regret the disappearance of Adolf Wohlbrück's expressive face from German screens after his great success in the film "Maskerade" (with Paula Wesseley)?'.[28] The promotional material carefully avoids the real reasons for his departure – by succinctly mentioning that after Hollywood had initially contracted him he continued his career in Britain – so as to avoid the sensitive subject. For the same reason Eagle-Lion-Film, as well as all the other private distributors, refrained from including anti-Nazi films in their catalogue, too. In the few cases in which such films were shown, they were substantially reedited or dubbed so as to remove all references to National Socialism. As Joseph Garncarz notes, 'the "nasty German" character was systematically eliminated from films until the end of the 1950s'.[29] What was a case of self-censorship by American and British film companies, made the promotion of émigrés as homecoming Germans possible to begin with. Whilst the star personae of Walbrook, Palmer and others took on strong anti-fascist and pro-Allied connotations in Britain through their role in wartime films, such images are largely unknown to the German public to this day, allowing public relations departments of British production companies to fill this void by presenting the German and Austrain public with an image of 'their' very own stars who, after an internationally successful career, return to their home country's screens.

It is difficult to determine whether British films with émigrés were more successful than those without in the western zones of the mid- to late 1940s because reliable box-office data is only available since the early 1950s.[30] Given that popular German cinema was, as can be inferred from the analysis of successful films in 1950s West Germany by Joseph Garncarz, relatively autonomous with a very high percentage of national film productions among the ten films of each year, the strategy by British distributors to foreground German-speaking actors in publicity campaigns might have worked as a sales argument. The émigrés Lilli Palmer and Peter van Eyck at least were repeatedly among the ten most famous stars in 1950s and 1960s West Germany respectively.[31]

Across the channel, anyhow, former refugees continued to have an impact on British film culture. As such they were involved in many of the seminal postwar films and television programmes – many of which included themes of displacement, cultural differences and border crossings.

Examples are the Powell and Pressburger productions *Black Narcissus* (1947, besides Pressburger, émigrés contributions include set design: Alfred Junge and William Kellner; and costume design: Hein Heckroth), *The Small Back Room* (1949), *Gone to Earth* (1950) and *The Tales of Hoffmann* (1951, all three films with Pressburger and Heckroth), *The Red Shoes* (again with Pressburger and Heckroth plus the actors Walbrook and Bassermann), John Boulting's *Brighton Rock* (1947, costumes: Honoria Plesch, music: Hans May, cast: Charles Goldner), *Queen of Spades* (1949, producer: Anatole de Grunwald, cinematographer: Otto Heller, set design: William Kellner, cast: Anton Walbrook), Carol Reed's *The Third Man* (1949, besides various German-speaking performances, émigrés contributed as co-producer: Alexander Korda, art director: Vincent Korda, Joseph Bato and Ferdinand Bellan, editor: Oswald Hafenrichter) and *Duel in the Jungle* (1954, producer: Marcel Hellmann, cinematographer: Erwin Hillier, music: Mischa Spoliansky). In addition to films, émigrés were also pivotal to development in early television as Rudolph Cartier's collaboration with the British writer Nigel Kneale's on the BBC's *The Quatermass Experiment* (1954), *Nineteen Eighty-Four* (1954) and *Quatermass II* (1955) illustrates.

Besides a number of émigrés who continued their career until well after the war, some like Cartier indeed only found real success after 1945. Among them were again many technicians and designers. The long list of cinematographers includes Erwin Hillier (who was, among other films, director of cinematography for *Shadow of the Eagle*, Sidney Salkow, 1950 and *The Dam Busters*, Michael Anderson, 1955), Otto Heller (e.g. *They Made Me a Fugitive*, Alberto Cavalcanti, 1947, *The Queen of Spades*, Therold Dickinson, 1949 and *The Ladykillers*, Alexander Mackendrick, 1955), Wolfgang Suschitzky (who worked as photographer and cinematographer, besides numerous documentary films. His name is perhaps best known for his bleak cinematography in *Get Carter*, Mike Hodges, 1971). Among the production designers were Hein Heckroth (who designed, for instance, the sets for several Powell and Pressburger productions in the late 1940s and early 1950s before returning to Germany), Ken Adam (who became one of the most sought-after international set designers ever since his work for the Bond film series) and William Kellner (who was, among other films, responsible for the designs in *Kind Hearts and Coronets*, Robert Hamer, 1949, *Women of Twilight*, Gordon Parry, 1952 and the Isherwood adaptation *I Am a Camera*, Henry Cornelius, 1955). Yet the list of notable émigré contributions well exceeds designers and cinematographers and also features actresses and actors, directors, writers and producers and also includes the children of émigrés film personnel who fled Germany in the 1930s. Here the writer and producer Wolf Rilla, son of German émigré actor Walter Rilla, serves an example. He worked for the film industry (*The*

Village of the Damned, 1960) and perhaps more notably for television (*The Avengers*, 1961–1969; *Zero One*, 1962–1965; and several productions for the BBC's Sundy Night Theatre). As with previous filmmakers, they incorporated aspects of their own lives into their stories. Cartier, for instance, repeatedly returned to the crucial topics of his life such as diaspora, holocaust, totalitarianism and fanaticism in his large oeuvre of television dramas. In so doing many of his theatre adaptations for the BBC – including *It is Midnight, Dr. Schweitzer* (1953), *The Devil's General* (1955), *The Mayerling Affair* (1956), *The Captain of Koepenick* (1958), *Cross of Iron* (1961) and *Dr. Korczak and the Children* (1962) – continued to differentiate between Germans and Nazis and reminded the British public (and his fellow émigrés) that democracy need to be defended to avert a repetition of history.

Owing to the various responsiblities of German-speaking émigrés in post-war British audio-visual culture their legacy well exceeded the actual period of exile that ended in 1945. Time and again they had been part of a vibrant media industry in various capacities, making it impossible to properly understand the history of British cinema without considering the mosaic picture of their contributions.

Notes

1 Naficy, p. 39.
2 See ibid., p. 5.
3 Ibid., p. 24.
4 See Robert Murphy, 'Strong Men: Three Forms of Magus in the Films of Powell and Pressburger', *Screen*, 46.1 (Spring 2005), 63–71.
5 Moor, 'Dangerous Limelight', p. 84.
6 See Tobias Hochscherf, 'From Refugee to the BBC: Rudolph Cartier, Weimar Cinema and Early British Television', *Journal of British Cinema and Television*, 7.3 (2010), 401–20.
7 See file on *Dead of Night* (German release title: *Traum ohne Ende*), German Filmmuseum, Frankfurt/Deutsches Institut für Filmkunde, Frankfurt/Main (hereafter DFF/DIF).
8 Exemplary of many of his fellow émigrés Cartier was eventually naturalised on 15 September 1949 following several unsuccessful earlier attempts. Personal staff file: Rudolph Cartier, BBC Written Archives Centre (WAC), L1/2177/1, 6 June 1952.
9 On the various continuities between Third Reich and postwar German cinema, see Hans-Peter Kochenrath, 'Kontinuität im deutschen Film', in *Film und Gesellschaft in Deutschland: Dokumente und Materialien*, edited by Wilfried von Bredow and Rolf Zurek (Hamburg: Hoffmann und Campe, 1975), pp. 286–92.

10 Claudia Dillmann, 'Treffpunkt Berlin: Artur Brauners Zusammenarbeit mit Emigranten', *FilmExil*, 3 (November 1993), 17–24.

11 Palmer, p. 280.

12 See Helmut G. Asper, 'Remigration und Remigranten im deutschen Film nach 1945', in *Zwischen den Stühlen? Remigranten und Remigration in der deutschen Medienöffentlichkeit der Nachkriegszeit*, edited by Claus-Dieter Krohn und Axel Schildt (= Hamburger Beiträge zur Sozial- und Zeitgeschichte, 39) (Hamburg: Christians, 2002), pp. 161–79 (p. 162).

13 Ibid., p. 174. Translated by Ronald Walker.

14 See Asper, 'Remigration und Remigranten', p. 165–68.

15 See Johannes von Moltke, 'Location *Heimat*: Tracking Refugee Images, from DEFA to *Heimatfilm*', in *Framing the Fifties: Cinema in a Divided Germany*, edited by John Davidson and Sabine Hake (New York and Oxford: Berghahn, 2007), pp. 74–90.

16 See, for instance, Jaimey Fisher's reading of *Der Ruf*, 'The Question of German Guilt and the "German Student": Politicizing the Postwar University in Kortner's *Der Ruf* and Von Wangenheim's *Und Wieder 48*', in *Framing the Fifties*, pp. 10–27 (pp. 16–19).

17 British films and television dramas revolving around émigrés' lives include *Frieda* (Basil Dearden, 1947), *Lost People* (Muriel Box and Bernard Knowles, 1949), *The Fool and the Princess* (William C. Hammond, 1948), *Refuge England* (Robert Vas, 1959), *Echo from Afar* (BBC, 1959) and *Return to Life* (John Krish, 1960).

18 See Hake, pp. 104–14.

19 'Regie, Horatio! „Die roten Schuhe", ein englischer Farbfilm', *Berliner Zeitung*, 1 February 1949 and 'Ein bunter Alpdruck', *Berliner Blatt/Die neue Zeitung*, 28 January 1949, unpaginated press clippings, DFF/DIF, file on *The Red Shoes*.

20 See unpaginated reviews collected in the text archive at the DFF/DIF, file on *The Red Shoes*; the Munich-based *Bayrisches Volks-Echo* from 14 January 1953, wrote 'There are few films as worthy of being called a work of art as this one', the *Allgemeine Zeitung* in Mainz emphasised the "visual effect of the sumptuous colour" and the superb performances (15 March 1950) and Wilhelm Mogge for the *Allgemeine Kölnische Rundschau* concluded – albeit with a minor curtailing that 'details were lovingly envisioned [by Powell and Pressburger] and colour effectively used as a means of artistic expression. "The Red Shoes" is a remarkable film for whose sake some of the sins of this young art form can be forgiven' (18 April 1950). Translated by Ronald Walker.

21 See '„Die roten Schuhe": Welterfolg eines englischen Farbfilms', *Allgemeine Zeitung*, 4 March 1950; and 'Andersens Märchen von den rotten Schuhen', *Nacht-Expreß*, Berlin, 28 January 1949, unpaginated press clippings, DFF/DIF, file on *The Red Shoes*.

22 Hans Wilfert, 'Kühnes Farbenspiel: „Die roten Schuhe" im Marmorhaus', *Neue Zeit*, 30 January 1949, unpaginated press clippings, DFF/DIF, file on *The Red Shoes*.

23 Asper, 'Remigration und Remigranten', pp. 163–4.

24 See Claus-Dieter Krohn and Axel Schildt, 'Einleitung', in *Zwischen den Stühlen?* pp. 9–17.

25 Political Welfare Executive: Control of propaganda and Publicity in Germany after the Cessation of Hostilities and During a period of Occupation, 1 June 1943, NA, FO 898/415. Cited in Gabriele Clemens, 'Remigranten in Kultur- und Medienpolitik der britischen Zone', in *Zwischen den Stühlen?*, pp. 50–65 (p. 56).

26 Clemens, p. 55.

27 Cited in Fisher, p. 27, endnote 5.

28 'Filmdienst: „Die Roten Schuhe"', unpaginated press release information and promotional brochure for *The Red Shoes* by Eagle-Lion-Film, circa 1949, DFF/ DIF, file on *The Red Shoes*.

29 Joseph Garncarz, 'Hollywood in Germany: The Role of American Films in Germany, 1925–1990', in *Hollywood in Europe: Experiences of a Cultural Hegemony*, edited by David W. Elwood and Rob Kroes (Amsterdam: VU University Press, 1994), pp. 94–135 (p. 107).

30 On the success of foreign films in Germany, see Joseph Garncarz, 'Populäres Kino in Deutschland. Internationalisierung einer Filmkultur, 1925–1990', unpublished post-doctoral dissertation (Habilitationsschrift) (Cologne: University of Cologne 1996).

31 Ibid., pp. 396–8.

Sources and Select Bibliography

Archives and Specialist Libraries:

Alfred Kerr Archive, Akademie der Künste, Berlin
British Film Institute (BFI) Library and Special Collections, London
CineGraph, Hamburgisches Zentrum für Filmforschung
Deutsches Filmmuseum Frankfurt (DFF)/Deutsches Institut für Filmkunde (DIF),
   Frankfurt/Main
Deutsches Literaturarchiv, Marbach
Deutsche Kinemathek, Berlin
National Archives, Kew, Richmond, Surrey
National Library of Scotland, Edinburgh

Surveyed Periodicals:

Cine-Technician
Kinematograph Weekly
Pem's-Privat-Berichte

Select Bibliography:

Albrecht, Gerd, *Nationalsozialistische Filmpolitik* (Stuttgart: Enke, 1969)
Aldgate, Anthony, and Jeffrey Richards, *Best of British: Cinema and Society from
   1930 to the Present* (London and New York: I. B. Tauris, 1999)
Asper, Helmut G., *Filmexil in Hollywood: „Etwas besseres als den Tod . . . " – Portraits,
   Filme, Dokumente* (Marburg: Schüren, 2002)
——, 'Film', in *Handbuch der deutschsprachigen Emigration 1933–1945*, edited by
   Claus-Dieter Krohn and others (Darmstadt: Wissenschaftliche Buchgesellschaft,
   1998), pp. 957–70
——, 'Remigration und Remigranten im deutschen Film nach 1945', in *Zwischen
   den Stühlen? Remigranten und Remigration in der deutschen Medienöffentlichkeit
   der Nachkriegszeit*, edited by Claus-Dieter Krohn und Axel Schildt (= Hamburger
   Beiträge zur Sozial- und Zeitgeschichte, 39) (Hamburg: Christians, 2002), pp.
   161–79

Aurich, Rolf, and Wolfgang Jacobsen, eds, *Werkstatt Film: Selbstverständnis und Visionen von Filmleuten der zwanziger Jahre* (Munich: text+kritik, 1998)

Balach, Helga, and others, eds, *Exil: Sechs Schauspieler aus Deutschland: Mit Beiträgen von Gero Gandert, Karsten Witte und Angelika Kaps*, 6 vols (Berlin: Stiftung deutsche Kinemathek, 1983)

Balcon, Michael, *Michael Balcon Presents . . . a Lifetime of Films* (London: Hutchison, 1969)

Bearman, Marietta, and others. *Wien – London hin und retour: Das Austrian Centre in London 1939–1947*, translated. by Miha Tavčar (Vienna: Czernin, 2004)

Benewick, Robert, *The Fascist Movement in Britain* (London: Allan Lane, 1972)

Bentwich, Norman, *The Rescue and Achievement of Refugee Scholars* (The Hague: M. Nijhoff, 1953)

Berger, Stefan, 'British and German Socialists Between Class and National Solidarity', in *Nationalism, Labour and Ethnicity, 1870–1939*, edited by Stefan Berger and Angel Smith (Manchester and New York: Man University Press, 1999), pp. 31–63

Bergfelder, Tim, 'National, Transnational of Supranational Cinema? Rethinking European Film Studies', *Media, Culture & Society*, 27.3 (2005), pp. 315–31

——, 'Negotiating Exoticism: Hollywood, Film Europe and the Cultural Reception of Anna May Wong', in *'Film Europe' and 'Film America': Cinema, Commerce and Cultural Exchange 1920–1939*, edited by Andrew Higson and Richard Maltby, Exeter Studies in Film History (Exeter: Exeter University Press, 1999), pp. 302–24

——, 'The Production Designer and the *Gesamtkunstwerk*: German Film Technicians in the British Film Industry of the 1930s', in *Dissolving Views: Key Writings on British Cinema*, edited by Andrew Higson (London and New York: Cassell, 1996), pp. 20–37

——, and Christian Cargnelli, eds, *Destination London: German-speaking Emigrés and British Cinema, 1925–1950* (Oxford and New York: Berghahn, 2008)

Berghahn, Marion, *Continental Britons: German-Jewish Refugees from Nazi Germany* (Oxford and New York: Berg, 1988)

——, *German-Jewish Refugees in England* (London: Macmillan, 1984)

——, 'German Jews in England', in *Exile in Great Britain: Refugees from Hitler's Germany*, edited by Gerhard Hirschfeld (Leamington Spa: Berg, 1984), pp. 285–306

Bock, Hans-Michael, and Michael Töteberg, 'A History of UFA', in *The German Cinema Book*, edited by Tim Bergfelder, Erica Carter and Deniz Göktürk (London: BFI, 2002), pp. 129–38

Brandlmeier, Thomas, '"Rationalization First": Deutsche Kameraschule im britischen Film', in *London Calling: Deutsche im britischen Film der dreißiger Jahre*, edited by Jörg Schöning (Munich: text+kritik, 1993), pp. 69–76

Brandt, Georg W., 'Thespis behind the Wire, or Entertainment in Internment: A Personal Recollection', in *Theatre and Film in Exile: German Artists in Britain, 1933–1945*, edited by Günter Berghaus (Oxford and New York: Berg, 1989), pp. 223–29

Brinson, Charmian, 'Facing the Facts: Relations with the "Heimat"', in *Changing Countries: The Experience and Achievement of German-speaking Exiles from Hitler in Britain from 1933 to Today*, edited by Marian Malet and Anthony Grenville (London: Libris, 2002), pp. 184–216

——, 'A Woman's Place . . .?: German-Speaking Women in Exile in Britain, 1933–1945', *German Life and Letters*, 51.2 (April 1998), 204–24

——, Richard Dove and Jennifer Taylor, eds, *'Immortal Austria?': Austrians in Exile in Britain* (= Yearbook of the Research Centre for German and Austrian Exile Studies, 8 (2006))

Brown, Geoff, *Michael Balcon: The Pursuit of British Cinema* (New York: The Museum of Modern Art, 1984)

——, 'Niederlage in Wembley: Tobis Klangfilm in England', in *Tonfilmfrieden/ Tonfilmkrieg: Die Geschichte der Tobis vom Technik-Syndikat zum Staatskonzern*, edited by Jan Distelmeyer (Munich: text+kritik, 2003), pp. 65–72

Burrows, Jon, 'Big Studio Production in the Pre-quota Years', in *The British Cinema Book*, edited by Robert Murphy, 2nd edn (London: BFI, 2001), pp. 20–7

Buxton, Dorothy Frances, *The Economics of the Refugee Problem* (London: Focus, 1939)

Cargnelli, Christian, 'Wien-Bilder: Paul L. Stein, Richard Tauber und das britische Kino', *'Immortal Austria': Austrians in Exile in Britain*, edited by Charmian Brinson, Richard Dove and Jennifer Taylor (= Yearbook of the Research Centre for German and Austrian Exile Studies, 8 (2006)), pp. 105–20

——, Brigitte Mayr and Michael Omasta, eds, *Carl Mayer – Scenar(t)ist: Ein Script von ihm war schon ein Film* (Vienna: Synema, 2003)

Cesarani, David, *Britain and the Holocaust* (London: Holocaust Educational Trust, 1998)

——, *Justice Delayed* (London: Heinemann, 1992)

Chanan, Michael, 'The Emergence of an Industry', in *British Cinema History*, edited by James Curran and Vincent Porter (London: Weidenfeld and Nicolson, 1983), pp. 39–58

Chapman, James, *The British at War: Cinema, State and Propaganda, 1939–1945* (London and New York: I. B. Tauris, 1998)

——, 'Why we fight: *Pastor Hall* and *Thunder Rock*', in *The Family Way: The Boulting Brothers and British Film Culture*, edited by Alan Burton, Tim O'Sullivan and Paul Wells (Trowbridge: Flicks Books, 2000), pp. 81–96

——, '"The true business of the British movie"? *A Matter of Life and Death* and British Film Culture', *Screen*, 46.1 (2005), 33–49 (p.35)

Christie, Ian, '*Blimp*, Churchill and the State', in *Powell, Pressburger and Others*, edited by Ian Christie (London: BFI, 1978), pp. 105–20

——, *A Matter of Life and Death*, BFI Film Classics (London: BFI, 2000)

——, ed., *Powell, Pressburger and Others*, edited by Ian Christie (London: BFI, 1978)

——, and Andrew Moor, eds, *The Cinema of Michael Powell: International Perspectives on an English Film-maker* (London: BFI, 2005)

Clarke, Alan, '"Theatre behind Barbed Wire: German Refugee Theatre in British

Internment", in *Theatre and Film in Exile: German Artists in Britain, 1933–1945*, edited by Günter Berghaus (Oxford and New York: Berg, 1989), pp. 189–222

——, "'They Came to a Country": German Theatre Practitioners in Exile in Great Britain, 1938–45', in *Theatre and Film in Exile: German Artists in Britain, 1933–1945*, edited by Günter Berghaus (Oxford and New York: Berg, 1989), pp. 99–119

Clemens, Gabriele, 'Remigranten in Kultur- und Medienpolitik der britischen Zone', in *Zwischen den Stühlen? Remigranten und Remigration in der deutschen Medienöffentlichkeit der Nachkriegszeit*, edited by Claus-Dieter Krohn und Axel Schildt (= Hamburger Beiträge zur Sozial- und Zeitgeschichte, 39) (Hamburg: Christians, 2002), pp. 50–65

Collinson, Naomi, 'The Legacy of Max Schach', *Film History*, 15.3 (2003), 376–89

Cook, Pam, *I Know Where I'm Going*, BFI Film Classics 65 (London: BFI, 2002)

Copsey, Nigel, *Anti-Fascism in Britain* (Basingstoke: MacMillan, 2000)

Corrigan, Philip, 'Film Entertainment as Ideology and Pleasure: A Preliminary Approach to a History of Audiences', in *British Cinema History*, edited by James Curran and Vincent Porter (London: Weidenfeld & Nicolson, 1983), pp. 24–35

Cull, Nicholas John, *Selling War: The British Propaganda Campaign Against American 'Neutrality' in World War II* (New York and Oxford: Oxford University Press, 1995)

Dillmann, Claudia, 'Treffpunkt Berlin: Artur Brauners Zusammenarbeit mit Emigranten', *FilmExil*, 3 (November 1993), 17–24

Distelmeyer, Jan, ed., *Alliierte für den Film: Arnold Pressburger, Gregor Rabinowitsch und die Cine-Allianz* (Munich: text+kritik, 2004)

——, ed., *Tonfilmfrieden/Tonfilmkrieg: Die Geschichte der Tobis vom Technik-Syndikat zum Staatskonzern* (Munich: text+kritik, 2003)

Dove, Richard, *Journey of No Return: Five German-speaking Literary Exiles in Britain, 1933–1945* (London: Libris, 2000)

——, ed., *'Totally un-English?': Britain's Internment of 'Enemy Aliens' in Two World Wars* (= Yearbook of the Research Centre for German and Austrian Exile Studies, 7 (2005))

Ede, Laurie, 'Capital and Creativity: Notes on the British Film Art Director of the 1940s', *Screen*, 45.4 (Winter 2004), pp. 367–74

Elsaesser, Thomas, 'A German Ancestry to Film Noir? Film History and its Imaginery', *Iris* 21 (Spring 1996), 129–44

——, 'Heavy Traffic: Perspektive Hollywood: Emigranten oder Vagabunden?', in *LondonCalling: Deutsche im britischen Film der dreißiger Jahre*, edited by Jörg Schöning (Munich: text+kritik, 1993), pp. 21–41

——, *Weimar Cinema and After: Germany's Historical Imaginary* (New York and London: Routledge, 2000)

——, with Michael Wedel, eds, *The BFI Companion to German Cinema* (London: BFI, 1999)

Falcon, Richard, 'No Politics!: "German Affairs" im Spionage- und Kostümfilm', in *London Calling: Deutsche im britischen Film der dreißiger Jahre*, edited by Jörg Schöning (Munich: text+kritik, 1993), pp. 77–88

Fisher, Jaimey, 'The Question of German Guilt and the "German Student": Politicizing the Postwar University in Kortner's *Der Ruf* and Von Wangenheim's *Und Wieder 48*', in *Framing the Fifties: Cinema in a Divided Germany*, edited by John Davidson and Sabine Hake (New York and Oxford: Berghahn, 2007), pp. 10–27

Fuchs, Christoph, 'In Labyrinth der Allianzen: Die Metamorphose des Fimenblabels "Cine-Allianz"', in *Aliierte für den Film: Arnold Pressburger, Gregor Rabinowitsch und die Cine-Allianz*, edited by Jan Distelmeyer (Munich: text+kritik: 2004), pp. 34–45

Garncarz, Joseph, 'Die Bedrohte Internationalität des Films: Fremdsprachige Versionen deutscher Tonfilme', in *Hallo? Berlin? Ici Paris!*, edited by Sibylle M. Sturm and Arthur Wohlgemuth (Munich: text+kritik, 1996), pp. 127–40

——, 'Hollywood in Germany: The Role of American Films in Germany, 1925–1990', in *Hollywood in Europe: Experiences of a Cultural Hegemony*, edited by David W. Elwood and Rob Kroes (Amsterdam: VU University Press, 1994), pp. 94–135

——, 'Populäres Kino in Deutschland. Internationalisierung einer Filmkultur, 1925–1990', unpublished post-doctoral dissertation (Habilitationsschrift) (Cologne: University of Cologne 1996)

Gemünden, Gerd, 'From "Mr. M" to "Mr. Murder": Peter Lorre and the Actor in Exile', in *Light Motives: German Popular Film in Perspective*, edited by Randall Halle and Margaret McCarthy (Detroit, MI: Wayne State University Press, 2003), pp. 85–107

——, and Anton Kaes, 'Introduction', *New German Critique*, 89 (Spring/Summer 2003), 3–8

Gilbert, Martin, *Auschwitz and the Allies* (London: Michael Joseph, 1981)

Gillman, Peter, and Leni Gillman, *'Collar the Lot!': How Britain Interned and Expelled its Wartime Refugees* (London: Quartlet Books, 1980)

Gledhill, Christine, *Reframing British Cinema 1918–1928: Between Restraint and Passion* (London: BFI, 2003)

Göktürk, Deniz, 'Transnational Connections – Introduction', in *The German Cinema Book*, edited by Tim Bergfelder, Erica Carter and Deniz Göktürk (London: BFI, 2002), pp. 213–16

Goergen, Jeanpaul, 'Entente und Stabilisierung: Deutsch-französische Filmkontakte 1925–1933', in *Hallo? Berlin? Ici Paris!*, edited by Sibylle M. Sturm and Arthur Wohlgemuth (Munich: text+kritik, 1996), pp. 51–62

Gough-Yates, Kevin, 'The BBC as a Source of Employment for Film Workers and Composers during the War', in *Literatur und Kultur des Exils in Großbritannien*, edited by Siglinde Bolbecher et al., Zwischenwelt, 4 (Vienna: Verlag für Gesellschaftskritik, 1995), pp. 215–40

——, 'Berthold Viertel at Gaumont-British', in *The Unknown 1930s: An Alternative History of the British Cinema, 1929–1939*, edited by Jeffrey Richards (London and New York: I. B. Tauris, 2000), pp. 201–17

——, 'The British Feature Film as a European Concern: Britain and the Emigré Filmmaker, 1933–45', in *Theatre and Film in Exile: German Artists in Britain,*

1933–1945, edited by Günther Berghaus (Oxford and New York: Berg, 1989), pp. 135–66

——, 'The European Filmmaker in Exile in Britain, 1933–1945' (unpublished doctoral thesis, Open University, UK, 1990)

——, 'Exiles and British Cinema', in *The British Cinema Book*, edited by Robert Murphy, 2nd edn (London: BFI, 2001), pp. 104–13

——, 'Jews and Exiles in British Cinema', *Leo Baek Institute Yearbook*, 37 (1992), 517–41

——, *Michael Powell in Collaboration with Emeric Pressburger* (London: BFI, 1971)

Guy, Stephen, 'Calling All Stars: Musical Films in a Musical Decade', in *The Unknown 1930s: An Alternative History of the British Cinema, 1929–1939* (London and New York: I. B. Tauris, 2000), pp. 99–118

Hampicke, Evelyn, and Jürgen Bretschneider, 'Biografie', in *Ewald André Dupont: Autor und Regisseur*, edited by Jürgen Bretschneider (Munich: text+kritik, 1992), pp. 111–26

Harper, Sue, '"Thinking Forward and Up": The British Films of Conrad Veidt', in *The Unknown 1930s: An Alternative History of the British Cinema, 1929–1939*, edited by Jeffrey Richards (London and New York: I. B. Tauris, 2000), pp. 120–37

Higson, Andrew, '"A Film League of Nations": Gainsborough, Gaumont-British and "Film Europe"', in *Gainsborough Pictures*, edited by Pam Cook, Rethinking British Cinema Series (London and Washington, DC: Cassell, 1997), pp. 60–79

——, 'FILM-EUROPA: Kulturpolitik und industrielle Praxis', in *Hallo? Berlin? Ici Paris!*, edited by Sibylle M. Sturm and Arthur Wohlgemuth (Munich: text+kritik, 1996), pp. 63–76

——, 'The Limiting Imagination of National Cinema', in *Cinema and Nation*, edited by Mette Hjort and Scott MacKenzie (London and New York: Routledge, 2000), pp. 63–74

——, 'Polyglot Films for an International Market: E. A. Dupont, the British Film Industry, and the Idea of a European Cinema, 1926–1930', in *'Film Europe' and 'Film America': Cinema, Commerce and Cultural Exchange 1920–1939*, edited by Andrew Higson and Richard Maltby (Exeter: Exeter University Press, 1999), pp. 274–301

——, 'Transnational Developments in European Cinema in the 1920s', *Transnational Cinemas*, 1.1 (2010), 69–82

——, and Richard Maltby, '"Film Europe" and "Film America": An Introduction', in *'Film Europe' and 'Film America': Cinema, Commerce and Cultural Exchange 1920–1939*, edited by Andrew Higson and Richard Maltby, Exeter Studies in Film History (Exeter: Exeter University Press, 1999), pp. 1–31

Hilchenbach, Maria, *Kino im Exil: Die Emigration deutscher Filmkünstler 1933–1945* (Munich: Saur, 1982)

Hirschfeld, Gerhard, 'Great Britain and the Emigration from Nazi Germany: A Historical Overview', in *Theatre and Film in Exile: German Artists in Britain, 1933–1945*, edited by Günter Berghaus (London and New York: Berg, 1989), pp. 1–14

Hochscherf, Tobias, 'From Refugee to the BBC: Rudolph Cartier, Weimar Cinema and Early British Television', *Journal of British Cinema and Television*, 7.3 (2010), 401–20

Holmes, Colin, *Anti-semitism in British Society, 1876–1939* (London: Edward Arnold, 1979), pp. 214–19

Horak, Jan-Christopher, 'Exilfilm, 1933–1945: In der Fremde', in *Geschichte des deutschen Films*, ed. by Wolfgang Jacobsen, Anton Kaes and Hans Helmut Prinzler (Stuttgart: Metzler, 2004), pp. 99–116

——, *Fluchtpunkt Hollywood: Eine Dokumentation zur Filmemigration nach 1933*, 2nd edn (Münster: MAkS, 1986)

——, 'German Exile Cinema, 1933–1950', *Film History*, 8.4 (1996), 373–89

——, 'On the Road to Hollywood: German-speaking Filmmakers in Exile 1933– 1950', in *Kulturelle Wechselbeziehungen im Exil – Exile Across Cultures*, edited by Helmut F. Pfanner (Bonn: Bouvier, 1986), pp. 240–8

——, 'Wunderliche Schicksalsfügung: Emigranten in Hollywoods Anti-Nazi-Film', *Exilforschung – Ein internationales Jahrbuch*, 2 (1984), 257–70

Howald, Stefan and Irene Wells, 'Everyday Life in Prewar and Wartime Britain', in *Changing Countries: The Experience and Achievement of German-speaking Exiles From Hitler in Britain From 1933 to Today*, edited by Marian Malet and Anthony Grenville (London: Libris, 2002), pp. 90–126

Jacobsen, Wolfgang, ed., *Conrad Veidt: Lebensbilder – Ausgewählte Fotos und Texte* (Berlin: Argon, 1993)

Joannou, Maroula, 'Powell, Pressburger, and Englishness', *European Journal of English Studies*, 8.2 (2004), 189–203

Kaes, Anton, 'A Stranger in the House: Fritz Lang's *Fury* and the Cinema of Exile', *New German Critique*, 89 (Spring/Summer 2003), 33–58

Klugescheid, Andreas, '"His Majesty's Most Loyal Enemy Aliens": Der Kampf deutsch-jüdischer Emigranten in den britischen Streitkräften, 1939–1945', in *Jüdische Emigration zwischen Assimilation und Verfolgung, Akkulturation und jüdischer Identität*, edited by Claus-Dieter Krohn (= *Exilforschung: Ein Internationales Jahrbuch*, 19 (2001)), pp. 106–27

Kochenrath, Peter, 'Kontinuität im deutschen Film', in *Film und Gesellschaft in Deutschland: Dokumente und Materialien*, edited by Wilfried von Bredow and Rolf Zurek (Hamburg: Hoffmann und Campe, 1975), pp. 286–92

Kracauer, Siegfried, 'National Types as Hollywood Presents Them', *Public Opinion Quarterly*, 13.1 (Spring 1949), 53–72

Krämer, Peter, 'Hollywood in Germany/Germany in Hollywood', in *The German Cinema Book*, edited by Tim Bergfelder, Erica Carter and Deniz Göktürk (London: BFI, 2002), pp. 227–37

Kreimeier, Klaus, *The UFA Story: A History of Germany's Greatest Film Company, 1918–1945* (Berkeley/Los Angeles/London: California University Press, 1999)

Kulik, Karol, *Alexander Korda: The Man Who Could Work Miracles* (London: W.H. Allan, 1975)

Kushner, Tony, 'The British and the Shoah', *Patterns of Prejudice*, 23.3 (Autumn 1989), 3–16

——, 'The Impact of the Holocaust on British Society and Culture', *Contemporary Record*, 5.1 (Autumn 1991), 349–75

——, *The Persistence of Prejudice: Antisemitism in British Society During the Second World War* (Manchester and New York: Manchester University Press, 1989)

——, 'Remembering to Forget: Racism and Anti-Racism in Postwar Britain', in *Modernity, Culture and 'the Jew'*, edited by Bryan Cheyette and Laura Marcus (Cambridge: Polity Press, 1998), pp. 226–41

Lafitte, François, *The Internment of Aliens* (London: Penguin, 1940; repr. London: Libris, 1988)

Lant, Antonia, *Blackout: Reinventing Women for Wartime British Audiences* (Princeton: Princeton University Press, 1991)

London, Louise, 'British Immigration Control Procedures and Jewish Refugees 1933–1939', in *Second Chance: Two Centuries of German-speaking Jews in the United Kingdom*, edited by Werner E. Mosse et al., (= Schriftenreihe wissenschaftlicher Abhandlungen des Leo Baeck Instituts 48) (Tübingen: Mohr, 1991), pp. 458–518

——, *Whitehall and the Jews, 1933–1948: British Immigration Policy, Jewish Refugees and the Holocaust* (Cambridge: Cambridge University Press, 2000)

Low, Rachael, *Filmmaking in 1930s Britain* (London: Allen & Unwin, 1985)

——, *The History of the British Film, 1918–29* (London: Allen & Unwin, 1971)

Lusted, David, '"Builders" and "The Demi-Paradise"', in *National Fictions*, edited by Geoff Hurd (London: BFI, 1984), pp. 27–30

Macdonald, Kevin, *Emeric Pressburger: The Life and Death of a Screenwriter* (London and Boston: Faber and Faber, 1994)

McLaine, Ian, *Ministry of Morale – Home Front Morale and the Ministry of Information in World War II* (London, Boston, MA and Sydney: Allen & Unwin, 1979)

Macnab, Geoffrey, *J. Arthur Rank and the British Film Industry* (London and New York: Routledge, 1993)

Malet, Marian, and Anthony Grenville, eds, *Changing Countries: The Experience and Achievement of German-speaking Exiles from Hitler in Britain from 1933 to Today* (London: Libris, 2002)

Moltke, Johannes von, 'Location *Heimat*: Tracking Refugee Images, from DEFA to *Heimatfilm*', in *Framing the Fifties: Cinema in a Divided Germany*, edited by John Davidson and Sabine Hake (New York and Oxford: Berghahn, 2007), pp. 74–90

Moor, Andrew, 'Dangerous Limelight: Anton Walbrook and the Seduction of the English', in *British Stars and Stardom: From Alma Taylor to Sean Connery*, edited by Bruce Babington (Manchester and New York: Manchester University Press, 2001), pp. 80–93

——, 'No Place Like Home: Powell, Pressburger Utopia', in *The British Cinema Book*, edited by Robert Murphy, 2nd edn (London: BFI, 2003), pp. 109–13

——, *Powell & Pressburger: A Cinema of Magic Spaces* (London and New York: I. B. Tauris, 2005)

Murphy, Robert, 'The Coming of Sound to the Cinema in Britain', *Historical Journal of Film, Radio and Television*, 4.2 (March 1984), 143–60

——, *Realism and Tinsel: Cinema and Society in Britain, 1939–49* (London and New York: Routledge, 1989; reprinted 1992)

——, 'Strong Men: Three Forms of Magus in the Films of Powell and Pressburger', *Screen*, 46.1 (Spring 2005), 63–71

Naficy, Hamid, *An Accented Cinema: Exilic and Diasporic Filmmaking* (Princeton, NJ: Princeton University Press, 2001)

Neugebauer, Rosamunde, 'Anti-Nazi-Cartoons deutschsprachiger Emigranten in Großbritannien: Ein spezielles Kapitel Karikaturengeschichte', in *Ästhetiken des Exils*, edited by Helga Schreckenberger (= Amsterdamer Beiträge zur neueren Germanistik, 54 (2003)), pp. 93–122

Oakley, Charles A., *Where We Came In: Seventy Years of the British Film Industry* (London: Allen & Unwin, 1964)

Omasta, Michael, Brigitte Mayr and Ursula Seeber, eds, *Wolfgang Suschitzky: Photos* (Vienna: Synema, 2006)

——, and Brigitte Mayr, eds, *Wolfgang Suschitzky: Films* (Vienna: Synema, 2010)

Panayi, Panikos, *Outsiders: A History of European Minorities* (London: Hambledon Press, 1999)

——, ed., *Germans in Britain since 1500* (London: Hambledon Press, 1996)

——, ed., *Immigration, Ethnicity, and Racism in Britain, 1815–1945* (Manchester: Manchester University Press, 1994)

——, ed., *Minorities in Wartime: National and Racial Groupings in Europe, North America and Australia During the Two World Wars* (Oxford and New York: Berg, 1993)

Petley, Julian, 'Film Policy in the Third Reich', in *The German Cinema Book*, edited by Tim Bergfelder, Erica Carter and Deniz Göktürk (London: BFI, 2002), pp. 173–81

Phillips, Alastair, *City of Darkness, City of Light: Émigré Filmmakers in Paris 1929–1939* (Amsterdam: Amsterdam University Press, 2004)

Political & Economic Planning (PEP), 'The British Film Industry – A Report on its History and Present Organisation, With Special Reference to the Economic Problems of British Feature Film Production' (London: PEP, 1952)

Powell, Michael, *A Life in Movies: An Autobiography*, 2nd edn (London: Faber and Faber, 2000)

Pross, Steffen, *„In London treffen wir uns wieder": Vier Spaziergänge durch ein vergessenes Kapitel deutscher Kulturgeschichte* (Berlin: Eichborn, 2000)

Ramsden, John, *Don't Mention the War: The British and the Germans Since 1890* (London: Little, Brown, 2006)

Reeves, Nicholas, 'Official British Film Propaganda', in *The First World War and Popular Cinema: 1914 to Present*, edited by Michael Paris (New Brunswick, NJ.: Rutgers University Press)

Richards, Jeffrey, *The Age of the Dream Palace: Cinema and Society in Britain 1930–1939* (London: Routledge and Kegan Paul, 1984)

——, 'The British Board of Film Censors and Content Control in the 1930s: foreign affairs', *Historical Journal of Film, Radio and Television*, 2.1 (1982), 39–48

——, 'National Identity in British Wartime Films', in *Britain and the Cinema in the Second World War*, edited by Philip M. Taylor (New York: St. Martin's Press, 1988), pp. 42–61

——, 'Wartime Cinema Audiences and the Class System – The Case of *Ships With Wings* (1941)', *Historical Journal of Film, Radio and Television*, 7.2 (1987), 129–41

——, ed., *The Unknown 1930s: An Alternative History of the British Cinema, 1929–1939* (London and New York: I. B. Tauris, 2000)

Richie, James Macpherson, 'German Refugees from Nazism', in *Germans in Britain Since 1500*, edited by Panikos Panayi (London and Rio Grande, OH: The Hambledon Press, 1996), p. 147–70

Robertson, James C., *The British Board of Film Censors: Film Censorship in Britain, 1896–1950* (London, Sydney and Dover, NH: Croom Helm, 1985)

——, 'British Film Censorship Goes to War', *Historical Journal of Film, Radio and Television*, 2.1 (1982), 49–64

——, *The Hidden Cinema: British Film Censorship in Action, 1913–1975* (London and New York: Routledge, 1993)

Rose, Sonya O., 'Sex, Citizenship, and the Nation in World War II Britain,' *American Historical Review*, 103.4 (October 1998), 1147–76

——, *Which People's War? Identity and Citizenship in Britain 1939–1945* (Oxford: Oxford University Press, 2004)

Rotha, Paul, *The Film Till Now: A Survey of the Cinema* (London: Jonathan Cape, 1930)

——, *Rotha on the Film: A Selection of Writings about the Cinema* (London: Faber and Faber, 1958)

Rubinstein, Bill, *The Myth of Rescue* (London and New York: Routledge, 1997)

Ryall, Tom, 'A British Studio System: The Associated British Picture Corporation and the Gaumont-British Picture Corporation in the 1930s', in *The British Cinema Book*, edited by Robert Murphy, 2nd edn (London: BFI, 2001), pp. 35–41

Schöning, Jörg, 'All Hands Abroad: Kleines Lexikon deutschsprachiger Filmschaffender in Großbritannien 1925–1945', in *London Calling: Deutsche im britischen Film der dreißiger Jahre*, edited by Jörg Schöning (Munich: text+kritik, 1993), pp. 99–150

——, ed., *London Calling: Deutsche im britischen Film der dreißiger Jahre* (Munich: text+kritik, 1993)

Sedgwick, John, 'Film "Hits" and "Misses" in Mid-1930s Britain', *Historical Journal of Film, Radio and Television*, 18.3 (1998), 333–51

——, 'The Market for Feature Films in Britain, 1934: a viable national cinema', *Historical Journal of Film, Radio and Television*, 14.1 (1994), 15–36

Shafer, Stephen C., *British Popular Films 1929–1939: The Cinema of Reassurance* (London and New York: Routledge, 1997)

Snowman, Daniel, *The Hitler Emigres: The Cultural Impact on Britain of Refugees from Nazism*, 2nd edn (London: Pimlico, 2003)

Steinbauer-Grötsch, Barbara, *Die Lange Nacht der Schatten: Film noir und Filmexil*, 2nd rev. edn (Berlin: Bertz, 2000)

——, '"Two shadowy figures framed à la Siodmak . . .": Der deutsche Stummfilm, die Filmexilanten und der amerikanische Film Noir', *FilmExil*, 6 (1995), 53–71

Stent, Ronald, *A Bespattered Page: The Internment of 'His Majesty's Most Loyal Enemy Aliens'* (London: André Deutsch, 1980)

Street, Sarah, 'Alexander Korda, Prudential Assurance and British Film Finance in the 1930s', *Historical Journal of Film, Radio and Television*, 6.2 (1986), 161–79

——, 'British Film and the National Interest, 1927–39', in *The British Cinema Book*, edited by Robert Murphy, 2nd edn (London: BFI, 2003), pp. 20–37

——, *British National Cinema* (London and New York: Routledge, 1997)

——, *Transatlantic Crossings: British Feature Films in the United States* (New York and London: Continuum, 2002)

Strickhausen, Waltraud, 'Großbritannien', in *Handbuch der deutschsprachigen Emigration 1933–1945*, edited by Claus-Dieter Krohn and others (Darmstadt: Wiss. Buchgesellschaft, 1998), pp. 251–70

Taylor, Philip M., ed., *Britain and the Cinema in the Second World War* (New York: St. Martin's Press, 1988)

Tegel, Susan, 'The Politics of Censorship: Britain's "Jew Suss" (1934) in London, New York and Vienna', *Historical Journal of Film, Radio and Television*, 15.2 (June 1995), 219–45

Thorpe, Francis, and Nicholas Pronay, *British Official Films in the Second World War* (Oxford: Oxford University Press, 1980)

Viertel, Salka, *The Kindness of Strangers* (New York: Holt, Rinehart and Winston, 1969)

Vietor-Engländer, Deborah, 'Alfred Kerr's Unknown Film Scripts Written in Exile: The Famous Critic and His Change of Genre', in *Ästhetiken des Exils*, edited by Helga Schreckenberger (= Amsterdamer Beiträge zur neueren Germanistik, 54 (2003)), pp. 123–39

Vincent, Jutta, *Identity and Image: Refugee Artists from Nazi Germany in Britain (1933–1945)*, Schriften der Guernica Gesellschaft: Kunst, Kultur und Politik im 20. Jahrhundert (Weimar: VDG, 2006)

Völker, Klaus, *Elisabeth Bergner: Das Leben einer Schauspielerin ganz und doch unvollendet*, (= Beiträge zu Theater, Film und Fernsehen aus dem Institut für Theaterwissenschaften der Freien Universität Berlin, 4) (Berlin: Edition Hentrich, 1990)

Walker, Greg, 'The Roots of Alexander Korda: myths of Identity and the International Film', *Patterns of Prejudice*, 37.1 (2003), 3–25

Wasserstein, Bernard, *Britain and the Jews of Europe, 1939–1945*, 2nd edn (London and New York: Leicester University Press, 1999)

Index

231

Barr, Charles 156–7
Bassermann, Albert 213, 215–16
Bato, Joseph 171, 216
Battle of Cable Street (4 October 1936)
 82, 109
BBC *see* British Broadcasting
 Corporation
Becker, Rudolph 25
Beery, Noah 129
Bell, George (Lord Bishop of
 Chichester) 83
Bellan, Ferdinand 75, 87, 123,
 216
Bells, The (Oscar Werndorff and
 Harcourt Templeman, UK 1931)
 25–6
Benjamin, Walter 98
Bentwich, Norman 117
Bergfelder, Tim 6, 8–9, 18, 28, 30, 35,
 46, 65, 73, 126
Berghahn, Marion 117
Bergner, Elisabeth 2, 34, 67–9, 74, 76,
 83, 121, 127
Bernauer, Rudolf 75, 83, 95–6, 105,
 121, 158
Bernelle, Agnes 83
Bettauer, Hugo 81
Betts, Ernest 192
Bhabha, Homi 8
Binder, Sybilla 60, 155, 182
BIP *see* British International Pictures
Biró, Lajos 1–2, 68–9, 74–5, 87, 95,
 121, 127
Bismarck (Wolfgang Liebeneiner,
 Germany 1940) 210
Blackguard, The (*Die Prinzessin und
 der Geiger*, Graham Cutts, UK/
 Germany 1925) 21
Black Narcissus (Michael Powell and
 Emeric Pressburger, UK 1947)
 177, 216
Blossom Time (Paul L. Stein, UK 1934)
 71
Bochmann, Werner 65
Bolvary, Geza von 30
Bomben auf Monte Carlo (Hanns
 Schwarz, Germany 1931) 81

Bond, Ralph 120
Bornemann, Ernst 74
Borzy (Gustav von Wangenheim, USSR
 1936), 4, 79
Boulting, John Edward 181
Boulting, Roy Alfred Clarence 181
Boyer, Charles 108
Brahm, Hans (John) 114–16
Brahm, John *see* Brahm, Hans
Brandes, Werner 2, 21, 29, 31–2, 38,
 41, 45, 205
Brandlmeier, Thomas 6
Brauner, Arthur 211
Brav, Ludwig 149
Brecht, Bertolt v, 64, 79, 112, 211
Breslauer, Hans Karl 81
Brighton Rock (John Boulting, UK
 1947) 216
British & Foreign Films (film
 company) 24
British Board of Film Censors (BBFC)
 47, 79–86, 89, 91–2, 94–5, 97,
 156–7, 160, 166
British Broadcasting Corporation
 (BBC) 2, 155, 216–17
British Chemicolour (film company)
 112, 124
British Cine-Alliance (film company)
 26
British International Pictures (BIP, film
 company) 1, 9, 17, 20, 22–3,
 29–33, 38, 44, 73, 78
British National Pictures (film
 company) 30, 155
British Talking Pictures (BTP, film
 company) 25
British Union of Fascists (BUF) 93,
 115, 117
 see also Mosley, Oswald
Brodsky, Nicholas 59, 76
Brodszky, Miklós/Nikolaus *see* Brodsky,
 Nicholas
Broken Blossoms (John Brahm, UK
 1936) 98, 114–15, 182, 207
Brunn, Fritz 64, 111, 121, 129
Buchan, John 84
Büchse der Pandora, Die (Georg

Lightning Source UK Ltd.
Milton Keynes UK
UKOW06f0941240515

252182UK00001B/3/P